FARM POLICIES IN SOCIALIST COUNTRIES

Farm Policies in Socialist Countries

DR THEODOR BERGMANN
*Department of Comparative
Farm Policies, University of
Hohenheim (Stuttgart-Hohenheim)*

Translated from the German by
LUX FURTMÜLLER

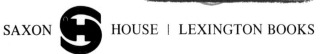

SAXON HOUSE | LEXINGTON BOOKS

First published as Agrarpolitik und Agrarwirtschaft sozialistischer Länder by
© Verlag 2000, Offenbach / M. 1973

Published by

SAXON HOUSE, D. C. Heath Ltd.
Westmead, Farnborough, Hants., England

Jointly with

LEXINGTON BOOKS, D. C. Heath & Co.
Lexington, Mass., U.S.A.

LC.

ISBN 0 347 01037 7
Library of Congress Catalog Card Number 74-25885
Printed by Tinling (1973) Limited
Prescot, Merseyside
(a member of the Oxley Printing Group Ltd)

Contents

List of tables

List of charts

List of figures

Abbreviations used

Most of the abbreviations used are in common usage and should require no explanation. However, the following abbreviations, used frequently in the course of the book, are likely to be less familiar and should be borne in mind from the outset:

ha   hectare(s) = 2·47 acres
q   quintal(s) (100 kg)
AL   agricultural land

xiv

Introduction

The material presented here is intended to be of use to all readers interested in agrarian policy — in particular, students of agriculture and young farmers — as a basis for the study of agrarian policy in socialist states. This book originated in the course, and as a result, of lectures and seminars given over several years at the Universities of Hohenheim, Göttingen and Armidale (Australia). It sets out to collect and correlate facts useful for the understanding and assessment of trends that are new and of long-term significance. While it does not claim to be a full scientific analysis, it may hopefully provide a critical digest of material not readily available to the student.

The first difficulties crop up as soon as we begin to collect and describe the facts. Wars and the destruction caused by them, revolutions and constitutional reorganisations play havoc with statistical investigations. There are linguistic obstacles, and, on top of these, the problems of comparing different social and economic systems employing different indicators to measure their performance, or else using indicators identical in name but at variance in substance. A further complication, closer to the heart of the matter, is the impossibility of viewing social upheavals such as the Russian Revolution of 1917 or the victory of the communists in Yugoslavia in 1944, in China in 1949 and in Cuba in 1959, with complete detachment. Nor is the distance in time great enough to enable the scholar to arrive at a balanced assessment, since the results and long-term effects of profound social changes do not become apparent until after a considerable lapse of time.

For the research worker who wishes to preserve his integrity and who strives to come as close as is humanly possible to attaining truly scientific standards, the best course to take is probably to recognise and openly declare his own point of view, which is bound to enter into his judgement of historical developments and may even affect his selection and description of facts. I approach my task as a critical Marxist — a statement which once upon a time, in the light of the pre-Stalinist understanding of Marxism, would have been pleonastic, unnecessarily repetitious, for Marxism is after all the critical analysis of society. Possible socialist forms of society were not exempted by Marx and Engels from the need for criticism. The present study, then, recognises the necessity of drastic social changes, with

1

all their consequences for the rural social structure, and looks upon social-ist economic planning as a necessary element of social progress. Yet the particular shape the transformation has taken in any one country cannot claim to be a universally valid, mandatory model to be copied by all, but must be understood in its specific historical, economic, socio-cultural and world-political context.

Socialism, especially in its difficult stage of construction, does not descend as a state of perfect harmony, like Pallas Athene, the Greek goddess of war, springing in full panoply from the head of Zeus. Far from it, socialism is the overcoming of the old order in a tough struggle, an experiment that constitutes a new departure in world history, and one for which there are no precedents or recipes. Achievements and mistakes, success stories and criticisms belong together and should not be selectively recorded, as the eulogists on the one hand and the cold warriors on the other have done for far too long.

There is no need to elaborate on the fact that there were gaps in the material at my disposal. Nor does this study cover all the socialist coun-tries. The intention was rather to avoid repetition and to present the several models of agrarian policy, together with their major modifications, adopted by socialist countries. In the first part developments and results are described and analysed country by country. The concluding sections attempt to arrive at a theoretical understanding of the problems of social-ist agrarian policies, to generalise the available experience as far as possible and thus contribute to a critical appreciation of the subject.

Critical observations from readers will be welcomed and may help to improve the book in the event of a second edition.

I have to thank my colleagues Onno-Hans Poppinga, for contributions to the text; Erich Roth, for preparation of the figures; Brunhilde Neef and Karla Maulbetsch for their indefatigable work in preparing clean copies of difficult texts. But the responsibility for errors and the opinions expressed is mine alone.

Theodor Bergmann
Stuttgart-Hohenheim, Spring 1973

1 Survey of the Socialist Countries

1.1 History of the system of socialist states

1917 ('October') Victory of the Social Democratic Workers' Party of Russia (Bolsheviks) in Russia's major cities; the October Revolution.

1917—1921 Civil war, massive intervention by many armies.

1918—1920 Unsuccessful revolutions in Germany and Hungary.

1924 After Lenin's death, Stalin assumes leading functions in Party and Government.

1936—1938 Civil war in Spain — ends with victory of Franco regime.

1936—1938 Sharp clashes between opposing factions within the Communist Party of the Soviet Union (CPSU) lead to a great 'purge', the destruction of the old guard of leading communists who were critical of Stalin's methods.

1939 (August) Stalin—Hitler Pact.

1939 (September) — 1945 (May) Second World War.

1941—1945 German—Soviet war, ending with the victory of the Soviet Union. The Red Army enters Bulgaria, Rumania, Hungary, Czechoslovakia, East Germany. Beginning of the gradual transformation of the social systems of these countries.

1944 Victory of the Yugoslav communists; formation of a communist government in Yugoslavia.

1948 Conflict between Yugoslavia and the Soviet Union and its allies; the first open split in the system of communist states. Yugoslavia is expelled from the community of socialist states and the Cominform.

1949 Victory of the Chinese communists after twenty years of civil war fought with varying fortunes.

1949 Formation of the Council for Mutual Economic Aid (Comecon or CMEA).

1953 Death of Stalin. Malenkov assumes the leadership.

1953 (June) Workers' rising in the GDR.

1954 Khrushchev assumes the highest political offices in the Soviet Union.

1955 Warsaw Treaty: military co-ordination of the European communist states.

1956 Twentieth CPSU Congress: official de-Stalinisation.

1956 Risings in Hungary and Poland.
1959 The Cuban Revolution is successful.
1960 First signs of Sino-Soviet tension.
1961 Albania breaks away from Warsaw Treaty and CMEA.
1964 (October) Khrushchev dismissed.
1965 Open breach between China and the Soviet Union.
1968 (August) Invasion of Czechoslovakia by Soviet Union and other
     Warsaw Pact countries ends the 'Prague Spring'.
1968 Romania loosens her ties with the Soviet Union and disowns Soviet
     foreign policy.
1970 Heightened tension between the Soviet Union and China; armed
     border clash on the Ussuri river.

1.2   Distinctions

While it is true that the socialist states have some socio-political features in common, it is equally certain that political and economic differences and conflicts of interest between them have become more clearly discernible.
      The communist countries belong to different agricultural zones:

Eastern Europe (temperate zone): mixed agriculture, including arable and
      stock farming.
East Asia (temperate to subtropical): rice cultivation predominates; spade
      husbandry.
Cuba (subtropical): sugar-cane monoculture.

      These countries are at various stages of economic development. Judged by such indicators as the relative strength of the agricultural population, the level of mechanisation and the consumption of fertilisers, they rank mostly with the developing countries, or at any rate did so at the time of their respective revolutions. However, social and economic stagnation has been overcome. The agricultural population is declining rapidly in relative terms, and literacy is attained before long. The first step on the road of economic and cultural development was taken with open eyes. That is to say: making up leeway and catching up with the industrial countries forms part of the social revolution. Nearly all the communist countries have made drastic changes in the agrarian structure and thus in the character of the rural population (see Table 1.1).

4

Table 1.1:   Characteristic data of communist countries

	Land area ('000 ha)	Agricultural land, 1967/68 ('000 ha)	Population, 1971 ('000)	Inhabitants per sq km	Inhabitants per ha, AL	Agricultural working population (%) 1950	Agricultural working population (%) 1965–67
Albania	2,875	1,244	2,230	78	0·6	70	58
Bulgaria	11,056	5,881	8,540	77	0·7	64	43
Czechoslovakia	12,590	7,117	14,500	113	0·5	38	18
GDR	10,829	6,302	17,041	158	0·4	29	15
Hungary	9,303	6,903	10,360	111	0·7	53	30
Poland	30,378	19,777	32,750	105	0·6	57	47
Romania	23,034	14,972	20,470	86	0·7	70	54
Yugoslavia	24,580	14,687	20,550	80	0·7	65	39[1]
USSR	2,233,770	204,619	241,748[2]	11	1·6	60	30[3]
Cuba	11,452	9,000? / 5,867?	8,550	75	1·1? / 0·7?	—	42
China	976,101	287,350	772,900	81	0·4	—	85
N. Korea	12,239	—	14,280	118	?	—	—
N. Vietnam	15,880	2,018[4]	21,600	136	?	—	78
Mongolia	153,100	80	1,280	1	?	?	59

[1] 1971.   [3] Equivalent in number of full-time workers, 1969: 25 per cent.
[2] 1970.   [4] Arable land.

Sources: Statistical Yearbooks of Federal Republic, Czechoslovakia, etc.

1.3 Data on agrarian structure and production

In most communist states private production in the sector of crop farming has been reduced to a minimum. In the Soviet Union the state farms are cultivating a large proportion of the acreage. The development of the socialist sector in crop farming, illustrated by the relative shares of the

Table 1.2

Percentage shares of social sectors in agricultural land, 1950–1969

	1950	1952	1954	1956	1958	1960	1961	1965	1969
1 Collective (co-operative) farms									
Albania	5	–	–	31	–	74	74	75	75
Bulgaria	11	45	46	63	84	93	93	84	84
Czechoslovakia	10	29	26	30	58	67	70	60	60
GDR	–	3	13	22	29	84	85	86	86
Romania	2	6	8	13	31	53	55	61	61
Hungary	6	20	21	25	16	61	76	78	78
USSR	–	–	–	–	80	56	49	42	40
Poland	1	3	7	1^1	1	2	2	1	1
Yugoslavia	18	14	2	2	2	1	1	1	1
2 State farms									
Albania	3	–	–	7	–	13	14	14	14
Bulgaria	3	4	5	6	5	5	5	14	14
Czechoslovakia	6	6	10	12	14	15	20	29	30
GDR	6	7	12	8	9	8	8	7	7
Romania	22	23	24	25	26	29	29	30	30
Hungary	5	13	14	14	14	13	14	16	16
USSR	–	–	–	16	19	42	50	57	58
Poland	9	12	12	13	12	11	11	14	15
Yugoslavia	3	3	4	4	5	7	8	12	12
3 Socialist sector (total)									
Albania	8	–	–	21	–	87	88	89	89
Bulgaria	14	49	51	69	89	98	98	98	98
Czechoslovakia	16	35	36	42	72	82	90	89	90
GDR	6	10	25	30	38	92	93	93	93
Romania	24	29	32	38	57	82	84	91	91
Hungary	11	33	35	39	30	74	90	94	94
USSR	–	–	–	–	99	98	99	99	98
Poland	10	15	19	14^2	13	13	13	15	16
Yugoslavia	21	17	6	6	7	8	9	13	13

[1] September 1956, 10; year end, 1.
[2] September 1956, 23; year end, 14.

Source: Statistical Yearbooks of socialist countries.

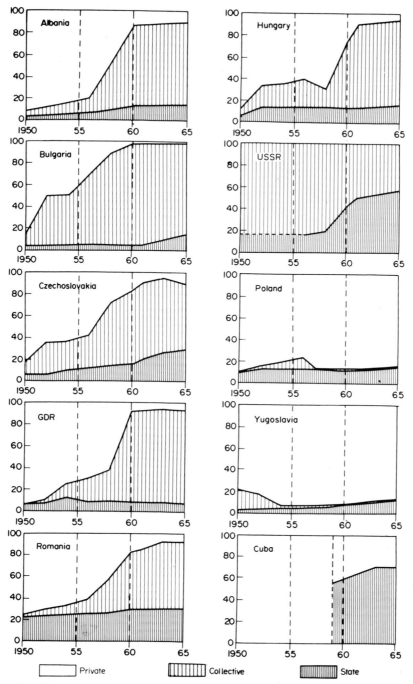

Fig. 1.1 Division of agricultural land between the social sectors, 1950–1965

7

social sectors in the total agricultural area (see Table 1.2 and Fig. 1.1), presents the fever chart of socialist agrarian policy; the struggle between the Soviet model (introduced on the strength of Soviet 'advice', meaning tutelage) and the specific conditions and needs of each country.

The development of the socialist sector in animal production shows even wider divergencies (see Table 1.3 and Fig. 1.2). The share of individual production is consistently higher than in arable farming, where mechanised methods are more easily introduced.

Table 1.3

Percentage shares of the social sectors in the livestock of some socialist countries

Country; type of livestock	Year end	State	Co-operatives (total)	Co-operatives (household plots)	Independent peasants	Total
Bulgaria						
Cattle	1950	0·3	36·1	16·6	63·6	100
	1955	1·1	38·7	8·7	59·2	100
	1963	7·9	87·9	18·1	4·2	100
Pigs	1950	2·5	45·7	33·6	51·8	100
	1955	5·1	64·2	31·4	30·7	100
	1963	5·3	90·8	29·4	3·9	100
Czechoslovakia[1]						
Cattle	1950	6·8	11·3	9·7	81·9	100
	1963	21·8	68·2	6·4	10·0	100
	1971[2]	27·5	64·0	4·6	8·5	100
Pigs	1950	15·6	9·6	8·4	74·8	100
	1963	21·7	67·6	12·8	10·7	100
	1971	23·0	68·3	9·9	8·7	100
Hungary						
Cattle	1950	2·5	0·9	–	96·6	100
	1955	9·9	13·3	4·8	76·8	100
	1963	13·3	80·1	36·5	6·6	100
Pigs	1950	10·3	0·8	–	88·9	100
	1955	20·5	14·6	6·3	64·9	100
	1963	18·9	69·4	35·7	11·7	100
GDR						
Cattle	1950	1·6	–	–	98·4	100
	1960	6·3	48·1	43·0	2·6	100
	1971	8·7	76·6	13·5	1·2	100
Pigs	1950	1·7	–	–	98·3	100
	1960	8·1	42·3	40·6	9·0	100
	1971	12·7	68·5	14·1	4·7	100

Poland					
Cattle	1950	5·1	0·5	—	94·4	100
	1963	13·0	0·9	—	86·1	100
	1972	17·3	1·5	0·1	81·1	100
Pigs	1950	5·9	0·4	—	93·7	100
	1963	11·1	1·0	—	87·9	100
	1972	12·1	1·1	0·2	86·6	100
Soviet Union					
Cattle	1950	7·4	91·9	42·7	0·7	100
	1963	28·2	71·8	28·2	—	100
	1968	30·0	70·0	28·0	—	100
Pigs	1950	14·9	84·1	33·7	1·0	100
	1963	28·6	71·4	32·2	—	100
	1968	30·0	70·0	26·0	—	100

[1] Figures for independent peasants include livestock kept without land.
[2] Figures for co-operatives include inter-co-operative enterprises.

Sources: *Zemědělská Ekonomika*; Brunner and Westen; Wädekin; and others.

The intensity of agricultural production (see Table 1.4) is also marked by large differences, due partly to ecological, partly to economic factors. The connection between yields and use of technical and chemical resources emerges clearly.

1.4 Common characteristics and differences

Some characteristics are, broadly speaking, common to all communist countries: notably, a centralised administration, economic planning, accelerated industrialisation, a radical transformation of the agrarian structure (excepting Yugoslavia, Poland and Cuba), and the rapid advance of literacy and expansion of the educational system. However, these characteristics are not everywhere developed to the same degree. In some of the countries the agrarian question was of great political and economic importance. Since the agricultural population formed a large majority in those countries, the revolutionaries needed their help. Accordingly, agrarian policy had to be designed to win over as many of the rural population as possible and to foster and mobilise their revolutionary energies. In addition, the agrarian sector had to provide the resources needed to ensure rapid economic development (factor contribution of agriculture).

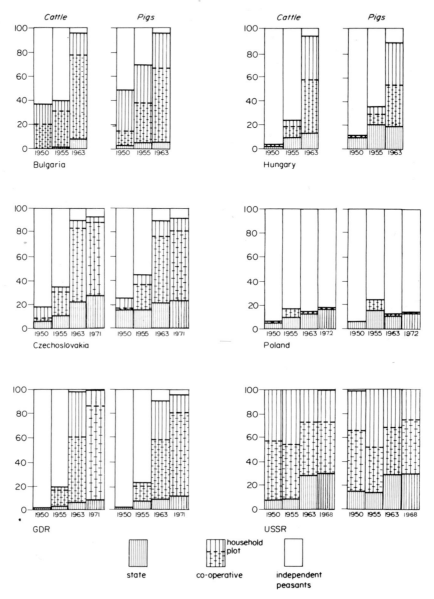

Fig. 1.2   Division of livestock numbers between social sectors, 1950—1963

The most important differences between the communist states consist in the following points:

(a)   level of economic development (indicated in part by the relative strength of the rural population engaged in agriculture);

Table 1.4

Comparative data on intensiveness of agricultural production of European communist states[1]

Yields (quintals per ha)	Year	Czecho-slovakia	Bulgaria	Hungary	GDR	Poland	Romania	Soviet Union
Wheat	1950	18·9	12·1	15·2	25·4	12·8	8·0	8·1
	1968	31·6	24·0	25·2	41·7	24·7	17·2	13·9
Barley	1950	16·8	12·5	12·6	22·5	12·9	6·1	7·4
	1968	29·7	20·0	23·4	35·6	23·6	20·2	15·0
Maize	1950	17·0	8·7	15·7	24·0	10·0	7·4	13·8
	1968	33·8	31·3	29·9	28·3	24·8	21·3	26·2
Potatoes	1950	124	49	48	181	138	70	104
	1968	176	119	89	188	185	117	123
Sugar beet	1950	285	85	146	273	222	88	159
	1968	377	343	324	333	358	218	229
Milk (kg per cow)	1950	1,634	425	1,243	1,891	1,648	894	1,370
	1968	2,309	2,541	2,389	3,313	2,293	1,794	2,033
Tractors[2] ('000)	1950	26	7	13	36	28	14	595
	1968	133	51	68	144	168	96	1,821
Combine harvesters	1950	392	13	25	389	84	118	211,000
	1968	14,395	9,137	10,418	17,923	10,290	47,092	580,600
Tractors[3] per 100 ha, AL	1968	2·9	1·4	1·5	3·0	1·0	1·1	0·7
Fertiliser consumption Pure nutrient per ha, AL	1950	34·8	1·1	—	104	17·7	5·6[4]	2·7
	1968	168·6	143·2	91·0	223·3	93·4	36·4	15·1

[1] Without Albania and Yugoslavia.
[2] Physical units.
[3] Equivalent of 15 hp units.
[4] 1960.

Source: *Statistické přehledy.*

(b)   level of cultural development (degree of illiteracy at the time of the revolution);

(c)   level of political-social development (democratic tradition in Czechoslovakia; autocratic tradition in Czarist Russia);

(d)   strength of Communist Party (Soviet Union, Czechoslovakia, Poland);

(e)   mode of planning (directive or indicative, centralised or decentralised);

(f)   degree of modification of Soviet model and extent of autonomy *vis-à-vis* the Soviet Union.

Combining the common basic model with the specific differences, the following main features emerge:

(a)   a differentiated agrarian structure;

(b)   the varying shares of the three social sectors in the total agricultural land, and in the output of arable farming and animal production;

(c)   the varying significance of private plots in collective or co-operative farms;

(d)   different trends of agrarian policy in present-day practice;

(e)   three communist-countries without collectivisation;

(f)   four distinct models of agrarian policy.

Whether, in the light of such substantial divergencies and the various conflicts of economic and political interests, the socialist countries can still be said to form a coherent system of states and economies, is open to question.

2 Countries with a Collectivised Agriculture

2.1 The Soviet Union: model of collectivisation

2.1.1 *History of Russian agrarian policy*

1606–1607 First peasant risings under Bolotnikov against the Government in Moscow.

1773–1774 Peasant revolt under Pugachov.

1861 First agrarian reform: abolition of serfdom; the peasants placed under the obligation of buying their greatly curtailed land holdings from their former masters, four-fifths of the purchase price being advanced by the state at a rate of interest of 6·5 per cent, to be paid off over 49 years.

1904–1905 Russo-Japanese war, Russia defeated.

1905 First major attempt at a revolution.

1906 Second agrarian reform introduced by Stolypin; dissolution of village communes ('mir').

1914 Entry into First World War.

1917 (February–March) Overthrow of Czar; democratic revolution.

1917 ('October') Second phase of revolution: victory of Bolsheviks. A decree issued, nationalising land; payments by peasants to landowners abolished; peasants seize land.

1921 End of war communism; under the NEP (New Economic Policy) private enterprise is admitted and encouraged, foreign capitalists are invited.

1929 First Five Year Plan of accelerated industrialisation.

1929–1933 Collectivisation of agriculture throughout the Soviet Union; establishment of machine and tractor stations (MTS).

1954–1958 Virgin lands campaign in Kazakhstan.

1958 Liquidation of MTS, machines sold off to kolkhozes.

1969 (November) Third Congress of Collective Farmers.

2.1.2 Regional differences*

In the Soviet Union's vast territory of 8·6 million square miles there are marked differences in agricultural performance between the various climatic zones. These differences, however, are hidden by the overall figures of Soviet statistics. If the figures are broken up according to regions (see in particular the works by Dumont and Schiller), large differences emerge as regards size of production units, intensity of exploitation, crop cultiviation, animal production and size of private plots (see Table 2.1 and Fig. 2.1).

In this section a survey is presented, first of the climate, soil and terrain in the natural landscape belts, and then of the crop farming zones, with reference to only the most important crops. Finally, the average size of production units in the various regions is shown. Only a few of the many connections and interrelations between these three factors can be indicated here.

From north to south, the Soviet Union can be divided into the following natural landscape belts:

tundra;
taiga (boreal coniferous forest);
mixed forest in European Russia;
forest steppe;
steppe;
semi-desert;
desert.

There are, moreover, small regions of a subtropical climate, chiefly in the Trans-Caucasus region, but also on the southern slopes of the Crimean coast. The most important mountain ranges are the Urals, the Greater and Lesser Caucasus, the mountains at the edge of Central Asia and on the southern borders of Siberia, and the mountains of East Siberia, especially in the south and north-east of that region. Finally, the mixed forests of the Far East have to be mentioned.

The tundra does not lend itself to agricultural utilisation, with the exception of the keeping of reindeer by nomadic tribes. In the taiga belt, the only substantial areas available for utilisation are in the western part of the region's southern fringe, and beyond the Yenisey only in river basins, due to the severity of the continental climate, which becomes progressively more extreme from west to east. In the north the boundary

---

* This chapter is based largely on the geographical works by Mellor, Pokšiševskij, Rauth, Wagener, and the thesis by Bossung.

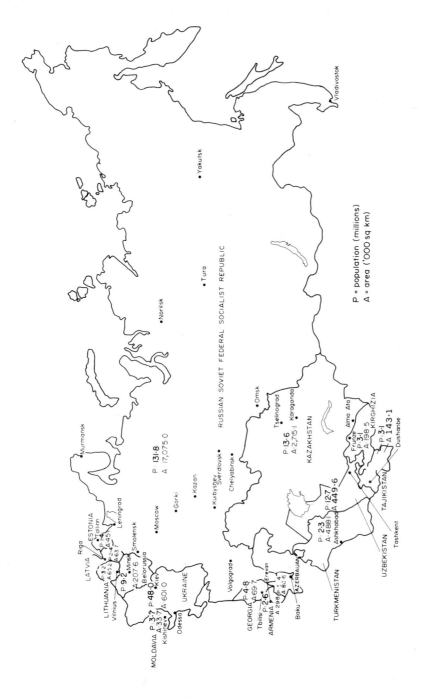

Fig. 2.1 Population and area of the republics constituting the Soviet Union, 1972

Table 2.1

Geographical, agricultural, economic data for Soviet republics

Republic	Area ('000 sq km)	Population, 1972 ('000 ha)	Inhabitants per sq km	No. agricultural kolkhozes		Household plots per kolkhoz		Sown area per kolkhoz[3]		Cattle[4]	
				1940	1971	1940	1971	1940 (ha)	1971 ('000 ha)	1940	1971
RSFSR	17,075·0	131,771	8	167,291	13,415	68	374	474	4·2	72	1,511
Armenia	29·8	2,635	88	1,030	475	174	221	398	0·5	280	526
Azerbaijan	86·6	5,375	62	3,416	948	105	279	311	0·8	173	519
Belorussia	207·6	9,171	44	10,237	2,174	75	378	283	1·6	75	1,258
Estonia[1]	45·1	1,395	31	2,213	215	55	287	263	1·7	100	1,307
Georgia	69·7	4,813	69	4,256	1,234	113	316	184	0·3	134	351
Kazakhstan	2,715·1	13,592	5	6,639[2]	425	97	485	724	9·6	257	2,080
Kirghizia	198·5	3,110	16	1,732	236	106	725	534	3·1	106	1,682
Latvia[1]	63·7	2,419	38	1,776	641	128	219	644	1·4	231	875
Lithuania[1]	65·2	3,219	49	4,500	1,384	73	185	330	1·0	34	600
Moldavia[1]	33·7	3,695	110	1,636	494	284	975	899	2·6	140	1,227
Tajikistan	143·1	3,149	22	3,093	265	64	848	248	1·8	37	1,325
Turkmenistan	488·1	2,328	5	1,540	327	87	490	245	1·8	44	618
Ukraine	601·0	48,048	80	28,374	8,981	141	560	784	2·7	122	1,557
Uzbekistan	449·6	12,731	28	7,499	1,042	107	785	365	1·8	66	835
USSR	22,402·2	247,451	11	236,900	32,256	81	439	492	3·0	85	1,337

1 1950 instead of 1940 throughout.
2 1945 instead of 1940.
3 Without collective farmers' household plots.
4 Kolkhoz-owned, at year end.

Table 2.1, continued

Republic	Population, 1972 (as percentage of total for USSR)	Sown area, 1970 (as percentage of total for USSR)	Urban population, 1972 (as percentage of total)	Wage and salary earners (percentage of population)	Gross product per inhabitant				Per capita national income (RSFSR=100)
					Industry 1968 Roubles	Index	Agriculture 1965 Roubles	Index	
RSFSR	53·2	59·3	64	38·4	1,430	100	218	100	100
Armenia	1·1	0·2	61	29·8	1,047	73	146	67	75
Azerbaijan	2·2	0·6	51	22·8	633	44	122	56	68
Belorussia	3·7	2·9	46	29·3	990	69	346	158	72
Estonia	0·6	0·3	66	44·5	1,839	128	381	179	112
Georgia	1·9	0·4	48	27·2	852	59	180	82	68
Kazakhstan	5·5	14·5	52	33·8	721	50	228	104	72
Kirghizia	1·3	0·6	38	23·5	731	51	227	104	60
Latvia	1·0	0·8	64	41·2	1,877	131	353	161	123
Lithuania	1·3	1·1	53	32·7	1,235	86	387	177	89
Moldavia	1·5	0·9	33	21·0	843	58	387	177	69
Tajikistan	1·3	0·4	38	17·8	527	36	206	94	51
Turkmenistan	0·9	0·2	48	20·7	473	33	208	95	62
Ukraine	19·4	16·2	56	30·4	1,405	98	300	137	87
Uzbekistan	5·1	1·6	37	20·5	524	36	205	94	58
USSR	100·0	100·0	58						
USSR less RSFSR					1,073	75	269	123	78
USSR less RSFSR and Ukraine					822	57	245	112	71

Source: *Narodnoe khozyaystvo.*

of the land suitable for cultivation is pushed southwards by the low prevailing temperatures and the shortness of the growing season. Stock farming can be maintained somewhat farther to the north, especially in the grassy lowlands in river valleys. Proceeding from north to south, the next three zones — mixed forest, forest steppe and steppe — make up the big agriculturally important regions; they constitute the so-called agrarian triangle. This is bordered in the south by a broad fringe (Volgograd, Uralsk, Tselinograd, Semipalatinsk) which marks the transition to the arid and desert regions. Other agriculturally important areas are the Caucasus region, the oases in Central Asia, and the zone of mixed forests found in the foothills and highland basins, along the desert rivers and in the Far East.

In the northern natural forest belt of the agrarian triangle atmospheric precipitation decreases from west to east (from 613 to 404 mm; 24·1 to 15·9 inches), with a maximum recorded in summer, while a winter minimum is clearly present only in Siberia. So there is no lack of snow in winter. The temperatures in the warmest month increase only slightly from west to east (17·5 to 18°C), while those of the coldest month show a steep decline (−4·3 to −18·5°). During the growing season, which diminishes from 134 days in the west to 112 days in the east, precipitation everywhere exceeds evaporation. In the moraine areas of the west (especially in the Baltic region and Belorussia) arable farming frequently requires soil improvement through drainage. The type of soil associated with this terrain both in the east and in the west is podzol soil, which is formed in humid conditions under forest vegetation (coniferous woods). These soils are poor in nutrients and produce low cereal yields (up to 10 quintals per hectare; 8 cwt per acre). There are production reserves in this area that could be mobilised by increased use of fertilisers; all the more so, as the more equable climate can be expected to produce steadier crops than the southern agricultural regions, where the soils are better but the climatic risks greater.

As regards arable farming, the months with below-zero mean temperatures and the duration of the frost-free period must be taken into account. In the west, four and a half months have mean temperatures below freezing point; in the east, the number is seven. The period free of frosts is three months in the west and slightly more in the east.

Continuing further south, the next zone is that of the forest steppes. Here optimal climatic and soil conditions coincide in an area extending from the north-eastern slopes of the Carpathians in the west to the Altai foothills in the east. Again, as can be seen by comparing the figures for Kiev, on the northern fringe of the forest steppe, and Omsk, precipitation decreases from west to east, (528 and 309 mm — 20·8 and 12·0 inches —

18

respectively). In the east, precipitation reaches its peak in summer, before the temperature peak; in the west, the two peak values coincide. Summer temperatures are high and change very little from west to east (mean temperatures of the warmest month respectively 19·5 and 19·1°), but the transition from winter to summer, and thus the melting of the snows, proceeds much more quickly in the east, winter temperatures for Omsk being much lower than those for Kiev (mean for the coldest month being −19·6 and −5·8° respectively), and the duration of the growing season correspondingly lower (126 as against 159 days). In the west, five months have negative mean temperatures, as against seven in the east. The frost-free period lasts three months in the west, over three and a half in the east. The correlation between precipitation and temperature does not preclude summer droughts, except in the West (northern Ukraine); in the Don and Volga regions and in the south of Western Siberia the danger of droughts is real, especially as the weather in these areas varies greatly from year to year. The size of the harvests here is decisively affected by the rapidity with which the snows melt (depth of soil humidity), by the volume and timing of precipitations in early summer, and by the occurrence of hot dust storms in summer. The primeval vegetation − oak forests petering out towards the south in the form of forest islands or narrow woodland strips surrounded by grassy steppes rich in meadow plants − has disappeared, apart from minor remnants. This is due to the high fertility of the forest steppe zone, where the soils − in the main various types of black earth − are particularly suitable for agriculture, provided they are formed on a substratum of glacial loess or similar horizons.

The southernmost zone of the agrarian triangle is the steppe zone, which in the course of the last 250 years has come to be utilised for agriculture. The last step in that direction was the virgin lands campaign of 1954 and the period following it, during which agriculture was extended to the dry southern part of the steppe zone beyond the Volga and the Urals. Fluctuations in the weather from year to year are particularly marked in the steppe zone and above all in its southern fringe area. This is of decisive importance for agriculture. All sub-regions are characterised by high summer temperatures (mean for the warmest month, 22 to 20·3°) and by a long growing season: as much as 200 days for Krasnodar in the extreme south of the zone; otherwise, decreasing from west to east, 150 to 138 days. In addition there is the danger of dry periods or even droughts, which progressively increases from north to south and west to east. This danger arises in the period after precipitation has attained its peak in the early summer. The volume of precipitation, incidentally, also declines eastwards. The soils of the steppe zone are chiefly black earths with a humus content decreasing from 6 to 10 per cent for the ordinary black earths in the north, to 6 per cent or less in the south. In the southern border fringe, soils of a dark-chestnut hue and with a humus content of 3 to 4 per cent predominate beside all types of saline soils. The black earth areas of the Soviet Union — in the forest steppe and steppe zones — total about 500 million acres (200 m. ha), about 2 acres (0·8 ha) per inhabitant. In the steppe zone even more than in the forest steppes, one must reckon with meteorological risks and fluctuating harvests. Spring wheat, for example, suffers damage through the hot and dry dust storms, called 'sukhovey', in three to five years out of ten in the southern Ukraine, and three to seven years out of ten in the virgin lands.

Where loess occurs at the foot of the mountains, in the region south of the deserts in Central Asia, irrigation can transform the area into fertile agricultural land. Favourable climatic conditions, comparable to those on the Nile, are found in many of the sheltered low-lying basins. Areas totalling over 10 million acres (4 m. ha) are being irrigated in Central Asia, chiefly with river water. The data for Tashkent convey an impression of the climatic conditions in the region. Annual precipitation reaches the fairly high figure of 371 mm (14·6 inches), which is partly explained by the altitude of Tashkent (1,590 feet). The mean temperature in January is −1·1°, in July 26·7° C. The greatest volume of precipitation occurs from January to April. Only in one month do temperatures fall below freezing point.

The mixed forests of the Far East lie within the range of the monsoon climate. The winter is similar to that in Central Siberia, with temperatures unusually low for those latitudes (January mean from −15 to −20° C). The summer is humid and warm, moderated by the influx of Pacific sea air (July mean 20° C). The monsoon rains start in May and continue till September, with the largest volume of rain falling in July (400 to 600 mm, 16 to 24 inches). Mixed deciduous forests thrive on various soils. There are also some areas in the Amur region with dark, black-earth type soils.

In the Trans-Caucasus region climatic conditions are completely different from those in the rest of Russia. On low ground, the climate is warm and humid with frequent cloudy days and heavy falls of rain, the annual figure being 600 mm (24 inches) or more. Precipitation reaches its seasonal peak in the autumn. There is no dry season in the proper sense. During the summer, humid, cool air from the sea blows over the land (July mean 24° C); in the winter the direction of the current is reversed, dry and warm air flowing from the interior regions (temperatures barely below zero). Daily temperature fluctuations are low by Russian standards. The Talysh basin in the vicinity of Lenkoran in the east has a climate similar to that of the Kolkhid lowlands, except that rainfall is less evenly distributed over the seasons, with a pronounced dry period in June. In both lowlands brown and red soils predominate. The Armenian highlands have a continental steppe climate. The winter is cold, with fairly heavy snow, although the largest volume of precipitation falls in spring and early summer. In the course of the summer the vegetation withers owing to the high rate of evaporation.

Natural conditions undoubtedly tend to promote the evolution of regional systems of soil utilisation, in the Soviet Union as elsewhere. Yet the optimum degree of specialisation is difficult to achieve, because the territories within which uniform natural conditions favour uniform production schedules, on the basis of specific crop rotation schemes, etc., are enormous self-contained zones, ranged in sequence from north to south (see Fig. 2.2). It follows that goods not produced in a particular specialised region would have to be brought in by long-distance transport, at a considerable cost that could not be ignored. Another point, applying to the Soviet Union in particular, is that its transport facilities would probably not be adequate to meet the requirements entailed by an extreme regional specialisation of agricultural production, and that in any case transport would not be rapid enough for the more perishable products. The transport problem, then, provides a weighty reason for the cultivation of large numbers of crops in each area, so that the agricultural regions, within the limits imposed by natural conditions, produce a broad range of products. Agricultural production on the fringe of the cities, in particular the growing of cucumbers in the vicinity of Leningrad, is an example.

The description of the agricultural regions must be confined here to a rough outline showing only the most typical features. Moving north towards the boreal coniferous forest taiga, arable farming progressively diminishes in importance. This tendency is well illustrated by the Vologda oblast 250 miles north of Moscow, where crops are grown on 5 to 6 per cent of the total area, with a slightly higher proportion of meadow and pasture land, and barely 20 per cent of the total area used for agriculture of any kind. Cereal harvests (rye and oats) produce low yields of 4 to 6 cwt per acre (5 to 7·5 q per ha). The cultivation of flax, a traditional crop in the area, and large-scale cattle breeding are well adapted to the humid climate with its short summers.

In the southern taiga of Western Siberia cattle breeding is prevalent (dairy cattle, partly on the basis of forest grazing), while in crop farming wheat predominates, though on account of the low winter temperatures

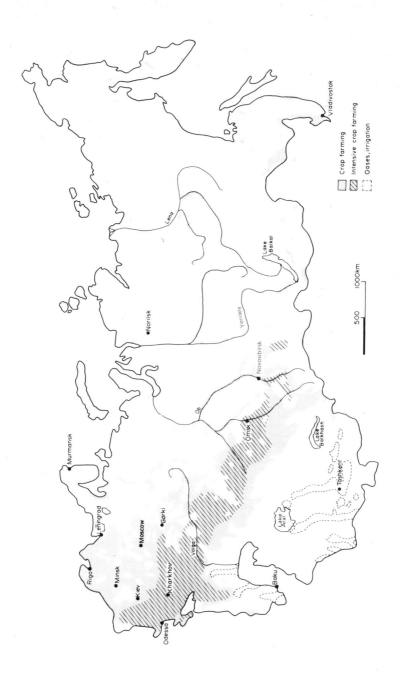

Crop farming
Intensive crop farming
Oases, irrigation

Vladivostok
Lena
Lake Baikal
Norilsk
Yenisey
1000km
500
Novosibirsk
Ob
Omsk
Lake Balkhash
Murmansk
Tashkent
Leningrad
Gorki
Lake Aral
Riga
Moscow
Volga
Minsk
Kiev
Kharkhov
Baku
Odessa

Fig. 2.2   Land use in the Soviet Union (Source: Mellor)

22

and the slight snow cover it has to be spring wheat, as is the case through-out Siberia.

In the east arable farming does not extend as far to the north as in the west, owing to the increasingly continental character of the climate. In Trans-Baikal, arable farming is confined to the lowland plains and their fringes and the total acreage is relatively small (in the Chita rayon, for instance, which is almost twice the size of the United Kingdom, it covers no more than 4·32 million acres (1·75 m. ha), or 4 per cent of the territo-ry). Cereal yields are also low, ranging from 4 to 6 cwt per acre (5 to 7·5 q per ha). Here again, stock farming — especially the keeping of sheep, which is well suited to the climate with its cold winters but extremely slight snowfall (20 cm, or 8 inches) — is of greater importance than arable farming.

Land utilisation in the mixed forest belt (where forest land accounts today for 20 to 40 per cent of the total area) is determined by both natural and historical conditions. In the humid and cool west (Baltic Republics, Karelian isthmus) stock farming is predominant — in particular cattle breeding, thanks to the favourable climate conditions — while the important pig farming industry of the Baltic countries follows a tradition established in the inter-war years, when the countries of the region special-ised in producing bacon for the West European, and above all the British, market. In Belorussia and northern Central Russia stock farming is still important, but arable farming (rye, oats, potatoes), dating back to the methods of peasant subsistence farming of the pre-Soviet era, also plays a substantial part in spite of poor soils. Potato growing in Belorussia forms the basis for intensive pig farming. In addition, Belorussia and the cool and humid north of European Central Russia are the chief flax growing areas not only of the Soviet Union but also of the whole world.

In the forest steppe zone, sugar beet growing has come to be most important in the area west of the Dnieper; east of the Dnieper wheat has displaced rye in the south. Hemp, tobacco and melon growing is impor-tant throughout the region, and orchards and vineyards form part of the cultivated rural landscape in the forest steppe zone. Stock farming is based on the cultivation of fodder plants, with ensilaged maize constantly growing in importance. In the forest steppe east of the Volga the share of crops preferring warm conditions and of rye is increasing. Beyond the Urals, land utilisation is comparable to that of the steppe zone further south.

In the steppe zone, production of cereals, especially wheat, predomi-nates: winter wheat in the west with its relatively warm winters and the protection of ample snow cover, spring wheat in the area east of the Volga

Table 2.2

Average sizes of kolkhozes and sovkhozes in the natural regions (1962)

	Mountain zone		Forest zone		Forest steppe and steppe zone		
	Armenia	Georgia	Latvia	North west of RSFSR	Ukraine	Central black-earth region	N. Caucasus
Sovkhozes							
AL ('000 ha)	2·9	3·3	4·0	6·1	5·9	11·4	19·1
Sown area ('000 ha)	0·8	1·0	2·1	2·4	4·6	9·5	9·2
Cows (no.)	300	200	500	700	700	800	800
Basic means of production[1] (million roubles)	1·1	1·6	1·4	1·9	2·1	2·1	2·6
Work force engaged in basic production	367	571	433	603	698	982	810
Kolkhozes							
AL ('000 ha)	1·4	1·3	2·1	3·1	3·3	5·1	10·1
Sown area ('000 ha)	0·5	0·4	1·2	1·3	2·6	4·1	5·6
Cows (no.)	149	100	264	269	450	354	606
Basic means of production[1] (million roubles)	0·3	0·4	0·6	0·4	0·7	0·6	1·0
Kolkhoz farmsteads	216	305	180	221	544	501	582

[1] Fixed assets (buildings and installations, machines and vehicles, livestock).

Source: Loncarevic.

and the Urals with its cold winters. Yields are around 13 cwt per acre (16 q per ha). Sugar beet benefits from the fertility of the soil; sunflowers – the Soviet Union's foremost oil crop – from the hot summers; maize and tobacco from the warm, long, cloudless autumn of the European Soviet Union. Fruit growing and viticulture are common on the northern slopes of the Yaila mountains and the Caucasus and have lately been extended on a considerable scale to the plains of the Pontic steppe. In the Trans-Volga steppes and the north of Kazakhstan, spring wheat and sunflower predominate. Stock farming, concerned mainly with cattle, sheep and pigs, is based in the humid west and north on the cultivation of fodder crops, in the dry south and east on natural pasture land. It is important throughout the region. The Caucasus region allows the cultivation of tea, citrus fruit and grapes. In the oases of Central Asia the leading crops are fruit, cotton and rice. The mixed forest region of the Far East produces chiefly cereals, soya and milk, as well as some potatoes and vegetables. In the southern part of the region rice, sugar beet and livestock come into the picture as well.

Differences in the average size of kolkhozes and sovkhozes in the various natural zones (see Table 2.2) cannot be attributed exclusively to differences in natural conditions; nevertheless, some correlations between natural location and size of production unit are indicated. Thus, in the mountain zones the low proportion of land suitable for cultivation has resulted in the establishment of relatively small kolkhozes and sovkhozes. The forest zone is dominated by large tracts of woodland, while the agricultural, and in particular arable, land is fragmented into small plots scattered among the forests and marshes. Wide variations in soil conditions occur within comparatively small areas. Accordingly, in the forest zone too, kolkhozes and sovkhozes are smaller than in the forest steppe and steppe zones, where large, compact areas of arable land are to be found.

2.1.3   *The economic system: methods and aims of central planning*

Agrarian policy is generally a sector policy placed within a wider framework of overall economic-social policy. The starting point of economic-social policy in the Soviet Union was an underdeveloped nation: the great majority of the population lived by agriculture and were illiterate; the industrial centres were new, and there were only a few of them. But the country had rich natural resources. The general aim, therefore, was to attain the same level of development as the industrialised and literate nations, and to this end all the country's domestic assets, physical and intellectual, had to be mobilised and concentrated on the strategically most important sectors. Specific aims were the achievement of general literacy, the building up of educational institutions, and the development of heavy industries. The development gap, the distance by which the country had fallen behind, was to be closed in the shortest possible time. It was intended to neglect the less important sectors. The abolition of all unproductive payments and of unproductive social strata in conjunction with the expropriation and nationalisation of the means of production and profits constituted the most important initial steps taken to get control of the decisive levers of economic development. The order of economic priorities was laid down as follows:

(i)   extraction of raw materials;
(ii)   development of heavy industries (steel works, oil refineries, generation and transmission of electric power);
(iii)   development of capital goods industries (heavy engineering);
(iv)   consumer goods industries;
(v)   agriculture.

As a result of the low priority accorded to consumer goods and agriculture, the consumers were forced to put up with a prolonged period of shortages and low-quality goods. The motives were political as well as economic; in real life the two aspects are closely connected. In the political sphere domestic and external factors have to be considered. The revolutionary domestic measures — expropriation of the capitalists' property and destruction of their political apparatus — aroused the hostility of most world powers, manifested in military intervention, economic boycott, cultural isolation and non-recognition. This, in turn, forced the Soviet leadership to rely exclusively on domestic resources. The wealth and variety of the country's natural resources and its size favoured autarchy and the 'building of socialism in one country'. Politically, the opposition of the former ruling classes was broken in the course of the social transformation, which wiped out several classes (see Table 2.7).

Planning means the concentration of the greatest possible efforts and resources on specified economic objectives, irrespective of considerations such as the lack of private economic profitability in the short term. Clear priorities were defined, so as to achieve a breakthrough and reach the 'economic take-off point' as rapidly as possible. During the initial phases of planning — and they were phases also of shortages and want — planning targets were set in physical terms (measured in tons of steel or oil, numbers of tractors and lorries, etc.). As diversification progresses and production capacities increase, and the wants and wishes of producers and consumers continue to grow, planning methods must be modified. Modern technologies (computers, cybernetics) and the availability of data make it possible to change over to a more general and indicative mode of planning, with planning targets given in terms of monetary units (measured and expressed in multiples of million roubles for each enterprise). Instead of applying the direct method of allocating raw materials or goods, planning can now operate by extending indirect guidance through financial instruments and by exercising indirect supervision, based on criteria such as the level of interest payments to the financial institutions and the profitability of the enterprises.

Efforts directed by planning make it possible to achieve quick economic results in the period of the 'take-off'. At the same time planning entails a number of problems, as for instance:

(a) ossification and self-interest of the planning bureaucracy;
(b) supervision of the planning mechanism;
(c) determination of targets and priorities;
(d) producers' participation in planning, democratisation of planning process;
(e) consideration of wants and wishes of consumers and producers;
(f) material incentives and their economically and socially constructive distribution;
(g) early discovery of planning errors and transition to new methods.

2.1.4 *Revolutionary transformation of the countryside and the agrarian structure*

The situation before the revolution was characterised by the presence of a large number of dwarf and smallholdings accounting for only a small proportion of the agricultural land; there was a polarisation of land ownership. The number of small peasant farms continued to rise after the revolution. In 1917 the last remnants of feudalism in the form of obligations and unproductive payments were abolished and a radical land reform was instituted, through which the land of the estate owners was distributed among the agricultural producers. The former landowners were forbidden to reside in their villages or to visit their former properties. The titles to the land were taken over by the state, but the peasants had no ground rent to pay. No further measures were taken by the state. Previously landless workers and enthusiastic communists set up voluntary communes and artels. By 1925 there were about 22,000 of these with 300,000 members. These experiments were tolerated but not encouraged by the Party. The communes held some 8 million acres (3·25 m. ha). By the end of 1928 the number of communes had risen to 33,000, with a membership of about

400,000 families. Each commune farmed on average 237 acres (96 ha). Thus, in an agricultural sector dominated by independent peasants, the communes were of only minor significance.

From 1929 to 1960 the agrarian structure of the Soviet Union was characterised by four institutions (see Fig. 5.1, p. 244):

(i)   collective farms (kolkhozes);
(ii)   household plots;
(iii)   state farms (sovkhozes);
(iv)   machine and tractor stations (MTS).

(i)   THE COLLECTIVE FARMS

Collectivisation was launched in 1929 at the same time as the programme of accelerated industrialisation. Attempts at persuasion and propaganda campaigns by the Party were followed in the end by coercive measures and the use of force against the peasants farming independently. In theory the peasants were to have joined the collective farms of their own free will. But compulsory membership – as it was to all intents and purposes – had two aspects: it meant on the one hand that every peasant had to join, and on the other hand that no one could be expelled because of bad work. Within four years – 1929 to 1933 – over 20 million Russian peasant households were merged into 237,000 collective farms. In the early stages of collectivisation only the cropland was brought into the kolkhoz. Vegetable and fruit growing and, above all, animal production remained within the scope of the individual household plots.

The following economic–rational motives for collectivisation can be discerned:

(a)   organisation of the amorphous peasant masses and utilisation of economies of scale, while avoiding the disadvantages of the big agricultural estates, since the kolkhozes, as co-operative ventures, would appeal to the members' self-interest;

(b)   forcing of grain cultivation, enabling the state to purchase the crops (thus assuring the population's supply of staple foods) at low prices (agriculture's production contribution to the economy);

(c)   movement of labour from the countryside into industry, partly voluntarily, partly – as far as the kulaks were concerned – involuntarily (factor contribution I);

(d)   rationing and economically optimal utilisation of agricultural machinery via machine-and-tractor stations;

(e)   simplified planning and organisation of agricultural advice, optimum use of scarce expert manpower;

(f) keeping direct and indirect investment in agriculture (production of capital goods and materials for agriculture) to a minimum, while concentrating the main effort of industrial development on basic industrial materials, investment goods, and the technical, social and cultural infrastructure;

(g) financing the social and economic construction effort from the proceeds of agriculture (factor contribution II).

The forced and accelerated amalgamations to which many millions of small independent peasant farms were subjected without economic or technological incentives aroused the resistance of the peasant population. This was manifested in

(a) non-delivery of agricultural produce;

(b) hiding away of grain;

(c) slaughtering of livestock;

(d) chasing away of state and Party officials visiting the villages on official business;

(e) assassination of state officials.

The silent, sometimes armed resistance offered by the peasants on the one hand, and the pressure brought to bear by the authorities on the other, led to a reciprocal escalation and to intervention by the police and the army.

After the Second World War the 237,000 collective farms were once again merged into large-scale agricultural enterprises, of which there were 35,600 in 1968. The membership of the new units averaged 420 families, as compared with 80 in 1940 (see Table 2.3 and Fig. 2.3).

The agricultural acreage per farm rose from 3,500 to 15,100 acres (1,400 to 6,100 ha). Half of it was cropland, the remainder partly grassland, partly fallow. The number of actively working kolkhoz members fell in the course of 28 years from 29 million to 18 million, a decline of 40 per cent, while the number of kolkhoz households fell by only 24 per cent, from 18·7 to 15·1 million. Thus the average number of workers supplied on a regular basis by each family dropped proportionately almost as fast as the number of families making up the membership of the collective farms. Although the ratio of agricultural population to agricultural land is still very high, labour productivity has markedly increased. While the total cropland of the kolkhozes declined by over 37 million acres (over 15 million ha), cattle raising increased several times over. The gradual transition to animal production on a large scale has been rendered possible by new developments in technology and veterinary medicine.

Remuneration was initially in terms of day-work units: the working

Table 2.3

Collective farms

	1940	1950	1953	1958	1961	1966	1971
Collective farms ('000)	235·5	121·4	91·2	67·7	40·5	36·5	32·8
Members' household plots (million)	18·7	20·5	19·7	18·8	16·4	15·4	14·1
Families per kolkhoz	81	165	220	275	399	417	439
Collective farmers engaged in agricultural work (average over year, million)	29·0	27·6	25·5	24·1	20·3	18·6	16·3
Arable land (million ha)	117·7	121·0	132·0	131·4	110·6	102·2	96·9
Arable land per kolkhoz ('000 ha)	0·5	1·0	1·4	1·9	2·7	2·8	3·2
AL per kolkhoz ('000 ha)	1·4	3·1	4·2	5·4	6·2	–	6·2
Cattle per kolkhoz	85	224	–	463	–	1,072	1,332

Sources: Rochlin and Hagemann; *Narodnoe khozyaystvo.*

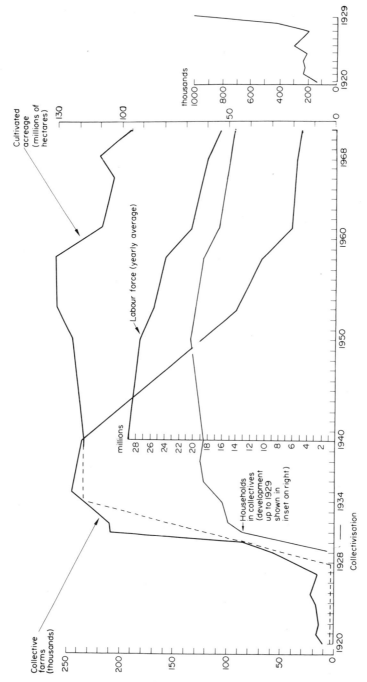

Fig. 2.3   Development of collective farms in the Soviet Union

days were recorded and each job classified according to the physical effort and qualifications involved. It is difficult in these circumstances to check on the quality of work done or to keep the labour record books accurately up to date. Wages were paid partly in advance, partly at the year end. But the year-end payments were only made after the MTS had been paid for its work, compulsory delivery targets had been met, contributions had duly been paid into the common fund, and so on. At this stage, then, wages are only a residual payment, coming at the bottom of the list after all the other obligations of the kolkhoz. Wages are in cash and in kind. Produce received in kind is converted into animal products on the household plots.

In some countries of the Eastern bloc there are three types of producer co-operatives, distinguished by the degree of integration and the valuation of the land brought into the co-operative by each member. Payments of ground rent are highest in type 1, lowest in type 3; conversely the proportion of the collective's profits paid out in wages is lowest in type 1 and highest in type 3. In this way differences in the level of landholdings before the formation of the co-operative are taken into account at first and only gradually levelled out. In the Soviet Union only one type exists, since all the land was nationalised in 1917. The ground rent is an element out of keeping with a co-operative; a kolkhoz paying ground rent becomes comparable to a joint stock company.

Formally and according to the statutes, the collective farm is a co-operative institution in which decisions on tillage, work plans, election of representative bodies and distribution of profits rest with the members. If that were carried out in practice it would represent an optimum form of large-scale enterprise adapted to the specific conditions of agricultural production: maximum economies of scale combined with the producers' self-interest, which ought to obviate the need for expensive supervision. What actually happened was that the collective farms were completely integrated with the general system of economic planning, in which all directives were issued by the central authorities and there was no chance of raising objections. The fulfilment of the planned quotas was overseen by the appointed chairmen and by officials who did not necessarily come from the village and who were in any case controlled by the Party. By these methods plan fulfilment and deliveries of the basic foodstuffs were safeguarded, but the co-operative atmosphere, the identification of the members with the enterprise, and incentives to high performance, initiative and supervision at local level were destroyed.

The collective farm places a large proportion of the risks of farming on the shoulders of the members. So long as the agricultural sector comprises the great majority of the population, that is economically unavoidable. Were it otherwise, the government would lose its capacity to finance industrial development.

(ii)   THE HOUSEHOLD PLOT

Beside the main, co-operative production unit, the household plots of the collective farmers continue to play a part. In the Soviet Union the household plots range from 0·6 to 1·2 acres (0·25 to 0·5 ha), supporting one to two cows, two calves, 12 to 25 sheep, etc.

The private sector is of substantial significance in the Soviet Union: 45 per cent of the potato and vegetable acreage are farmed privately, and the same applies to one-third of cattle stocks, including in particular half the cows, one-fifth of the sheep, and half the fruit trees. The collective farmers market their products themselves, sometimes in places thousands of miles away; alternatively they sell to the state purchasing organisations, which pay higher prices for these products than the kolkhoz receives for its compulsory deliveries.

The collective farmers and members of their families work partly in the kolkhoz, partly on the household plot. In 1959 9·9 million members of families worked on those privately farmed plots. At the outset, the kolkhoz grows only field crops; vegetable and fruit growing and, above all, animal husbandry, including dairy farming, remain predominantly in private hands.

The household plot has the following tasks:

(a)   supplementing the output of the large-scale units by supplying products which cannot, or cannot yet, be produced by mechanical methods;
(b)   diversification of market supplies by deliveries to local and regional markets;
(c)   utilisation of surplus labour at times when the seasonal demand for labour is lowest;
(d)   utilisation of surplus fodder crops produced by the collective farm;
(e)   additional income for the families of kolkhoz members, intended to safeguard their standard of living (see Fig. 2.4).

By utilising the factors of production and assuring food supplies for the population, the household plot complements the big socialist farms, with which it lives in a sort of symbiosis, even while competing with them for the factors of production. If the kolkhoz remunerates the labour of its members at a low rate, the individual member will seek to concentrate more on farming his household plot and to supplement his store of feed-

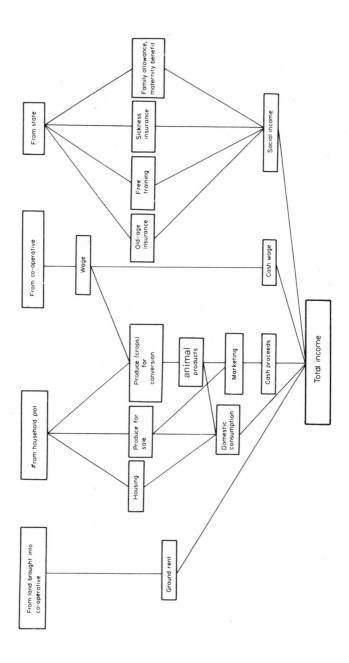

Fig. 2.4   Income of co-operative peasant

34

ing stuffs from the collectively grown fodder crops. In that way the household plot is the last refuge of the members in their confrontations with a strict and unscrupulous planning bureaucracy and an unfeeling kolkhoz chairman.

The attitude of the government and the Communist Party towards the household plot has varied widely from period to period. At times there was a movement towards abolishing the household plot altogether, or at any rate curtailing it severely. At other times the household plot was in official favour and its extension was encouraged. At present the latter view is predominant. Today it is understood and appreciated that the household plot can discharge functions complementary to the basic planning. Previously, official 'Marxist' theory in the Soviet Union maintained that the household plot ought to be abolished, at least gradually and in the long term. Now it is recognised and accepted. Its abolition would create a difficult economic problem. The factors of production (farm buildings, areas of marginal land) would be devalued at a stroke. Large new public investments would become necessary. Underemployment would turn into unemployment, or the wages funds of the collective farms would have to be substantially increased. If the household plot is to be abolished at some distant future stage, it can only be done step by step, to an extent depending on the parallel development of technological progress, accompanied by the production of more agricultural machinery and the supply of more, as well as more varied, goods to the urban and rural markets.

The ruling official view has been formulated as follows in the theoretical journal of the CPSU:

> In its decision on the household plot the Congress of Collective Farmers has taken account of the actual conditions and recognised the household plot as useful. It was decided not to break with a practice established over decades and to take the peculiarities of the individual republics and of the various ecological and economic zones into account. Now and in the future the collective farmer's household plot has an important part to play in expanding the general resources governing the country's food supplies. It would be a great mistake to ignore this fact. The model statutes of the kolkhozes have set a standard for the delimitation of the household plots, which will effectively prevent their unchecked growth on the one hand and their decline on the other (*Kommunist* 17, 1969).

Collective farming, then, does not involve the complete integration of all the elements of production — as it does in the kibbutz, for example —

but a symbiosis between co-operative and private-enterprise elements. The same can be said about the West German co-operatives, except that the relative importance of the two elements is here reversed. In West Germany it is the individual farm that matters most, and the co-operatives are in general only secondary institutions set up for the purpose of supporting and complementing the individual production units of the members. In the Soviet Union the co-operative farm matters most, with the household plots playing no more than an auxiliary part.

In view of this mutual complementarity the productivity of Soviet collective agriculture is difficult to measure, and comparisons with agricultural productivity in the USA or West Germany make no sense. In assessing productivity per unit area, consideration must be given to the climate, the use of chemical fertilisers and the supply of fodder crops to the household plots. In assessing labour productivity, the factors to be considered are: intermittent employment owing to the predominance of arable farming, with full-year working feasible only for small groups (engaged, for instance, in repairing machines), on both climatic and operational grounds. The relative shares of the co-operative and private components in the total income of the collective farmer cannot be disentangled, since the produce supplied to the household plot by the kolkhoz by way of renumeration in kind enters into the home consumption of the individual household as well as into its stock-raising activities and its private marketing efforts.

Despite the relatively high level of mechanisation of tillage, productivity remains low, because the private sector does not work productively and the peasants spend much time on their trips to market. As is invariably the case before the introduction of intensive animal husbandry with a high conversion factor and before the existence of local industries, the agricultural population is underemployed. In January 1959, for example, 18 million persons were employed in the kolkhozes, as against 30·7 million in July of the same year. In 1967 men were employed for periods varying from 158 days during the whole year in the central black-earth region, to 254 days in the north-west. For women the corresponding figure varied from 184 to 262 days. The variations reflect the relative share of animal production in the various regions; also, women do more work in the animal sheds than men.

(iii) STATE FARMS

The state farms are the second pillar of the communist agrarian structure. They require no special explanation in terms of agrarian sociology. Their acreage increased particularly steeply during the years 1956 to 1961; that is to say, during the virgin lands campaign. The number of state farms has constantly risen in relation to their total area: a fact which indicates a trend towards decentralisation and a reduction in the size of the production units. While arable farming, in terms of acreage, increased nearly eightfold, cattle raising rose more than tenfold, as shown in Table 2.4.

Table 2.4

Development of state farms

(a) *Absolute values*

Year	Number	Labour force ('000)[1]	Arable land (million ha)	Cattle (million)
1940	4,159	1,373	11·6	2·5
1953	4,857	1,844	15·2	3·4
1958	6,002	3,835	37·1	8·2
1962	8,570	6,893	86·7	20·9
1964	10,078	7,268	87·3	22·2
1968	13,398	7,459	89·2	25·8
1971	15,502	9,212	94·4	30·7

(b) *Average per state farm*

Year	Labour force	Arable land ('000 ha)	Cattle	Pigs	Tractors (at 15 hp)
1928	134	0·8	97	31	2
1940	330	2·8	592	459	24
1950	334	2·6	562	500	26
1953	380	3·1	700	—	—
1958	639	8·7	1,370	1,355	90
1962	804	10·1	2,439	—	—
1964	721	8·6	2,201	1,144	121
1968	623	6·7	1,927	865	116
1971	594	6·1	1,980	1,200	125

[1] Annual average.

Sources: Strauss; Rochlin and Hagemann; *Narodnoe khozyaystvo.*

Table 2.5

Percentage shares of the sectors, 1950 and 1968

	Kolkhozes	Sovkhozes	Social sector, total 1950	Household plots	Kolkhozes	Sovkhozes	Socialist sector, total 1968	Household plots
Land								
Agricultural land	79	19	98	2	40	58	98	2
Sown area	83	11	94	6	50	47	97	3
Livestock								
Cattle	49	7	56	44	42	30	72	28
Pigs	50	15	65	35	44	30	74	26
Sheep	74	11	85	15	40	39	79	21
Goats	46	1	47	53	11	6	17	83
Vegetable products								
Grain	82	11	93	7	53	45	98	2
Sunflower	91	5	96	4	80	18	98	2
Potatoes	23	4	27	73	24	14	38	62
Sugar beet	97	3	100	–	92	8	100	–
Vegetables	45	11	56	44	26	33	59	41
Cotton	96	4	100	–	80	20	100	–
Fruit[1]	20	13	33	67	29	26	55	45
Grapes[1]	51	25	76	24	37	43	80	20
Animal products								
Meat	22	11	33	67	32	30	62	38
Milk	19	6	25	75	35	27	62	38
Eggs	9	2	11	89	14	26	40	60
Wool	67	12	79	21	39	41	80	20

[1] 1959 instead of 1950.

Sources: Wädekin; Brunner and Westen; and others.

Apart from the sovkhozes producing staple foods for the market, there are two further groups of state enterprises in agriculture:

(i) auxiliary farms for factory canteens, sanatoria and army units — these are exempt from quota deliveries to the state;
(ii) experimental and training establishments.

Both were last included together in detailed official statistics in 1963, when they comprised 85,555 farms with an average of 701 acres (284 ha) of agricultural land each. According to the overall figures for 1967, they accounted then for 4·6 per cent of the agricultural land, but for over 14 per cent of the total horse-power capacity. So they are well equipped.

The relative shares of the three sectors have slightly shifted over the years (see Table 2.5). In absolute terms, the kolkhozes have retained almost their entire agricultural area, but their share declined owing to the vast tracts of virgin lands brought into cultivation by the state farms. The share of the private sector in the total agricultural land is very small, but its share in animal production is still important, declining in the case of cattle and pigs, increasing in respect of sheep and goats. Their share in industrial crops (sugar beet, cotton) is negligible; in crops reaped with combine harvesters very small; in the case of labour-intensive crops still relatively high. While declining, the share of the private sector in animal production still represents a significant contribution to market supplies, and is at any rate substantially higher than its share in agricultural land. There is in fact no correlation between acreage and livestock holdings. This is a case of production independent of acreage, supported by fodder supplies from the large-scale enterprise. The two principal forms of large-scale agricultural enterprise — the kolkhoz and sovkhoz — vary greatly in relative importance from region to region. The kolkhozes predominate in the long-settled densely populated and intensively exploited lands, whereas sovkhozes hold the major share of agricultural land in, above all, the recently settled regions, where the prevailing ecological and economic conditions are marginal (see Fig. 2.5).

(iv) THE MACHINE AND TRACTOR STATIONS (MTS)

Collectivisation went hand in hand with the establishment of the machine and tractor stations. The entire technical equipment assigned to the collective sector, as well as the staffs of tractor drivers, mechanics, etc., were concentrated there. The collective farms had to negotiate with the machine and tractor stations about every tillage job. The payment for contract work was in kind. In that way the scant material was used to the best

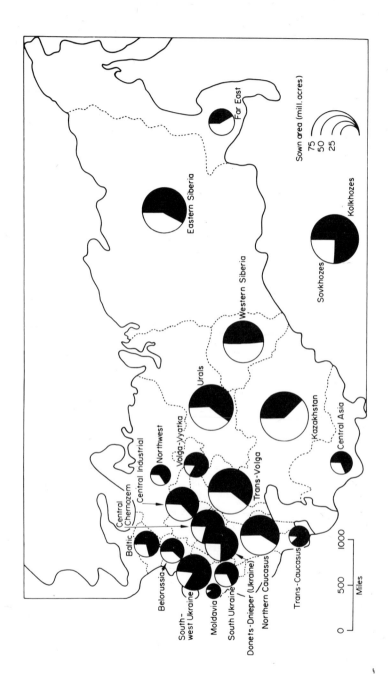

Fig. 2.5 Soviet Union: share of state farms and collective farms in regions (Source: Taaffe, *Atlas of Soviet Affairs*)

advantage, the few technically qualified people were deployed according to plans drawn up at higher levels, and staple products were collected for the state. The MTS also had advisory and planning functions. In 1958 all the stations were disbanded, their equipment was sold off to the kolkhozes and their personnel were integrated with the collective farms. A limited number of stations was retained to cope with special tasks, such as repair of heavy machinery, hiring out of, and contract work with, new machines designed for operating over vast areas. The winding up of the MTS had become possible at this stage as more agricultural machines were now being manufactured and could be bought by the collective farms, thus dispensing with the need for administrative allocation. Moreover the collective farms had more experienced and trained manpower than in the past. The liquidation of the MTS had two main consequences:

(i)   improved internal organisation and operational planning of the collective farms;
(ii)   end of compulsory deliveries in kind from the kolkhoz to the MTS in payment for work done.

2.1.5   *Development and structure of the population*

Population growth is substantial, but has slowed down in recent years. There are wide variations in the density of the settlement. The population is concentrated in the west and north-west (see Fig. 2.6). Attempts to settle remote eastern territories require large investments and have so far been only moderately successful. The new agrarian structure engendered rapid population shifts. One-quarter of the population is still engaged in agriculture. The rapid progress of urbanisation has led to an acute housing shortage in the towns (see Table 2.6).

The proportion of workers and salaried employees (inclusive of those employed in state farms) rose from 17 per cent before the First World War to almost 78 per cent in 1967. The collective farmers make up 22·3 per cent of the gainfully employed population. The percentage representing the relative strength of the collective farmers was highest in 1939, since when it has been steadily declining (see Table 2.7 and Fig. 2.7).

Thus three interlinked demographic processes have been at work:

(i)   population growth;
(ii)   numerical decline of the rural and agricultural population;
(iii) social transformation of independent into collective farmers, liquidation of the capitalist class and an independent middle class, increase in the number of people dependent on wages.

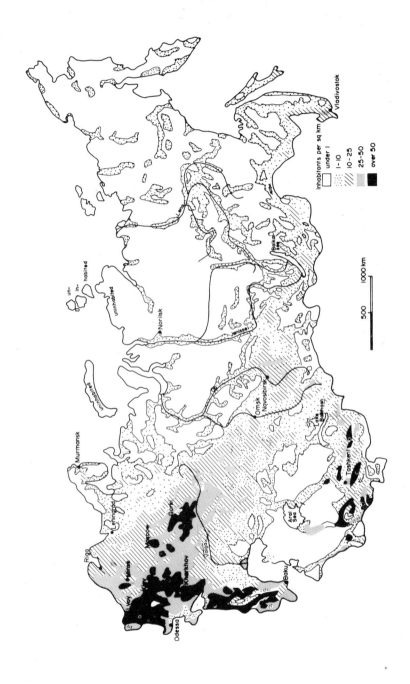

Fig. 2.6   Population density in the Soviet regions, 1965 (Source: Mellor)

Table 2.6

Population growth and population changes — urbanisation

	Population (millions)	Agricultural population (as percentage of total)	Village population
1913	159·2	75	82
1939	170·6	62	68
1956	200·2	43	55
1959	208·8	39	52
1961	216·1	35	50
1963	223·1	33	48
1966	231·9	28	46
1969	238·9	25	44
1972	247·5	—	42

Sources: *Informationen zur politischen Bildung; Narodnoe khozyaystvo.*

Table 2.7

Social change (relative strengths of various strata in percentage of total population)

Class	1913	1928	1939	1959	1967	1972
Factory and office staffs	2·4	5·2	16·7	18·8	} 77·7 {	20·9
Factory and office workers	14·6	12·4	33·5	49·5		59·8
Co-operative peasants and artisans	—	2·9	47·2	31·4	22·3	19·3
Independent peasants and artisans	66·7	74·9	2·6	0·3	—	—
Bourgeoisie, landowners, merchants and kulaks	16·3	4·6	—	—	—	—
	100	100	100	100	100	100

Source: *Narodnoe khozyaystvo.*

The data in Table 2.7 are rather general and say nothing about stratification and income differentials within the two main groups. The technical intelligentsia — sprung from the working class and the peasantry and comprising economists, agronomists, zootechnicians, engineers, mecha-

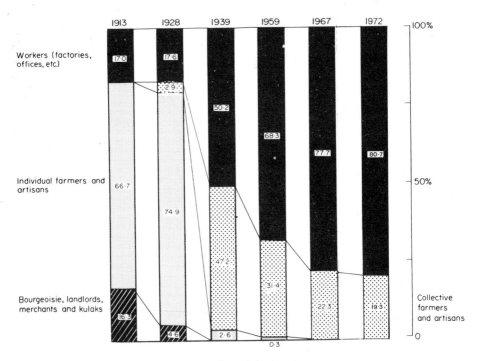

Fig. 2.7   Soviet Union: change of social structure

nisers, administrators — constitutes a numerically small but socially relevant grouping within the agricultural population.

2.1.6   *Agrarian policy of the post-Stalin era and the new economic system*

The new era began at about the time of Stalin's death — that is to say at the end of the period of reconstruction which followed the devastation of large areas of the country in the Second World War — and lasted into the early 1960s, when the introduction of the new economic system may be considered to have marked the opening of a new chapter of Soviet economic history. Changes were effected in four spheres:

(i)   structure,
(ii)   production and its requirements,
(iii) market and price policies,
(iv)   welfare policy for the collective farmers.

44

(i)   STRUCTURAL MEASURES

Size of production units. In the past the medium-sized farms had been amalgamated into ever larger units. Now production units of many thousands of acres may make sense in the thinly populated, arid steppes of Asia, but outside the gates of Moscow market gardening enterprises of 125 to 250 acres are the most economical units. Scientific investigations were launched to ascertain the optimum size. Moreover, no further amalgamations were undertaken; instead, attempts were made to link numbers of collective farms through schemes of economic co-operation and the formation of kombinats (in which the powers of the central administration are limited), and decentralisation was fostered by the establishment of semi-autonomous sub-units. Large working groups were divided into smaller units: the brigade gave way to the 'link' (tsveno). The individual workers in sovkhozes and kolkhozes were given more responsibility. All jobs concerned with any one particular crop or livestock were assigned to particular workers on a permanent basis. These workers were to be replaced only in emergencies.

Changes in the household plot. There was a tendency towards abolishing them, then again a tendency to enlarge them. At present the latter prevails. The function of the household plot as a factor complementing the instrument of basic central planning is now recognised and appreciated. Past theory looked askance at the household plot and wanted it gradually abolished; now its communist credentials have been discovered.

The machine and tractor stations were wound up in 1958 and their machines were sold off to the collective farms. See subsection 2.1.4(iv).

Collective farms into state farms? This transformation of agrarian structure is a most controversial subject. The political-ideological interpretation (as given, for instance, by O. Schiller) regards it as a last step completing the development by which the once independent peasant is to be turned into an agricultural worker employed by the state. A very different picture emerges from an economic interpretation (such as expounded by Weinschenck, Schlesinger, Sakoff, and to some extent Wädekin), which considers this demand as inspired by the wish of the collective farmers, especially in economically weak kolkhozes, to get away from seasonal unemployment in winter and to pass their own risks on to the state. It is in fact the latter thesis which has been borne out by the events of agrarian policy since 1965: the twenty-third CPSU Congress ordered new kolkhoz statutes to be drafted; a confirmatory statement was made by Brezhnev;

and a Congress of Soviet Collective Farmers was held in November 1969, the first in 34 years.

In the past, agriculture was equipped with a minimum of production aids. Deliberately and methodically the scarce investment resources were concentrated on other sectors. For a long period agriculture was not only denied all development finance but actually subjected to disinvestment by the exaction of a financial contribution to the development of the other economic sectors. In the end the stagnation of agriculture endangered the expansion of the rest of the economy. On the other hand, the successful expansion of industry provides the basis for new large-scale investments for the benefit of agriculture: agricultural machines, fertilisers, plant protection agents, buildings, land improvement, supply of consumer goods to the rural population. Thus industry has paved the way for the transition from extensive to intensive agricultural production: less reclamation of virgin lands, more investments in land already under cultivation. In the first phase all the forces of society were concentrated on the transformation of the agrarian structure. The undeniable advantages of large-scale production were overrated. Indeed, as Dumont has pointed out, large-scale production without technology is not industry at all, but belongs to the pre-industrial stage of manufacture.

Communist critics of Stalin declared, 'The collectivisation of wooden ploughs is a fraud'. Perhaps a virtue was made here of necessity, and a theory was devised to rationalise the shortage of productive equipment. Accordingly, the role of technology in transforming the agrarian structure and influencing the attitude of the peasants was underestimated to begin with and subsequently replaced by administrative measures. Today, the significance of machines and fertilisers is recognised and taken into account by communist planners (notably by men like Kardelj). The same quarrel over the relative importance of productive forces versus production relations took place in China at a later date (see section 4.1).

(iii)   MARKET AND PRICE POLICY

In the first phase agriculture was disadvantaged through the price scissors, that is to say price differentials, which were strictly maintained by rigorous price controls on goods sold through official channels combined with the rationing of important products. By contrast, the policy now is to cheapen the peasants' productive equipment and consumer goods, but not foodstuffs. Producer prices were raised by several methods:

(a)   compulsory delivery quotas were repeatedly reduced (since July 1957, the products of the household plots can be sold freely);
(b)   the prices for the remaining quota deliveries were brought closer to the free market prices;
(c)   price controls on non-staple foods sold at the kolkhoz markets were lifted.

One side effect of the improved supply situation was that it prompted many collective farmers to make long, uneconomic trips to market. In summer this practice means lost working days; in winter it is of no economic importance. In 1966 products of the household plots were sold at 7,260 kolkhoz markets with a total sales area of over 500 million square feet; each month an average of 17·7 million producers offered their wares.

The remaining compulsory deliveries were abolished in 1959. The delivery quotas and the fixed prices associated with them were supplanted by delivery contracts concluded between the kolkhozes and the marketing and processing enterprises, which are predominantly state-managed. Lately, marketing organisations have also been formed jointly by groups of several kolkhozes. In contrast to the former one-sided delivery obligations, the determination of quantities, delivery dates, prices and quality is now hammered out in negotiations between equal partners at regional level. Perhaps this will lead to flexible planning without market chaos, instead of the rigid planning of the past, accompanied by delivery chaos. Failure to perform the contractual obligations entails fines on the defaulting side, whichever it may be. Compulsory deliveries at prices fixed substantially below the level of market prices are equivalent to a tax levied in kind. If that method is abandoned some other form of taxation, openly visible and subject to inspection, must be found.

(iv)   WELFARE POLICY FOR THE COLLECTIVE FARMERS

Successive improvements were made first in the assessment, then in the payment, of the trudoden, the work unit. In the early days remuneration for work was paid out only or predominantly after the harvest. Later that method of computing wages was abolished altogether. Gradually payments for work were made more and more frequently, till in the end the collective farmers received fixed monthly payment at roughly the level of the wages of sovkhoz workers. This development depended on an increase in revenue and greater independence of the collective farms. The aim was gradually to introduce a guaranteed remuneration for the working collective farmers. On 1 June 1966, a guaranteed minimum wage was actually laid down for all collective farms. In the past, the wage received by the collective farmer had been a residual payment, entirely dependent on crop yields and harvest results, while all other commitments and items of expenditure of the collective farms had to be settled first in a definite order of priorities laid down by finance directives (quota deliveries, payment of MTS, allocations to the statutory funds of the collective farm). Now wages have a higher priority; the livelihood of the collective farmer is assured.

Social insurance. The free health service was available from the outset for all inhabitants of the Soviet Union. The collective farmers also received children's allowances and maternity grants. However, they were excluded from the general old-age insurance. Instead, the kolkhozes were obliged to maintain funds of their own, out of which old age allowances had to be paid. Gradually the kolkhoz members were integrated into the general old-age insurance scheme. This process began in 1965 and was completed in 1970. Now the collective farmers qualify for old-age pensions under virtually the same conditions as apply to all workers and salaried employees: men receive the old-age pension from the age of 60, women from 55, but the amount of their pensions is only 85 per cent of what industrial workers get. The 15 per cent is intended to take account of the lower cost of foodstuffs and the income from the household plots. It is the intention of the authorities to take action in the future to bring agricultural pensions more closely into line with the rest.

(v)   CHANGES UNDER THE NEW ECONOMIC SYSTEM

Work on the elaboration of a new economic system has been in progress for about ten years, but no clear definitions or comprehensive descriptions have so far been issued. The central planning system of the past was suitable for the initial stages of economic development, characterised by a relatively small number of big, centrally managed projects and a low level of consumer goods supplies. Diversification of production and consumption renders detailed old-style central planning difficult and, in part, superfluous. Planning methods and controls are being refined, but their role is also elevated — or relegated? — to the level of outline planning and long-term trend planning. Decisions of detail, concerning for instance the production plan, are left to the industrial and agricultural enterprises, and in particular to their managers. New prices and basic indices are being introduced. The number of indices is being reduced, and rigid adherence to them is no longer enforced. Indices of physical planning (in tons or

Table 2.8
Land use (million ha, 1 November 1971)

	Land area	AL	Arable less permanent fallow	Meadows	Pastures
Kolkhozes	337·8	204·7	107·2	14·5	79·9
collectively farmed	332·8	200·1	103·3	14·3	79·9
privately farmed	4·6	4·3	3·6	0·2	–
Sovkhozes and other state enterprises	701·8	337·7	114·0	24·9	195·1
Privately farmed outside kolkhozes	3·7	3·5	2·5	0·4	–
Total used by agricultural production units	1,043·3	545·9	223·7	39·8	275·0
State forest and land fund	1,124·1	41·1	0·4	5·6	34·8
Other areas	60·1	20·3	0·5	1·1	18·4
Total area	2,227·5	607·3	224·8	46·5	328·2

Source: *Narodnoe khozyaystvo.*

other units referring to quantities) are replaced by those of indirect, financial planning (turnover in terms of money). The supply of materials to the enterprises is organised as a continuous process. A limited decontrol of prices and production programmes adds to the material incentives of managers and workpeople. Greater flexibility is allowed in fixing wages.

Market elements take effect to a limited extent. The market is no longer looked upon as the antithesis of socialist economic planning, but as a complement and corrective. Only if the market is satisfied, at least in the long term, can there be a question of rational and successful planning. It was the original idea of planning, after all, to ascertain and satisfy the aggregate needs of consumers and society. Economic and financial instruments of guidance are brought into play, while administrative measures are reduced. The new economic system builds on the achievements of the past, while replacing its methods by new ones.

2.1.7   *Production problems*

(i)   FOUNDATIONS OF AGRICULTURAL PRODUCTION (INPUTS)

Over large sections of agricultural land in the Soviet Union the value of production cannot be compared with conditions in Western Europe. Marginal production conditions necessitate extensive exploitation. Yields are correspondingly low.

Irrigable land totalled in 1968 about 25·2 million acres (about 10·2 million ha), of which 24·2 million acres (9·8 million ha) was actually irriga-

Table 2.9

Fertiliser production (in thousand tonnes[1])

	Nitrogen	Phosphate	Potash
1940	789	1,844	526
1950	1,497	2,838	1,015
1960	3,749	5,795	1,842
1965	11,132	11,290	4,547
1970	22,463	16,943	6,187
1971	25,279	18,500	6,741

[1]   Gross weight, not pure nutrient.

Source: *Narodnoe khozyaystvo.*

50

Table 2.10

Use of fertilisers, 1968

	Kg pure nutrient per ha AL	Arable land
Nitrogen	6·3	15·7
Phosphate	4·8	12·0
Potash	4·0	10·0
Total	15·1	37·7

Source: *Narodnoe khozyaystvo.*

ted (i.e. 1·8 per cent of the agricultural land, 4·6 per cent of cropland). In the same year open-ditch drainage systems operated on 17·5 million acres (7·1 million ha corresponding to 1·3 per cent of the agricultural land), tile-line drainage on 6·4 million acres (2·6 million ha, or 0·5 per cent of the agricultural land).

Fertiliser production was neglected for decades, and it was only under Khrushchev that the development of the fertiliser industry was begun. Output has risen, but so far not enough to fulfil plans and meet requirements (Table 2.9). The use of fertilisers per acre is correspondingly low (Table 2.10). However, a comparison with Western Europe is not appropriate here, owing to the abundance of land and the low population density in the Soviet Union. The use of fertilisers at Western European levels would not make economic sense.

Mechanisation was started as early as 1930, but its progress was held up by the needs of the arms industry and by the Second World War. After 1958 large investments were made to increase the production of agricultural machinery (Table 2.11). Production (in thousand units) rose as follows:

	1962	1966	1969	1971
Tractors	287·0	382·5	442	472·0
Tractor ploughs	146·6	177·5	197*	220·1
Seed drills	162·5	219·5	174*	140·6
Combine harvesters	79·8	92·0	94·5	102·0

* 1968

Table 2.11

Machinery stock (in thousands)

Year	Tractors		Combine harvesters	Lorries
	No.	Nominal 15 hp units		
1928	27	–	2	0·7
1940	531	684	182	228
1950	595	933	211	283
1960	1,122	1,985	497	778
1962	1,329	2,400	520	875
1962[1]	–	2,696	845	1,650
1966	1,660	3,233	531	1,017
1970	1,977	4,343	623	1,206
1970 (Plan)	2,490	–	530	1,012
1971	2,046	4,530	639	1,243

[1]   Number required to ensure completion of work on schedule.

Source: *Narodnoe khozyaystvo.*

Agricultural manpower. It will be seen from Table 2.12 that the number of persons employed in agricultural enterprises is high. The figure was 26·6 million in 1971. To see this figure in proportion, the following facts must be considered:

1   Owing to the climate and the insignificant part played by intensive animal husbandry in the large-scale enterprises, there is a marked seasonal unemployment or underemployment.
2   The functions of the agricultural sector are different and more comprehensive than in the agriculture of capitalist societies (construction brigades, repair work, advice services). All the services for agriculture are carried out by the large-scale enterprises for themselves. There are hardly any non-agricultural enterprises undertaking contract work or providing services for agriculture.

During the period 1940–1971 the total agricultural manpower gradually declined by 15 per cent; but the number of persons working in the kolkhozes alone dropped during the same period by no less than 43 per

Table 2.12

The agricultural labour force (seasonally adjusted average) in millions

	1940	1950	1960	1968	1971
Kolkhozes	29·0	27·6	22·3	18·1	16·5
no. engaged directly in agriculture	26·1	25·1	20·1	16·5	—
All agricultural production units	31·3	30·9	29·4	27·5	26·6
no. engaged directly in agriculture	28·1	27·9	26·1	24·6	23·4
Kolkhoz labour force as a percentage of total agricultural labour force	92·6	89·3	75·8	65·8	62·0
Kolkhoz workers directly engaged in agriculture as a percentage of the total work force so engaged	92·8	90·0	74·0	67·1	—

Source: *Narodnoe khozyaystvo.*

cent. In other words, the state farms' proportion of the total agricultural manpower has increased. The great efforts made over the years to promote the general education and specialised training of the agricultural population have resulted in a generally higher level of qualification.

(ii) THE VIRGIN LANDS CAMPAIGN: SOCIAL-ECONOMIC PROBLEMS

Efforts to raise agricultural production resulted only in slow progress in the long-settled areas. That is why the decision was taken in 1954 to bring vast tracts of virgin land in Kazakhstan under cultivation. The intention was to ensure a rapid increase in grain production by extending the acreage. Young people, equipped with new machines, were sent into the region with the task of establishing new settlements and vast new state farms. After several good harvests, the yields fell owing to the vagaries of natural conditions. The scheme was also handicapped by the region's remoteness from the centres of consumption. The campaign achieved a limited success at best. Investments were high, but the results were uncertain and mediocre. Everything had to be built from scratch: roads, farm buildings, dwelling houses, schools, hospitals, silos, storage depots. Tractors and equipment had to be brought in. The extension of the cultivated acreage beyond the limits of established settlements meant that, while agricultural land had been gained, marginal soils had now to be tilled under marginal ecological conditions.

The cultivation and settlement of the virgin lands was not abandoned, but after this experiment measures were taken to advance and intensify production in the regions with established settlements by the increased use of machines, fertilisers and plant protection agents, and by expanding animal production, introducing drainage schemes, and so on. In the course of the virgin lands campaign the area of the state farms was substantially increased. This was due above all to the cultivation of new lands, and only to a lesser extent, if at all, to the liquidation of collective farms and their conversion into state farms. As can be seen from Table 2.13, the yields in

Table 2.13

Results of the virgin lands campaign, 1954—1958

	USSR (total)		Virgin lands		Remainder	
	1953	1958	1953	1958	1953	1958
Sown area						
(million ha)						
Wheat	48·3	66·6	20·8	43·5	27·5	23·1
Grain (total)	106·7	125·1	36·7	60·1	70·0	65·0
Other crops	50·5	70·5	11·3	20·6	39·2	49·9
Total	157·2	195·6	48·0	80·7	109·2	114·9
Gross production						
(million tonnes)						
Wheat	41·3	76·6	15·9	43·3	25·4	33·3
Grain (total)	82·5	141·2	26·9	58·4	55·6	82·8
Yields (q per ha)						
Wheat	8·6	11·5	7·7	10·0	9·2	14·4
Grain (total)	7·8	11·3	7·3	9·7	7·9	12·6

Source: Strauss.

the virgin land regions were lower than in the rest of the Soviet Union, and so depressed the average.

Despite the large investments and the tremendous human exertion involved, this campaign can be justified economically, at least in the long run. In the regions with old-established settlements, planning can to a certain extent draw on existing assets — farm buildings, dwelling houses, drainage installations and the whole infrastructure — accumulated by peasant investment over the centuries. But it is in most cases difficult to extend the agricultural area, because of the shortage of land and existing user rights. In order to modernise and intensify production, an administrative and advisory apparatus is required, and this finds itself face to face with the peasant masses who are attached to their ancient customs and age-old experience and who resist rapid innovation and quick changes. If production rises, the additional produce reaches the market only slowly and in part, the remainder being diverted to higher local consumption, and partly to the household plots. In the virgin land territories, on the other hand, new planning cannot benefit from the fruits of former investment, but neither is it hamstrung by long-standing user rights and the rigidity of an established social structure. Once the large investments have been made, production can be rapidly increased, and there is no difficulty in ensuring that all of it reaches the market. Thus the 'incubation period' from new investments to increased market deliveries can be considerably shortened, though at some economic cost. Cultivation of new lands, therefore, is a venture more easily embarked upon in rich and highly developed economies.

(iii) PRODUCTION TRENDS

In arable farming, acreages were substantially increased (see Table 2.14). Spring wheat ranks before winter wheat in terms of acreage (119 as against 44·5 million acres; 48·2 as against 18·0 million ha). This results in low average wheat yields. Winter rye is still an important crop, with an acreage of 30·1 million acres (12·2 million ha). Substantial increases have been registered in the acreages of new industrial crops and of fodder crops. Yields have increased gradually, but are still mediocre by Western European standards. It must be borne in mind, however, that average figures for the Soviet Union as a whole are of limited value. In the densely populated regions yields are likely to be far above the average. Differences in yields are no doubt as wide within the Soviet Union as they are between Western Europe and the Soviet Union as a whole.

In animal husbandry progress has been slow in overcoming the conse-

Table 2.14

Trends of agricultural production and use of means of production

	1913	1940	1950	1960	1968	1971
Crop farming (million ha)						
Grain	104·6	110·7	102·9	115·6	121·5	117·9
Commercial crops (total)	4·9	11·8	12·2	13·1	14·6	14·3
cotton	0·7	2·1	2·3	2·2	2·5	2·8
sugar beet	0·7	1·2	1·3	3·0	3·6	3·3
sunflower	1·0	3·5	3·6	4·2	4·9	4·5
Potatoes	4·2	7·7	8·6	9·1	8·3	7·9
Fodder crops	3·3	18·1	20·7	63·1	60·7	65·2
All crops	118·2	150·6	146·3	203·0	207·0	207·3
Gross production (million tonnes)						
Grain	86·0	95·6	81·2	125·5	169·5	181·2
Sugar beet	11·3	18·0	20·8	57·7	94·3	72·2
Potatoes	31·9	76·1	88·6	84·4	101·6	92·6
Yields (q per ha)						
Grain	8·2	8·6	7·9	10·9	14·0	15·4
Sugar beet	168	146	159	191	266	219
Potatoes	76	99	104	92	123	117

56

	1916	1941	1951	1961	1968	1972
Animal production						
Meat (million tonnes)	5·0	4·7	4·9	8·7	11·6	13·3
Milk (million tonnes)	29·4	33·6	35·3	61·7	82·3	83·2
Eggs ('000 million)	11·9	12·2	11·7	27·4	35·7	45·1
Milk yield per cow (kg per year)	982	1,185	1,370	1,779	2,033	2,281
Means of production						
Chemical fertilisers (million tonnes)	0·2	3·2	5·4	11·4	36·2	50·5
Pure nutrient (kg per ha arable)	0·03	3·7	7·3	12·2	37·7	—
Tractors ('000)	27[1]	531	595	1,122	1,821	2,046
Livestock (millions)						
Cattle	58·4	54·8	57·1	75·8	95·1	102·4
cows	28·8	28·0	24·3	34·8	41·2	41·2
Pigs	23·0	27·6	24·4	58·7	49·0	71·4
Sheep	89·7	80·0	82·6	133·0	138·7	139·9
Horses	—	—	13·8	9·9	8·0	7·3

[1] 1928.

Sources: ADSL, after *Ökonomik der Landwirtschaft* no. 11, 1967; *Agriculture of the Soviet Union*; Schinke; *Narodnoe khozyaystvo*.

57

Table 2.15

Demand for, and production of, selected agricultural products in 1961–1963 with estimates for 1975 (in million tonnes)

	Total demand				Domestic production			
	1961–63	1975 (high)	(low)	Average percentage increase per year	1961–63	1975 (high)	(low)	Average percentage increase per year
Grain[1]	95·4	126·3	124·6	2·1	98·5	137·2	127·7	2·3
Sugar	8·0	12·3	11·7	3·2	6·3	12·0	12·0	5·1
Cotton	1·33	1·61	1·53	2·8	1·59	2·37	2·28	6·5
Fats and oils	3·7	6·3	5·9	4·1	3·75	6·2	5·8	3·7
Meat[2]	7·46	11·6	11·0	3·2	7·46	10·9	10·4	2·8
Milk[3]	62·0	85·2	85·2	2·5	63·3	87·1	87·1	2·5
Eggs	1·63	2·4	2·3	2·8	1·62	2·4	2·3	2·8
Wool	0·25	0·38	0·38	3·3	0·23	0·42	0·39	4·6

[1] Including rice.
[2] Not including offals.
[3] Not including butter (recorded under 'fats and oils').

Source: FAO, *Agricultural projections*.

quences of collectivisation, when stocks were depleted by large-scale slaughter. Cattle stocks are gradually being expanded; yields are rising, but still mediocre.

Development of production and demand. The development of production can barely keep up with the population growth and the qualitative changes in demand. Production is still largely dependent on natural conditions. Owing to the low capital intensity of agriculture, harvests are fluctuating from year to year by wide margins. From time to time foodstuffs are imported on a large scale, then again food is exported. According to FAO estimates (Table 2.15), demand is expected to increase considerably up to 1975, especially in respect of products with a high conversion factor. This suggests the need for a steep long-term increase in production.

2.1.8   *Social issues*

(i)   INCOMES OF THE COLLECTIVE FARMS AND THEIR MEMBERS

The cash income of the collective farmers is derived from two sources: from the collective farm and its revenues, and from the individual household plots. Kolkhoz revenues (shown in Table 2.16) have increased more than sevenfold from 1950 to 1967 as a result of the large price increases introduced by the state. The share of animal production went up from 24·4 per cent in 1940 to 43·2 per cent in 1965, and thus continues to be comparatively low. Revenue from sales to the state rose sixfold owing to the large increase of official purchasing prices, but revenues from the kolkhoz markets appear to have been stagnating. There are two possible explanations for this trend:

(i)   incomplete records of turnover;
(ii)   joint interest of producers and planners in understating the volume of such sales.

The average revenue per kolkhoz rose during the 27 years from 1940 to 1967 from R 9,000 to R 688,000. In assessing the reasons for this steep increase – in particular the official price increases, changes in the value of money and increases in production – it must be noted that as a result of amalgamations the number of collective farms was reduced almost to a seventh of the figure at the beginning of the period (see Table 2.3). A more direct indication of the trend is provided by the figure of kolkhoz revenue per household, that is to say per kolkhoz family; this increased to almost 15 times the figure in 1950.

The cash income derived by the collective farmers from their household

Table 2.16

Cash income of collective farmers, 1940–1967 (thousand million roubles)

	1940	1950	1953	1958	1964	1965	1967
Plant production							
Deliveries and sales to state and co-operative	0·69	1·81	2·24	6·67	9·8	—	—
Sales at kolkhoz markets	0·45	0·58	0·68	0·97	1·1	—	—
Plant production total	1·14	2·39	2·92	7·64	10·9	10·4	—
Animal production							
Deliveries and sales to state and co-operative	0·22	0·34	1·00	4·18	5·5	—	—
Sales at kolkhoz markets	0·29	0·34	0·70	0·60	0·5	—	—
Animal production total	0·51	0·68	1·70	4·78	6·0	8·6	—
Subsidiary enterprises and other sources	0·42	0·11	0·34	0·78	1·0	0·9	—
Total revenues	2·07	3·42	4·96	13·20	17·9	19·9	24·9
Revenues per kolkhoz ('000 roubles)	9·0	28·0	54·0	195·0	476·0	550·0	688·0
Revenue per kolkhoz household (roubles)	110·7	166·8	251·8	701·5	1,130·0	1,293·0	1,646·0

Source: Rochlin and Hagemann.

plots by sales to official organisations did increase markedly — more than fourfold between 1952 and 1964 — while their income from kolkhoz markets remained static. The share of public trade (sales to official organisations) as a proportion of the total income derived from household plots went up from 15 per cent in 1952 to 51 per cent in 1964 (see Table 2.17).

Cash wages (see Table 2.18) of workers at state farms rose from 1958 to 1964, but reached no more than 70 per cent of the average wages paid in industry. According to a computation by Erich Strauss, the earnings of the collective farmer averaged in 1964 about 80 per cent of the average wage received by kolkhoz workers; that is, roughly 55 per cent of the

Table 2.17

Cash income of collective farmers from household plots, 1952–1964

| | Public trade[1] | Kolkhoz market | Total | Public trade | Kolkhoz market | Total | Public trade as percentage of total trade |
	('000 million new roubles)				(1952 = 100)		
1952	0·68	3·90	4·58	100	100	100	15
1958	2·56	3·29	5·85	377	84	127	44
1960	3·28	2·84	6·12	482	73	133	52
1962	3·91	4·04	7·95	575	103	173	50
1964	3·70	3·60	7·30	544	92	159	51

[1]   Comprises state purchases and co-operatives.

Source: Strauss, and others.

Table 2.18

Average monthly earnings (in new roubles)

	Industry	State farms	State farms as a percentage of industry
1958	87·1	53·1	61
1960	91·3	53·9	59
1963	98·4	67·1	68
1964	100·5	70·6	70

Source: Strauss.

Table 2.19

Average monthly wages (in roubles)

	1965	1968	1971
Workers and salaried employees	96·5	112·6	126·0
Workers and salaried employees in state farms and similar establishments	74·6	92·1	106·0
Collective farmers	52·3	66·2	77·5

Source: Brunner and Westen.

average industrial wage. More recent data are not available. Brunner and Westen, however, have calculated that in 1968 the collective farmer was paid an average monthly wage of R 66·2, an increase of R 14 over 1965. The differentials by which his income fell below those of the sovkhoz worker and those of the urban and industrial worker were calculated at 28 and 41 per cent respectively (Table 2.19). It must be realised, however, that in view of the large regional variations such overall figures for the major sectors of the Soviet Union as a whole have a very limited informative value. They may reflect trends but not real life.

Such very sketchy calculations indicate a threefold social gradient between town and country, between industry and agriculture, and, within agriculture, between state farm workers and collective farmers. Income in kind and the lower cost of food in the village cannot entirely compensate for these differentials. Thus the disparity in the status of the rural population continues, though it is somewhat less acute than it used to be. Official policy strives to end this discrimination against the agrarian sector, but so far has not fully realised this aim. Perhaps it is necessary for some disadvantages to remain, in order to encourage the flow of manpower away from agriculture, a trend that is closely connected with social mobility, social change and economic development. Not until the agricultural population has dropped to about 10 per cent of the total population, as is the rule in modern countries, will society be in a position to abolish the underpayment of the villagers. The elimination of the discrepancy will then become economically possible and socially necessary.

In the early stages planning was inevitably focused on the need to mobilise the factor contribution of agriculture (labour and capital) for the general economic take-off. The effects of that policy are clearly visible; they are still felt by the peasant population even now.

(ii) DEMOCRATISATION OF THE COLLECTIVE FARMS

The dismantling of central dirigism and central controls permits and indeed demands the more active participation of the kolkhoz members, whose share in decision-making had previously existed only on paper. Originally the co-operatives were democratic bodies, and there were formal safeguards to protect that democracy. But the speed and harshness with which the agrarian structure was transformed in the Stalin era led to resistance on the part of the peasants. They were made to conform not by persuasion but by coercion and terror. The spontaneous beginnings of co-operative democracy were trampled under foot and perished, victims of the barbarity of the social transformation. Now official policy vigorously calls for democracy, as instanced by Brezhnev's statement in 1966 and the Congress of Collective Farmers at the end of 1969. Perhaps democracy comes in the wake of rising standards of living and better education. The new generation is free of bitterness. It did not witness the grim sequence of feudal oppression up to 1917, peasant revolution and land seizure between 1917 and 1920, the New Economic Policy in 1920—1928, collectivisation and coercion in 1929—1934. It is able to demand co-operative democracy and to work it, without resentment or psychological inhibitions.

The fact that the peasants did not join voluntarily but under coercion becomes less painful and less important as time goes on. Today's members were born into the kolkhoz. The labour market, now almost free, enables them to leave the farms and forces the authorities to improve working and living conditions at the kolkhoz. Loss of manpower to the towns and the predominance of older age groups among those remaining behind have become urgent problems. In the past nobody could be expelled from a collective farm; the kolkhozes were compelled to keep their members. Now expulsion is to be permitted so as to promote the mobility of labour.

Democratisation has the dual function of (a) giving more responsibility to the members, thus stimulating their identification and interest, and (b) putting the managers on their mettle through sharper local supervision by the rank and file.

(iii) SOCIAL CHARACTERISTICS OF THE COLLECTIVE FARMER; COMPARISON WITH THE STATE FARM WORKER

In terms of agrarian sociology, the kolkhoz peasant represents a special category, as typical of his sphere as the Western European farmers, the North American wheat growers, the share croppers of the rice-growing areas, and the plantation labourers of the monocultures are typical of theirs. The collective farmer works in the ambience of a new technology in relatively large production units and relatively large working groups, not so far in his capacity as an individual worker. Within the limits defined by state planning and direction he has the statutory right to participate in the running of the enterprise. In his social status the collective farmer differs from the state farm workers in several ways, which are summed up in Chart 2.1.

Chart 2.1
Social status of sovkhoz worker and kolkhoz peasant

Aspect	Sovkhoz	Kolkhoz
Employment	more regular, all the year round	more seasonal
Remuneration		
(a) mode	assured, regular wage	originally: residual payment; now: assured income, more closely in line with sovkhoz wage
(b) amount		
in cash	higher	lower
in kind	less	more
household plot	less	more extensive and free
Social security		
(a) health service	yes	yes
(b) maternity grant and children's allowance	yes	yes
(c) old-age pension	yes	originally: only from local kolkhoz funds; since 1970: included in comprehensive state insurance scheme
Vocational and social promotion	more effective	originally: less opportunity; now: almost equal opportunity
Professional representation	trade union	1935–1970: none; now: attempt in progress to establish representative bodies at all levels
Participation in decision-making	not provided for	complete if and when co-operative democracy has been restored

In terms of numbers these two groups are the most important in the socialist agriculture of the collectivised economic systems. Their social status differs in many respects. A third group, numerically smaller but socially of extreme importance, is that of the technical intelligentsia: economists, agronomists, zootechnicians, engineers, administrators, etc.

No data are available about seasonal fluctuations of employment at the state farms. Probably employment there is more even than at the collective farms. Since the effective work load in agriculture is subject to seasonal fluctuations, it means that this 'natural loss' is transferred to the state. This state of affairs provides an additional impulse for promoting the diversification of the work of the state farms by animal production, processing of crops, auxiliary industries, and so on.

The worker at the state farm receives his regular wage, irrespective of the harvest results, in accordance with the collective agreement negotiated between his union and the Ministry of Agriculture. The collective farmer used to be much more dependent on the year's harvest and on the farm management. This changed only in recent years, when the remuneration of the collective farmer was brought more closely into line with that of the sovkhoz worker.

As regards education, vocational training and social betterment, the state farm workers were in a somewhat more favourable position. Having all along been in charge of their technical equipment, the state farms were able to train and encourage their workers, and they were serving their own interests in doing so. The collective farms did not reach a similar position until 1958, when the machine and tractor stations were wound up, and their machines disposed of to the kolkhozes.

To begin with, social security was more comprehensive at the state farms. Their workers and salaried employees were from the outset included in the health service, old-age insurance, maternity and family allowances as well as accident insurance. The collective farmers were at the beginning only included in the health service — even there they did not qualify for the payment of sickness benefit — and they received maternity and children's allowances. Old-age pensions and other social policy benefits were left to the discretion, and the resources, of each individual collective farm, which was supposed to finance those benefits out of its social fund, the maintenance of which was mandatory. After 1965 the collective farmers were included in the general old-age insurance scheme. The gradual narrowing of the gap in social security and social policy benefits will eventually lead to full equality if the relative size of the agricultural population continues to drop to the level of other industrial societies.

On paper the collective farmers have greater rights to a say in the management and production programme of their farm, in the activities of the chairman and the elected committees, in the distribution of any surplus, and so on, than are enjoyed by the sovkhoz workers. Those rights, however, were substantially curtailed through central planning, the statutes and administrative supervision. The sovkhoz worker has no share in the management of his farm; but the kolkhoz peasants and their farms have no one to represent them in their dealings with the state administration, the purchasing enterprises, and so on. There is no peasant association nor any organisation speaking on behalf of the collective farms as a whole and putting forward their views, wishes and demands. Only the chairman can try to discuss the case of his particular kolkhoz with the state administration.

At the end of the 1920s there were beginnings to democratic organisations in this sphere. During the hard struggle for collectivisation they were destroyed. The official thesis was that peasants and workers were working and fighting side by side in their alliance, since their interests were identical. That may be true in the long run, but it is certainly not the case in the short run. However, on the basis of that contention the peasants were not allowed to form organisations of their own. From the point of view of macro-economics, the government's policy on this point paid off. But the social cost was, and still is, high and must not be ignored. A new attempt is being made at present to re-establish some representation for the collective farmers. As for the employees of the sovkhozes, they are members of their trade union and can let the union act on their behalf in putting forward their demands.

The collective farm ought to be democratically organised, with open communication between the elected management and the working members. Official guidelines must be discussed, and the members have to be persuaded to accept them and act on them. At the same time the members should exercise supervision over the leadership and re-elect or dismiss it. In the special case of co-operative production, the co-operative system implies the identity of members and workers: in the co-operative all members work and all workers are members. This leads to the complete identification of the co-operators with their enterprise. Such an attitude is supported and reinforced by economic incentives. But the more the free decisions of the members are circumscribed by state directives and planning regulations, the harder it is for them to identify with their enterprise and to exercise the statutory local supervision. Conversely, a more strongly developed co-operative democracy provides the members with a motivation for improved performance and intensive participation and supervision at their farm.

In modern industrial states the shift of population away from the countryside is effected by the pressure of economic forces and the attraction of industry. In the developing countries it is hardly possible to exert economic coercion, nor is there any scope for offering material incentives. Political coercion acts more harshly, as it is experienced more consciously and leaves the victim no alternative. Perhaps the motivation of the kolkhoz members will now be effectively stimulated by

(a)   training, prospect of rising socially to the rank of qualified technician, higher responsibility, democratic management;
(b)   a modern wage system;
(c)   higher income through an increase in production and the closing of the price scissors;
(d)   inclusion of the collective farmers in the state social insurance scheme.

Since the labour market is being liberalised, young people can leave the farms. Accordingly, work in the co-operative *must* be made more attractive. Underemployment causes some concern. Establishment of industry in the village, diversification of the village economy, closer dovetailing of industry and agriculture, and extension of high-grade animal husbandry are the kind of measures that may eliminate underemployment.

(iv)   AGRARIAN INSTITUTIONS

The changes in the agrarian structure in conjunction with strict central planning were bound to affect the forms of the institutions and the methods and tools of agrarian policy.

Planning. Although no provision is made for the direct representation of the interests of the agricultural producers in the planning organisation, the producers have had some influence on planning decisions in recent years. Decisions both on production and on the allocation of production equipment and materials have been affected in this way.

Administration is rigorously centralised, but operates through two parallel chains of command: state and party each have their own departmental offices for agriculture. Khrushchev's attempt at decentralising agricultural administration was reversed after his overthrow. The tasks of the administration comprise production planning and guidance, checks on performance and deliveries, allocation of production equipment and materials. There is no need for organising advice on production and management problems on Western European lines, as the experts are in any case working in the large-scale enterprises.

Services are mostly integrated within each farm. Since the winding up of the machine and tractor stations, the use of most of the technical equipment falls into the same category. Advice is given by experts on the staff of the farm: economists, crop farming specialists, zootechnicians, mechanisers. No separate organisation is therefore required for these functions. Production and work organisation are planned by the senior officials at both state and collective farms, unless kolkhoz members state their wishes and assert their influence.

Training is highly specialised. There is a large demand for experts; accordingly the number of students is high. A substantial and growing proportion of the people working in agriculture have undergone some vocational training.

Professional representation for the collective farms and their members was abolished at the beginning of the 1930s. Its gradual re-establishment appears to have been taken in hand after the Congress of Collective Farmers in 1969. At present its competencies are still limited. State farm workers are represented by their trade union.

2.1.9   *Assessment of long-term production trends*

The problems involved in comparing economic performance in different social systems are discussed below in Chapter 7. A picture of the long-term production trend of Soviet agriculture as compared with population growth is presented in Table 2.20 and Fig. 2.8.

After a period of great upheavals and severe crises — the First World War and its aftermath, collectivisation, the Second World War and its aftermath — production rose steeply, considerably faster than the population. Whereas from 1913 to 1971 the population rose by 53 per cent, total agricultural output increased by 212 per cent; in other words, output per inhabitant more than doubled. The setbacks to animal production were much more severe and lasted longer than those affecting arable farming. In the livestock sector it took a long time to overcome the consequences of the mass slaughter of cattle that had been the peasants' response to collectivisation. Cattle stocks are on the increase. Productivity in the livestock sector is being improved, but performance so far is still indifferent. Horses are being used on a very large scale and it will not be possible to reduce their numbers substantially until more tractors are available. Table 2.20 clearly illustrates the positive effect which some mea-

Table 2.20

Trends of agricultural production and population of Czarist Russia and Soviet Union, 1913–1971 (1913 = 100)

Year	Crops	Animal products	Agricultural production	Population
1913	100	100	100	100
1917	81	100	88	103·0
1920	64	72	67	98·2
1921	55	67	60	–
1922	75	73	75	–
1923	84	88	86	–
1924	82	104	90	–
1925	107	121	112	–
1926	114	127	118	92·3
1927	113	134	121	–
1928	117	137	124	–
1929	116	129	121	96·1
1930	126	100	117	–
1931	126	93	114	–
1932	125	75	107	–
1933	121	65	101	–
1934	125	72	106	–
1935	138	86	119	–
1936	118	96	109	–
1937	150	109	134	117·6
1938	120	120	120	119·9
1939	125	119	121	–
1940	155	114	141	120·4
1941	–	–	87	–
1942	–	–	54	–
1943	–	–	52	–
1944	–	–	76	–
1945	93	72	86	–
1946	100	87	95	–
1947	140	89	122	–
1948	158	96	136	–
1949	156	109	140	–
1950	151	118	140	114·1
1951	133	126	130	116·0
1952	148	129	142	118·0
1953	148	141	146	120·0
1954	153	153	153	122·0
1955	175	160	170	124·1
1956	201	177	193	125·8
1957	198	196	197	–
1958	227	205	218	131·2
1959	215	221	219	133·4
1960	226	219	224	135·7
1961	230	229	230	–
1962	229	235	233	140·1
1963	209	221	216	142·1
1964	270	217	247	144·0
1965	247	254	252	145·9
1966	281	264	274	147·5
1967	281	271	279	148·7
1968	299	278	290	150·1
1969	280	278	280	151·8
1970	313	302	309	153·2
1971	309	313	312	–

Sources: Strauss; *Informationen zur pol. Bildung; Narodnoe khozyaystvo.*

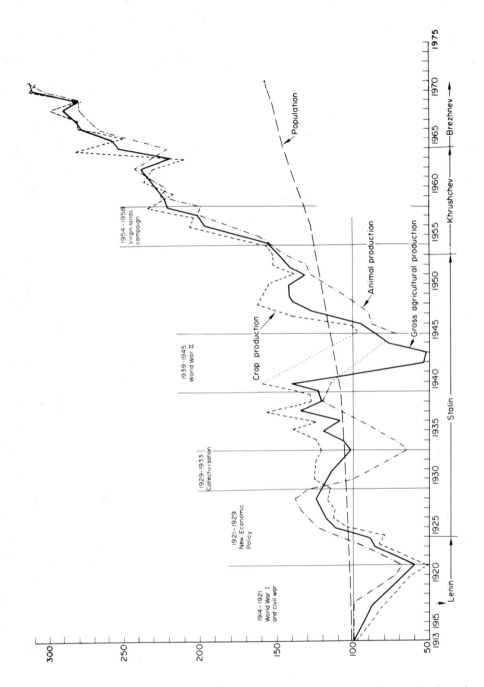

Fig. 2.8   Soviet Union: trends of population growth and gross agricultural production

sures of agricultural policy had on production. Lenin's NEP, Khrushchev's virgin lands campaign and the priorities recently laid down for industries serving agriculture all show up in the production curves. The negative short-term effect of collectivisation on production is also manifest.

Every social transformation is painful and exacts social costs. If it is gradual, spread over a long period of time, and if the price is exacted from individuals, the cost is not readily discernible. It may also happen that production losses incurred as a result of the transformation are outbalanced by a general trend of rising production. The radical transformation of the agrarian structure, embracing the entire agricultural population and effected in a minimum of time, compresses all the negative social and production effects into that brief period, while the positive effects do not appear till later. Whether or not it would have been possible without collectivisation to have brought about a production increase of the same magnitude with equally low inputs in the agrarian sector is a question that will never be settled. The answer will depend entirely on the observer's point of view.

Table 2.21 and Fig. 2.9 illustrate the development of animal stocks. It appears that here the effects of both internal and external factors are longer lasting than in crop farming. Moreover, it is in the nature of things that rises or falls in animal production occur with a certain time lag after the corresponding development in plant production.

2.1.10 *Prospects of structural development*

Three roads are conceivable:

1 First extreme: back to the many millions of undersized peasant farms. This is impossible on economic as well as political grounds. It is a course that would solve the problems neither of production nor of social and economic change. Vast additional investments would be required to equip millions of individual farms with separate farm buildings and separate machines, on top of the investments for fertilisers, etc. Some of these investments would not be rational macro-economically. The establishment of family farms in the Soviet Union would not constitute a return to things as they were in the past; rather it would signal the adoption of a Western European precept that has become questionable even in the region where it originated.

2 Second extreme: collective farms to be transformed into state farms. There is little likelihood of this happening on economic grounds (as ex-

Table 2.21
Numbers of livestock, 1916—1972 (in millions)

Year	Cows	Cattle	Pigs	Sheep	Horses
1916[1]	28·8	58·4	23·0	89·7	38·2
1928[1]	33·2	66·8	27·7	104·2	36·1
1929	29·2	58·2	19·4	97·4	32·6
1930	28·5	50·6	14·2	85·5	31·0
1931	24·5	42·5	11·7	62·5	27·0
1932	22·3	38·0	10·9	43·8	21·7
1933	19·4	33·5	9·9	34·0	17·3
1934	19·0	33·5	11·5	32·9	15·4
1935	19·0	38·9	17·1	36·4	14·9
1936	20·0	46·0	25·9	43·8	15·5
1937	20·9	47·5	20·0	46·6	15·9
1938	22·7	50·9	25·7	57·3	16·2
1939	24·0	53·5	25·2	69·9	17·2
1940	22·8	47·8	22·5	66·6	17·7
1941	27·8	54·5	27·5	79·9	21·0
1942	15·0	31·6	8·3	70·5[2]	10·0
1943	13·9	28·3	6·1	61·4[2]	8·2
1944	16·5	33·8	5·5	63·2[2]	7·8
1945	21·4	44·1	8·8	70·5[2]	9·9
1946	22·9	47·6	10·6	58·5	10·7
1947	23·0	47·0	8·7	57·7	10·9
1948	23·8	50·1	9·7	63·3	11·0
1949	24·2	54·8	15·2	70·4	11·8
1950	24·6	58·1	22·2	77·6	12·7
1951	24·3	57·1	24·4	82·6	13·8
1952	24·9	58·8	27·1	90·5	14·7
1953	24·3	56·6	28·5	94·3	15·3
1954	25·2	55·8	33·3	99·8	15·3
1955	26·4	56·7	30·9	99·0	14·2
1956	27·7	58·8	34·0	103·3	13·0
1957	29·0	61·4	40·8	108·2	12·4
1958	31·4	66·8	44·3	120·2	11·9
1959	33·3	70·8	48·7	129·9	11·5
1960	33·9	74·2	53·4	136·1	11·0
1961	34·8	75·8	58·7	133·0	9·9
1962	36·3	82·1	66·7	137·5	9·4
1963	38·0	87·0	70·0	139·7	9·1
1964	38·3	85·4	40·9	133·9	8·5
1965	38·8	87·2	52·8	125·2	7·9
1966	40·1	93·4	59·6	129·8	8·0
1967	41·2	97·1	58·0	135·5	8·0
1968	41·6	97·2	50·9	138·4	8·0
1969	41·2	95·7	49·0	140·6	8·0
1970	40·5	95·2	56·1	130·7	7·5
1971	41·0	99·2	67·5	138·0	7·4
1972	41·2	102·4	71·4	139·9	7·3

[1]   Within the frontiers of the year concerned.   [1 2]   Sheep plus goats.
Sources: Strauss; Rochlin and Hagemann; *Narodnoe khozyaystvo.*

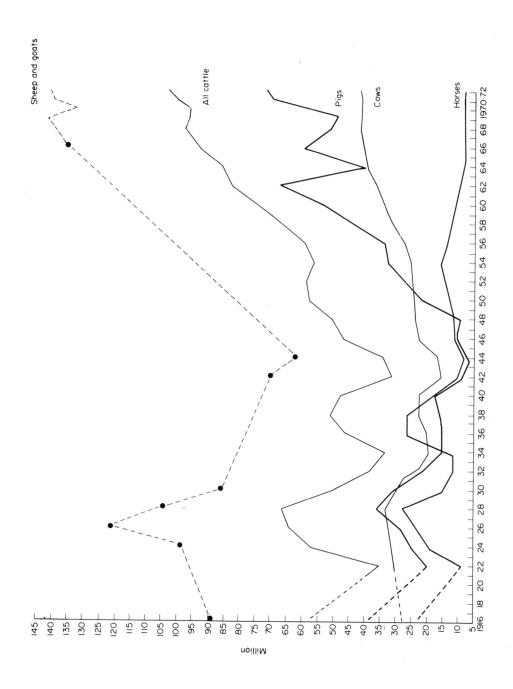

Fig. 2.9   Soviet Union: trends in animal husbandry

plained above). It is a hypothetical policy that plays a greater part in Western than in Soviet thinking.

3 A possible middle way: decentralisation, limitation of central production management to indicative outline planning, delegation of responsibility, priority in investment planning for industries manufacturing agricultural production equipment and materials, fostering of increased agricultural production, changes in work organisation, formation of smaller production teams, adjustment to new technology, gradual democratisation of the kolkhozes. All this adds up to retaining the new structure, while modernising it and providing it more effectively with production equipment and materials.

Under Stalin, the importance of structure was overrated, that of the means of production underrated. Private enterprise elements have survived in the Soviet economic system and are now being tolerated, because it has been recognised that it is not only possible, but also easier to direct the economy through a small number of levers. The planners' tool box, too comprehensive and unwieldy at first, is now being adapted. The planners are learning to confine themselves to the use of the decisive control instruments and have given up the ambition of completely integrating all the means of production into their central plans.

The new model statutes and the other results of the Congress of Collective Farmers held at the end of 1969 indicate that collective farms will continue to exist for a long time to come. Their methods are to be adjusted to changed conditions; the internal organisation is to be democratised. Or, as Soviet theoreticians put it, 'from the point of view of the development of the socialist society, co-operative ownership of the means of production is equal in value to state ownership'.

Several problems remain:

1 Agricultural production cannot be raised at the same rate as industrial output. Industrial development stimulates the demand for agricultural products: more city dwellers means more cash, higher demand per consumer, increased raw material needs on the part of the factories. Market relations and organisation are still rudimentary. The producers are not inclined to deliver more foodstuffs so long as they cannot get industrial goods in return. Many production problems are inherent in the accelerated transition from an agrarian to an industrial state. The building up of industry is followed by increases in agricultural investments. But this is not possible until industry produces the requisite agricultural production

74

equipment and materials; neither is it necessary before the non-agricultural population reaches a phase of rapid growth. Harmonising the interlocking economic processes in the various spheres is an unceasing and difficult task.

2   Underemployment exists on a large scale in agriculture. Further modernisation is liable to aggravate the situation, especially under extreme climatic conditions. However, the expansion of animal production and the associated industry tends to stabilise the demand for labour and to iron out the seasonal fluctuations.

3   Industrialisation of the village. The establishment of industries in rural areas is facilitated by the size of the settlements, but hampered by the long lines of communication and the low overall density of population.

2.1.11 *Summary*

1   Collectivisation means a rapid transition from subsistence farming to market production, but without the market mechanism.

2   Soviet policy is beset by dogma in so far as it insists that the precepts and motivations of Soviet agricultural policy that were rational in 1929 under the special world-political conditions prevailing then must be upheld for all time and all peoples as the universal norm governing the building up of a socialist economy and society. Both the changes within the Soviet Union and the specific circumstances of other countries were ignored when the Soviet model was imposed on those countries after 1945.

3   The structural change was positive and may have created a pattern of farming for the future. The production relations were revolutionised. But their importance was overrated and the requisite means of production were not forthcoming. Not until much later was it realised that modern production relations can only be fully effective and carry conviction if modern means of production are available in adequate quantities. This was a contributory factor in the emergence of disproportions in the economy, so that agrarian policy came to act as a brake on the processes of economic growth.

4   The attempt to enforce the Soviet dogma throughout the European 'Soviet bloc' helped to bring on political crises and disintegration. Punctuated by convulsions and bouts of fever, a differentiated development — including decollectivisation in Yugoslavia and Poland — gradually emerged.

Chart 2.2

Phases of collective farming and their aspects

Aspects	Phase I	Phase II
Material production factors		
Means of production	scant, allocated	ample, bought
Ownership of machines	MTS	co-operative
Operations		
Sphere of operations	exclusively or predominantly arable farming	gradual diversification, high-grade animal products
Operational and crop planning	centralised	within co-operative
Supervision	strict, centralised	gradually relaxed and decentralised
Management	Party official	agronomist
Distribution of proceeds		
Compulsory deliveries	high	progressively reduced, finally abolished
Remuneration	residual payment, governed by work units	guaranteed, regular monthly pay
Household plot	tolerated, held down	accepted, encouraged
Members and kolkhoz		
Membership	*de facto* compulsory	gradually relaxed, now truly voluntary
Resignation	economically impossible	possible
Leaving the village	officially encouraged, but controlled by state	spontaneous, unsupervised
Specialised training	rare	common
Co-operative democracy	repressed	encouraged
Social policy		
Old-age insurance	financed by co-operative	part of nation-wide social insurance scheme

2.2 Modification of the Soviet model in industrial countries

2.2.1 *Czechoslovakia: collectivisation without peasant resistance*

(i) HISTORY

1919 After 300 years of national and cultural oppression Czechs and Slovaks form an independent state in the aftermath of the First World War. T.G. Masaryk becomes President of the new republic. The first agrarian reform distributes a number of large estates of Austrian and Hungarian landowners.

1921 Czechoslovakia, Romania and Yugoslavia form the Little Entente, a defensive alliance against demands of their neighbours for a revision of the post-war frontiers and against the possibility of a future resurgence of German imperialism.

1935 Eduard Benes elected President of the Republic as Masaryk's successor.

1938 (September) Munich Agreement: France, Britain and Italy accept Hitler's demands for a German occupation of vital parts of Czechoslovakia. Chamberlain, the British Prime Minister, claims to have assured 'peace in our time'. The Soviet Union is excluded from the negotiations, in order to divert Hitler's might and ambition against the east. Czechoslovakia is prevented from stating its point of view and is forced to submit to the Munich Agreement.

1938 (1 October) Hitler's armies march into the border regions of the country. Benes is replaced by Hacha and leaves the country.

1939 (14 March) Hitler occupies the remainder of the country and proclaims Slovakia an 'independent state' with a puppet government. Bohemia and Moravia lose their sovereign status and are turned into a Reich Protectorate with a German Governor.

1939 (1 September) Hitler starts the Second World War.

1942 Heydrich, SS leader and Governor of the Protectorate, is assassinated by partisans. In retaliation the village of Lidice is destroyed, all men executed, women and children deported.

1944 Abortive partisan rising.

1945 Hitler defeated; Soviet and Czechoslovak forces coming from the east, and US forces advancing from the west liberate the country; a coalition government of communists and Czechoslovak socialists takes over.

1945–1948 Second agrarian reform, distribution of private estates and the land of expelled German farmers.

1948 The Communist Party seizes power in a bloodless coup.

1950 Beginning of collectivisation.

1951 Stalin's advisers demand purges and show trials; 12 Party leaders are sentenced in a big show trial and executed.

1968 The 'Prague Spring': the old leadership is deposed and replaced by Dubcek, Smrkovsky, Svoboda and Šik; internal reforms on the basis of the communist system are foreshadowed and proclaimed.

1968 (21 August) The armies of the Soviet Union, Bulgaria, Hungary, Poland and the GDR invade the country to put an end to the strivings after modernisation. No armed resistance; the leaders are dismissed step by step and replaced by neo-Stalinists.

(ii)   THE AGRARIAN STRUCTURE BEFORE THE COMMUNIST TAKE-OVER

The first agrarian reform of 1919 had expropriated the property of most of the big landowners, who by virtue both of their culture and their citizenship were mostly foreigners (German and Austrian noblemen in Bohemia and Moravia, Hungarian noblemen in Slovakia). For the rest the German minorities among the peasantry retained their social status and their property. In part they benefited from the land distribution. The new agrarian system, which remained substantially unchanged till 1949, was characterised by small and middle-sized units. Holdings of over 124 acres (50 ha) accounted for 9 per cent of all arable land (see Table 2.22). The agricultural sector was helped by a large number of service co-operatives.

Table 2.22

Sizes of production units, 1 March 1949

Category (ha)	No. of units	Percentage of total	Cropland		AL	
			ha	%	ha	%
up to 0·5	297,046	19·7	50,999	1·0	74,503	1·0
0·5−2	398,299	26·4	315,316	6·1	428,875	5·8
2−5	350,904	23·3	879,135	17·0	1,155,465	15·8
5−10	255,293	16·9	1,332,997	25·8	1,734,704	23·7
10−20	158,874	10·6	1,539,767	29·9	1,996,114	27·3
20−50	35,159	2·3	570,501	11·1	780,174	10·7
over 50	11,489	0·8	468,991	9·1	1,149,924	15·7
Total	1,507,097	100	5,175,706	100	7,319,759	100

Source: *Economic policy... .*

(iii) THE NEW AGRARIAN STRUCTURE

After the Second World War the first steps towards social change were taken with much circumspection. The tenant farmers' rents were substantially reduced and smallholders were helped in various ways by the introduction of differential prices. All German and a large part of the Hungarian peasants were expelled, and Czech and Slovak settlers were sent into the border areas. After that, all farms of over 124 acres (50 ha) were expropriated. During the various stages of that second agrarian reform 5·2 million acres (2·1 million ha) of agricultural land and 4·9 million acres (2·0 million ha) of forest land was expropriated and redistributed, mostly to state and collective farms. Machine co-operatives were encouraged.

After 1948 the Soviet model of agrarian policy was adopted. But Czechoslovakia is technically, culturally and politically more advanced than the Soviet Union. From 1950 to 1961 collectivisation was slowly carried through, without meeting more than moderate resistance on the part of the peasants. Topographically unfavourable areas were exempted. The new agrarian policy was intelligently adapted to the traditions and the natural conditions of the country (see Tables 2.23 to 2.26 and Figs 2.10 and 2.11).

Table 2.23

Development of the unified co-operatives according to type

Year	Number of co-operatives	Percentage belonging to:		
		type 1	type 2	types 3 and 4
1949	2,098	96·1	3·9	—
1950	7,110	45·7	28·4	25·9
1952	8,636	15·7	27·4	56·9
1953	8,388	12·5	8·0	79·5
1954	6,745	—	5·6	94·4
1955	6,795	—	3·2	96·8
1956	8,072	—	2·0	98·0
1957	11,090	—	—	100·0

Source: *Economic policy... .*

To make it easier for the formerly independent peasants to adjust to the new system, four different types of collective farms were introduced.

Table 2.24

Sizes of production units, 1 January 1972

Sector	No. of units	AL ('000 ha)	Percentage of total AL	ha per production unit
State	38,855	2,082	29·7	–
state farms	324	1,428	20·3	4,408
Co-operatives				
(less household plots)	5,859	3,954	56·3	675
Household plots	659,778	287	4·1	0·4
Joint co-operative enter-				
prises	34	0·8	–	–
Peasant farms				
up to 0·5 ha	626,741	163	2·3	0·3
over 0·5 ha	196,201	464	6·6	2·4
total	822,942	627	8·9	0·8
Allotments and holdings				
managed by joint heirs	1,947	68	1·0	–
		7,020	100·0	

Source: *Statistika ročenka.*

In fact, they represented four successive stages in the process of integrating the factors of production:

Type 1: The members did not pool their land holdings, but tillage was carried out jointly. Machines were used partly on an individual, partly on a co-operative basis.

Type 2: The land passed into co-operative ownership; boundaries were ignored during tillage work. Crops were harvested co-operatively, while animal production continued on an individual basis. The proceeds of the joint harvest were distributed largely according to the land brought by each member into the co-operative.

Type 3: Both crop farming and animal husbandry were collectively organised. A household plot with a few animals was left to each member to be farmed as an individual holding. The proceeds were distributed partly according to work done, partly according to the land contributed. Members were paid both in cash and in kind.

Type 4: The integration of production was similar to that in type 3, but

Table 2.25

Social sectors' shares in agricultural land, by region, 1 January 1972

	Socialist sectors			Household plots	Independent peasants	All sectors
	Total	State	Co-operative[1]			
In '000 ha						
Prague and						
Central Bohemia	679	224	436	19	26	705
Southern Bohemia	569	172	376	21	26	595
Western Bohemia	516	291	216	9	18	534
Northern Bohemia	387	258	123	6	19	406
Eastern Bohemia	643	171	442	30	38	681
Southern Moravia	866	181	631	54	57	923
Northern Moravia	509	214	270	25	61	570
Western Slovakia	930	212	654	64	60	990
Central Slovakia	571	179	365	27	231	802
Eastern Slovakia	655	181	442	32	159	814
Czechoslovakia	6,325	2,083	3,955	287	695	7,020
As a percentage of the AL in each region						
Prague and						
Central Bohemia	96·3	31·8	61·8	2·7	3·7	100
Southern Bohemia	95·6	28·9	63·2	3·5	4·4	100
Western Bohemia	96·6	54·5	40·4	1·7	3·4	100
Northern Bohemia	95·3	63·5	30·3	1·5	4·7	100
Eastern Bohemia	94·4	25·1	64·9	4·4	5·6	100
Southern Moravia	93·8	19·6	68·4	5·8	6·2	100
Northern Moravia	89·3	37·5	47·4	4·4	10·7	100
Western Slovakia	93·9	21·4	66·1	6·4	6·1	100
Central Slovakia	71·2	22·3	45·5	3·4	28·8	100
Eastern Slovakia	80·5	22·2	54·3	4·0	19·5	100
Czechoslovakia	90·1	29·7	56·3	4·1	9·9	100

[1]   Less household plots.

Source: *Statisticka ročenka*; author's own calculations.

remuneration was no longer dependent on the land contributed by each member on joining.

Table 2.23 shows how the 'lower' types 1 and 2 gradually disappeared.

A reorganisation of the united agricultural co-operatives was started in 1959. It involved the establishment of larger units by amalgamation, a

81

Table 2.26

The agricultural labour force according to sectors and regions, 1 February 1970

| | Permanently employed | | | | Independent peasants | Seasonal helpers on co-operatives and peasant farms |
	Total	State sector total	State farms	Unified co-operatives		
Number of workers						
Prague	1,965	1,932	1,175	–	33	395
Central Bohemia	111,266	32,913	25,264	75,320	3,033	44,037
Southern Bohemia	83,110	21,044	13,025	56,244	5,822	19,509
Western Bohemia	61,881	28,292	16,676	30,860	2,729	11,433
Northern Bohemia	52,827	30,278	23,824	21,309	1,240	38,504
Eastern Bohemia	111,141	24,333	14,425	81,045	5,763	42,179
Southern Moravia	171,588	29,605	17,250	134,218	7,765	161,615
Northern Moravia	94,648	26,709	18,400	55,176	12,763	101,830
Western Slovakia	179,542	36,356	21,094	132,439	10,747	164,498
Central Slovakia	134,367	16,856	12,863	58,314	59,197	150,645
Eastern Slovakia	130,018	18,938	14,011	72,754	38,326	66,608
Czechoslovakia	1,132,353	267,256	178,007	717,679	147,418	801,253

As a percentage of the total regular agricultural labour force in each region

Prague	98·3	59·8	—	1·7
Central Bohemia	29·6	22·7	67·7	2·7
Southern Bohemia	25·3	15·7	67·7	7·0
Western Bohemia	45·7	26·9	49·9	4·4
Northern Bohemia	57·3	45·1	40·3	2·4
Eastern Bohemia	21·9	13·0	72·9	5·2
Southern Moravia	17·3	10·1	78·2	4·5
Northern Moravia	28·2	19·4	58·3	13·5
Western Slovakia	20·2	11·7	73·8	6·0
Central Slovakia	12·5	9·6	43·4	44·1
Eastern Slovakia	14·6	10·8	55·9	29·5
Czechoslovakia	23·6	15·7	63·4	13·0

Source: *Statisticka ročenka*; author's own calculations.

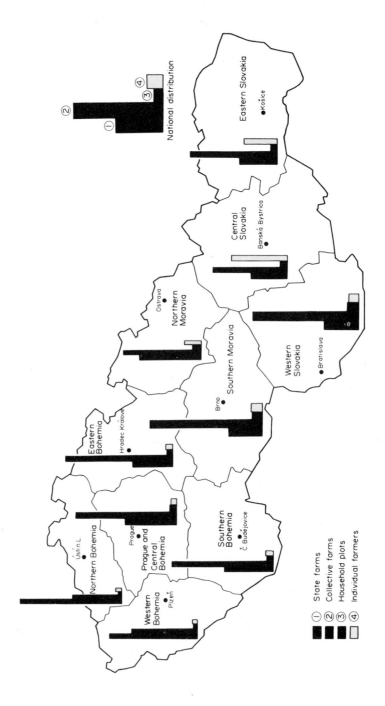

Fig. 2.10   Czechoslovakia: share of social sectors in agricultural land in the regions, 1970

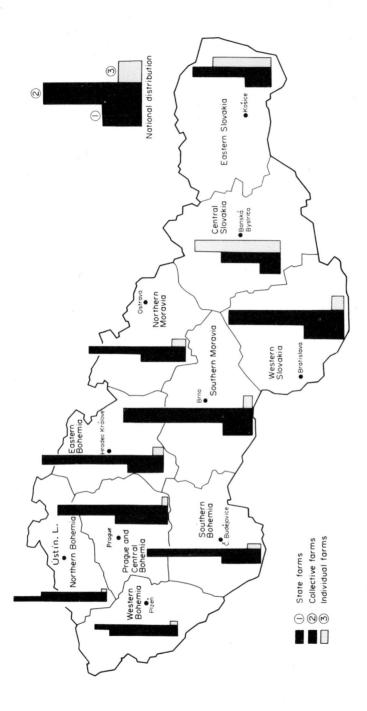

Fig. 2.11   Czechoslovakia: share of social sectors in the agricultural labour force in the regions, 1970

85

decrease in membership figures and, to a minor extent, transfer of land to state farms (see Table 2.27 and Fig. 2.12). State farms were established especially in thinly populated areas, notably border areas from which national minorities had been expelled after 1945.

Table 2.27

The unified agricultural co-operatives, 1955–1971 (end of year figures)

	1955	1959	1960	1965	1971
Number	6,795	12,560	10,816	6,704	5,871
AL, including household plots ('000 ha)	1,947	4,793	4,903	4,277	4,241
Percentage of total AL	26·7	63·8	67·5	60·2	60·4
Membership	329,500	970,100	994,400	877,500	876,245
Regular labour force	327,700	909,600	878,600	725,900	715,770[1]
AL per permanent worker (ha)	6·0	5·3	5·6	5·9	5·9[1]
AL per co-operative (ha)	270	354	420	608	675
Number of members per co-operative	48	77	92	131	149

[1]   1969 instead of 1971.

Source: *Statisticka ročenka*; author's own calculations.

Private sector:
1   Independent peasants are particularly numerous in Central and Eastern Slovakia, the reasons for this being both historical and topographical. Vertical integration with the state farms is being attempted in these areas.
2   Household plots are of varying importance in the different regions as regards their share in total agricultural production and their contribution to the population's food supplies. Their importance is proportionally small in farms with efficient market outlets and in areas where the villages are well supplied, but in Slovakia their share is substantial (see Table 2.28).

(iv)   POPULATION AND OCCUPATIONAL STRUCTURE

The population – 14·3 million in 1970 – is almost stationary, but still growing fairly fast in Slovakia. The proportion of the population gainfully employed in agriculture declined from 40 per cent in 1948 to 16·8 per cent in 1970. In absolute figures the number of those working on the land

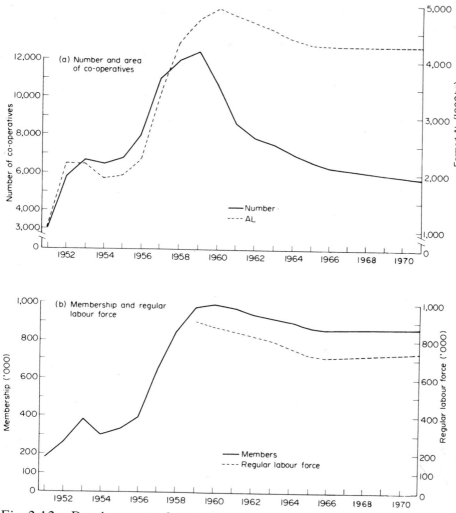

Fig. 2.12   Development of agricultural producer co-operatives in Czecho-slovakia

fell from 1,839,000 in 1955 to 1,132,000 at the beginning of 1970, a decline of over 38 per cent in 14 years.

The process of social restructuring over the two decades 1950–1969, as illustrated in Table 2.29 and Fig. 2.13, was rapid and far-reaching:

(a)   the number of workers increased, both in absolute and relative terms;

(b)   the same applies, more emphatically still, to the remaining salaried employees;

Table 2.28

Percentage shares of social sectors in livestock holdings and gross production

	State	Co-operatives	of which household plots	Independent peasants and others[1]
Cattle				
1950	6·8	11·3	9·7	81·9
1963	21·8	68·2	6·4	10·0
1970	27·4	58·6	4·9	9·1
Cows				
1967	24·7	54·7	9·5	11·0
1970	27·4	55·1	8·1	10·5
Pigs				
1950	15·6	9·6	8·4	74·8
1963	21·7	67·6	12·8	10·7
1967	21·7	54·7	12·2	11·4
1970	22·3	55·4	11·8	10·5
Sheep and goats				
1967	20·1	45·7	14·8	19·4
1970	20·3	44·2	14·4	21·1
Gross production at current prices				
1968	25·1	54·0	9·1	11·8
1969	24·8	54·5	9·5	11·2
1970	26·6	54·1	8·8	10·5
1971	24·9	54·6	9·4	11·1

[1]   Including livestock held by non-agricultural establishments.

Source: *Statistické prehledy.*

(c)   the peasants' share was halved, and four-fifths of those who remain-ed joined co-operatives;
(d)   self-employed professional people and tradesmen were decimated, many of them becoming state employees;
(e)   the capitalists were liquidated as a class.

    Distinct shifts are taking place within the agricultural population. The

Table 2.29

Social structure of the population of Czechoslovakia

	No. ('000)			Percentage of total		
	1950	1961	1969	1950	1961	1969
Workers	6,950	7,738	8,378	56·4	56·3	58·2
Other employees	2,028	3,834	4,275	16·4	27·9	29·7
Small peasants	2,510	484	317	20·3	3·5	2·2
Co-operative peasants	2	1,466	1,191	0	10·6	8·3
Other co-operative producers	0	164	165	0	1·2	1·1
Professions	} 470	{ 9	13	} 3·8	{ 0·1	0·1
Artisans and traders		51	50		0·4	0·4
'Capitalists'	378	–	–	3·1	–	–
Total	12,338	13,746	14,389	100·0	100·0	100·0

Source: *Statisticka ročenka.*

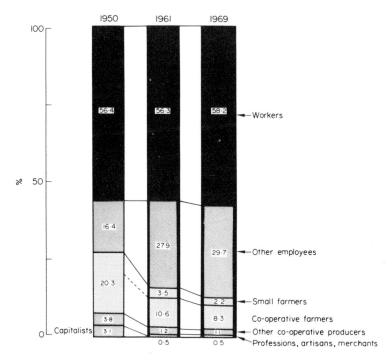

Fig. 2.13   Change of social structure in Czechoslovakia

89

proportion of men is highest in the state farms, somewhat lower in the co-operative farms and smallest among the independent peasants (see Table 2.30 and Fig. 2.14). The growing proportion of those belonging to the older age groups is also more marked in the private sector than in the co-operative and state sectors. That is to say, collectivisation and the social transformation of agriculture are reflected in a number of separate trends:

(a)   population drift away from the land, providing manpower for the further development of industry;

(b)   running down of the smallholdings, which become places of retreat for older working people and secondary enterprises of industrial workers, run by their wives;

(c)   transformation of independent peasants into co-operative peasants and pooling of their production equipment.

The social condition of the small peasant farms in West Germany is

Table 2.30

The regular agricultural labour force according to sector, age and sex

	State sector	Unified co-operatives	Independent peasants	All sectors
Age groups at 1 February 1973 (figures as percentages)				
15 – 19	5·1	2·3	1·1	2·9
20 – 24	10·8	7·0	1·8	7·5
25 – 29	12·3	9·3	3·0	9·5
30 – 34	11·3	8·0	4·6	8·6
35 – 39	11·1	8·5	6·5	9·0
40 – 44	12·0	11·2	9·4	11·2
45 – 49	11·9	13·5	12·6	13·0
50 – 54	9·9	12·1	11·8	11·5
55 – 59	6·1	8·4	11·4	8·0
60 – 64	5·1	9·6	15·9	9·0
65 –	4·4	10·1	21·9	9·8
	100·0	100·0	100·0	100·0
Sex (figures at 1 February 1970)				
Men	153,296	360,581	50,623	564,500
Women	113,960	357,098	96,795	567,853
Total labour force	267,256	717,679	147,418	1,132,353
Men (percentage of total)	57·4	50·2	34·3	49·9

Sources: *Statisticka ročenka; Statistické prehledy.*

90

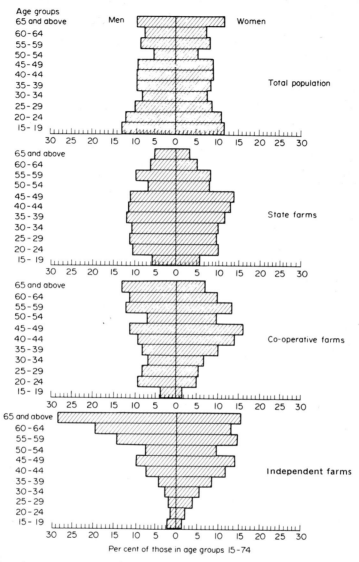

Fig. 2.14 Age structure of agricultural labour force in Czechoslovakia, 1970

reproduced on a large scale — magnified and thus clarified — in Czechoslovakia's unified agricultural co-operatives. But the gap left by the departure of some individuals is felt much less acutely in a co-operative than in an individual peasant farm. Even though the rate of substitution of capital equipment for manpower is low, the co-operatives can maintain the level of production.

(v)   INPUT AND OUTPUT

The utilisation of agricultural land at the end of 1971 is shown in Table 2.31. It will be seen that well over two-thirds of the acreage is cropland, compared with under one-seventh taken up by meadows and one-ninth by pasture land.

The most important crops (Table 2.32) were fodder crops, accounting for over 30 per cent of the cultivated area, followed by wheat with roughly 22, barley 17, oats and potatoes 7 per cent.

Table 2.31

Land use at the end of 1971

	'000 ha	As percentage of AL
Arable	4,989	70·5
Hop gardens	10	0·1
Vineyards	36	0·5
Meadows	961	13·6
Pasture land	787	11·1
Other areas	294	4·2
Total agricultural land	7,077	100·0

Source: *Statisticka ročenka.*

Table 2.32

Acreages of major crops, 1971 (thousand hectares)

Wheat	1,103·1	Fodder root crops	65·4
Rye	233·7	Herbaceous fodder crops	1,532·8
Barley	850·6	Rape and rape seed	51·5
Oats and mixtures	343·7	Linseed	25·7
Maize	142·3	Sugar beet	188·9
Pulses	47·5	Tobacco	3·6
Potatoes	332·2		

Source: *Statisticka ročenka.*

Table 2.33

Intensiveness of agricultural production, pre-1938 to 1971

| | Czechoslovakia | | | | | | West Germany |
	1934–38	1948	1955	1960	1965	1971	1969
AL ('000 ha)		7,548	7,414	7,327	7,160	7,077	13,848
Yields							
Wheat (q per ha)	17·1	16·4	20·4	23·3	24·2	35·3	40·2
Barley (q per ha)	17·0	15·4	20·1	24·8	21·4	33·6	32·9
Sugar beet (q per ha)	286	236	285	346	261	313	458
Potatoes (q per ha)	135	110	127	90	85	139	271
Milk (kg per cow)	2,164	1,334	1,660	1,862	2,015	2,553	3,760
Fertiliser consumption (kg pure nutrient per ha)							
N		4·9	13·4	20·1	34·7	59·5	68·4
P_2O_5		7·9	13·2	21·9	35·8	49·7	58·8
K_2O		5·6	20·1	26·3	55·6	73·2	76·7
N + P + K	22·3	18·4	46·7	68·3	126·1	182·4	203·9
Tractors ('000)		25·8[1]	33·5	74·9	125·4	137·5	1,293·0
AL per tractor (ha)		207[1]	162	72	43	51	10·7

[1] 1950.

Sources: *Statisticka ročenka* and others.

Table 2.34

Agricultural production, 1948–1971

	1948	1955	1960	1965	1971
Agricultural gross production					
(in million Kcs at 1967 prices)	40,084	50,324	54,645	53,013	69,267
percentage vegetable	57·3	53·0	50·6	44·0	45·2
percentage animal	42·7	47·0	49·4	56·0	54·8
Agricultural gross production (1936=100)	73·0	91·7	99·5	96·6	126·2
Vegetable products (1936=100)	78·5	91·1	94·4	79·6	106·9
Animal products (1936=100)	66·8	92·4	105·5	116·0	148·3
Agricultural market production					
(million Kcs at 1967 prices)	15,209	22,813	27,656	29,747	44,710
Gross production (1936=100)	66·4	99·7	120·8	129·9	195·3
Vegetable products (1936=100)	89·5	103·2	119·2	99·2	190·3
Animal products (1936=100)	52·7	97·5	121·8	148·2	198·3
Gross production					
per permanent worker (1936=100)	107·6	156·4	223·6	252·4	353·5
per ha AL (1936=100)	76·4	98·3	106·0	105·3	139·3

Source: *Statisticka ročenka.*

The total area of agricultural land is slowly decreasing. Yields stagnated for a long time and have risen only during the last five years, but are still substantially lower than in Western Europe. The use of capital equipment and materials is considerably lower, but is gradually increasing. Gross production per unit area rose by under 40 per cent from 1936 to 1971, whereas production per head of the permanent labour force more than trebled (Tables 2.33 and 3.34 and Fig. 2.15).

The share of animal production has somewhat increased, even though stocks of cattle, pigs and chickens registered only moderate growth figures (see Table 2.35). The cattle and pig populations have been static since 1966. The annual milk yield amounted to 2,500 kg per cow in 1970.

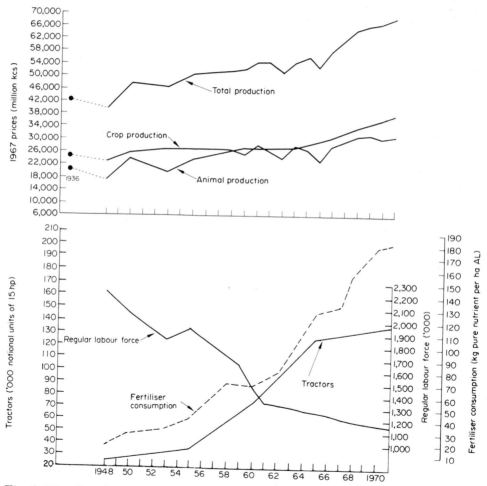

Fig. 2.15   Czechoslovakia: agricultural production and input of production factors

95

Table 2.35
Livestock numbers (thousands), 1948–1971 (end of year figures)

	1948	1955	1960	1965	1970	1971
Horses	628	543	330	188	131	118
Cattle	3,663	4,107	4,387	4,389	4,288	4,349
cows	1,871	2,084	2,047	1,948	1,881	1,900
Pigs	3,242	5,285	5,962	5,544	5,530	5,935
Sheep and goats	459	1,000	646	614	981	932
Poultry	16,393	23,367	28,157	27,752	39,187	38,238

Sources: *Statisticka ročenka* and others.

(vi) ASSESSMENT AND CRITICISM OF AGRICULTURAL PERFOR-MANCE

If the development in Czechoslovakia (Table 2.36) is compared with the rising production trends, say, in the Netherlands or in West Germany, the result is catastrophic. A different result is obtained, however, if Czechoslo-vakia's agricultural production figures are assessed in the light of the aims of the country's economic policy. What happened was that industry con-tinued to be developed, while agriculture was maintained with declining manpower and minimum inputs and supplied maximum factor contribu-tions to the rest of the economy. This relationship made sense during the

Table 2.36
Crop and animal production, pre-1938 to 1971 (in thousand tonnes)

	1934–38	1955	1960	1970	1971	1967–71
Wheat	1,513	1,473	1,503	3,174	3,878	3,196
Rye	1,577	968	895	454	619	643
Barley	1,109	1,291	1,745	2,280	2,851	2,336
Oats and mixtures	1,212	974	1,020	776	902	897
Maize	225	391	572	513	524	481
Potatoes	9,635	7,905	5,093	4,793	4,621	5,431
Sugar beet	4,664	6,152	8,368	6,644	5,832	6,809
Meat		767·9	929·5	1,233·9	1,304·7	
Milk		3,445	3,715	4,650	4,776	
Eggs (millions)			2,267	3,733	3,996	

Source: *Statisticka ročenka.*

phase of original accumulation, but it has ceased to serve a useful purpose in the new phase where industry is able to provide its own capital.

In his criticism of the system, Šik points out that labour productivity in agriculture was raised by drawing off latent reserves of manpower and developing large-scale collective farming, while total output remained almost unchanged. But now there is a shortage of manpower and the labour force has too few young workers and too many old ones. These are great obstacles to production, especially as mechanisation makes only slow progress. Supply difficulties necessitate increased food imports.

In Mysliveček's view, state interference in the management of a co-operative and the imposition of detailed production quotas and delivery obligations cannot be reconciled with the co-operative principle and genuine economic independence. As production enterprises, agricultural co-operatives must seek to maximise their income while reducing costs to a minimum. However, that is made impossible by official regulations, which therefore run counter to the principles of co-operative ownership. This gives rise to antagonisms which are reflected in the attitude to co-operative ownership and in the social position of the co-operatives.

Sagara and Kohn say that the members fail to identify with the co-operative because they have so little say in its running. As a result, intellectual and material performance falls short of the optimum. There is a clear connection between democracy in a co-operative and the performance of the members.

The critique of the system by reformists and other economists within the country is based on an acceptance of the fundamental principles of the socialist economy and planned development. These critics hold that there is a close correlation between economic stagnation on the one hand and the neglect of the social needs on the other, between political pressure, lack of initiative and poor performance.

Karcz and other critics outside Czechoslovakia adopt a different approach. They argue that before the communists seized power and embarked on their economic policy the starting position of the country was equal to that of West Germany in every respect — climate, technical equipment, types of crops, yields, etc. — the sole difference lying in the social structure of agriculture: collectivisation in Czechoslovakia, individual production in West Germany. In their view the lower production and productivity of Czechoslovak agriculture is due to this factor alone.

(vii) SOCIAL SECURITY AND INCOMES

Formally, that is to say as regards the scope of social insurance, the

97

agricultural population enjoys nearly the same terms as other wage and salary earners. Old-age insurance is compulsory for co-operative peasants and agricultural workers. However, the old-age pensions of the co-operative peasants are substantially below those of the workers, because the first peasants to qualify were credited with very few contribution years. Health care is extended to all citizens. However, the co-operative peasants are not eligible for sickness benefit. Accident insurance is compulsory. There is no unemployment insurance. Children's allowances are paid to all families.

It is true that some social problems have so far remained unsolved. Nevertheless, the social and working conditions of the former small peasants have been greatly improved as a result of collectivisation; for example, by vocational training, social advancement, regular working hours, days free of work in animal production, and incomes approaching the wages of industrial workers.

As can be seen from Table 2.37, incomes were lowest in the co-operative farms. On top of the income differential between industry and agriculture, there was a second differential within the agricultural sector between state farms and co-operative farms. Attempts were made in the 1960s to reduce these disparities and bring the co-operative peasants more closely into line with the other groups.

(viii) OUTLOOK

In 1968, when the attempt was made to democratise and reform the communist system, the peasants showed no inclination to return to the old system of individual farming. They feel that their social position has improved and they are aware of being somewhat better equipped with machines than they used to be. The pace of collectivisation was comparatively slow and so gave the peasants time to become accustomed to the new ways.

It appears possible — with all due reservations — to discern a number of trends in agriculture. These are described below.

Fundamental changes in the agrarian structure are not to be expected. Transfers from the co-operative to the state sector may occur on a limited scale where co-operatives are not viable and large investments are required. Instead of continuing to increase the size of production units, attempts are now being made to effect decentralisation by forming estate administrations equipped with limited powers, which are to organise the division of labour in production and the co-ordination of effort in repair work and processing operations. As regards equipment, the various production units

Table 2.37

Average monthly incomes according to economic sector

| Year | All sectors | | Agriculture | | | | | |
| | | | State farms | | | Co-operatives | | |
	Kcs (1)	1960=100 (2)	Kcs (3)	1960=100 (4)	As % of (1) (5)	Kcs (6)	1960=100 (7)	As % of (1) (8)
1960	1365	100	1113	100	81·5	853	100	62·5
1961	1398	102·4	1147	103·1	82·0	893	104·7	63·9
1962	1407	103·1	1181	106·1	83·9	832	97·5	59·1
1963	1409	103·2	1187	106·6	84·2	956	112·1	67·8
1964	1456	106·7	1246	111·9	85·6	1053	123·4	72·3
1965	1493	109·4	1308	117·5	87·6	1102	129·2	73·8
1966	1534	112·4	1396	125·4	91·0	1177	138·0	76·7
1967	1618	118·5	1483	133·2	91·7	1342	157·3	82·9
1968	1750	128·2	1647	148·0	94·1	1492	174·9	85·3

Source: *Economic policy…*.

preserve their independence, buying their own machines and turning to the repair-technical stations only for specialised jobs. The household plots and independent peasant farms are to remain for the foreseeable future. Efforts are being made to bring the small peasant farmers into the system of market production. Agriculture is supplied on a growing scale with industrial production equipment and materials and with modern farmbuildings.

Under a resolution of the Co-operative Congress of 1968, an autonomous organisation of the unified agricultural co-operatives has been formed. This organisation is to negotiate with the government, for instance on problems of prices or old-age pensions, and to hold responsibility for lectures, training and club activities. Furthermore it is planned to set up a marketing organisation for the co-operatives, which is to purchase, market and export the products. Attempts to correct the lopsided age structure of the agricultural labour force are no longer made by the administrative manipulation of the labour market but by the recruitment of young people through special bonuses and allowances.

The agricultural price policy was modified for the first time in 1960, when differential price levels were abolished and uniform purchasing prices were fixed at a level averaging about 15 per cent above the previous split prices. Further changes are to be expected. They are likely to affect the ratio between the prices of agricultural production equipment and materials and the prices of agricultural products, as well as the relative price levels of various agricultural products. The aim is to raise agricultural incomes and improve social conditions for the agricultural population.

A new system of differential delivery premiums and differential taxes has been introduced for the agricultural enterprises. It makes allowance for the more or less favourable character of local production conditions in 142 locations. The tax ranges from Kcs 10 to Kcs 960 per hectare (Kcs 4–385 per acre), the delivery premium from Kcs 0·50 to Kcs 55 per Kcs 100 of market production under contract. As an incentive for production and marketing an additional premium is offered for deliveries in excess of the quantity contracted for.

2.2.2 GDR: resistance to the adoption of the Soviet model

(i) THE MAIN EVENTS OF POLITICAL AND AGRARIAN POLICY

1944—45 The Red Army of the Soviet Union defeats Hitler's Germany and advances from the east as far as the Elbe.

1945 The Potsdam conference of the four victor powers – the Soviet

Union, USA, Britain and France — provides for the severance of the former German eastern territories and the forcible resettlement of the Germans who had remained there and confirms the division of the truncated Germany into four parts. A Soviet military administration takes charge in the Soviet Zone of Occupation.

1945 A land reform is ordered; about 230,000 small and medium peasant farms with up to 49 acres (20 ha) of agricultural land emerge from the carving up of the big estates. Gradually the other components of a socialist social system on the Soviet model are also being introduced: expropriation of factories and banks, central planning.

1946—48 Establishment of Peasant Mutual Aid Associations and machine and tractor stations.

1949 Foundation of the GDR.

1952 (July) Decision of the Central Committee of the SED (Socialist Unity Party) on reorganisation of small peasant farms within the framework of producer co-operatives; after two pauses in 1953—54 and 1956—58, collectivisation is completed in 1960.

1953 (17 June) Workers' rising in Berlin and other cities; the Red Army intervenes.

1956 The GDR joins the Warsaw Treaty.

1961 (August) Erection of the Berlin Wall: end of unchecked mass migration from the GDR.

1963 Introduction of the New Economic System for the modernisation of economic planning.

1971 (3 May) Walter Ulbricht resigns from his post of First Secretary of the SED and is succeeded by Erich Honecker.

1972 The Basic Treaty between the West German Federal Republic and the GDR recognises the standing of the GDR as a state in its own right; two German states with different social systems exist side by side 'on German soil'.

(ii) AGRARIAN STRUCTURE AT THE OUTSET; TRANSFORMATION IN THREE STAGES

The position before the land reform of 1945 — as shown in Table 2.38 — was characterised by a pronounced polarisation of land ownership. At the one end of the scale there were 318,000 smallholders with less than 12·4 acres (5 ha), and at the other 6,300 large production units exceeding 247 acres (100 ha). The position was markedly different in the Western occupation zones. Such regions of big landed estates as remained in the truncated Germany lay mostly in the Soviet Zone.

Table 2.38

Number and size of agricultural production units in the GDR

Size of unit (ha)	1939	1946	1951	Increase or decrease 1939–1951	
				absolute	%
0·5 – 5	317,998	332,026	369,247	+ 51,249	+16·1
5 – 20	188,685	353,613	370,445	+181,760	+96·3
20 – 50	48,548	50,926	43,354	– 5,194	–10·7
50 – 100	8,098	7,618	4,406	– 3,692	–45·6
Over 100	6,292	1,260	941	– 5,351	–85·0
Total	569,621	745,443	788,393	+218,772	+38·4

Source: Kramer.

During the first 15 post-war years three successive stages can be discerned in East German agricultural policy.

First stage: expropriation of big landed estates. The first development was the land reform of 1945, in the course of which 4,278 farming enterprises of leading members of the National Socialist Party and another 7,112 estates of over 247 acres (100 ha) were expropriated without compensation. The expropriated land, together with state lands comprising 4·15 million acres (1·68 million ha) cropland and 840,000 acres (340,000 ha) grassland, constituted the land fund. Out of this fund the land was provided for the rapid settlement of 210,076 resettlers, who received on average 20 acres (8 ha) of agricultural land, 4·19 million acres (1,696,000 ha) in all. Another 670,000 acres (271,000 ha) were allocated for housing and amenities in the new settlements. The remainder was used for the establishment of 540 publicly owned estates (VEG) intended to be, or to become, model enterprises for research, breeding and development tasks.

In its early stages, this drastic restructuring of the ownership of agricultural land was launched on orders from the Soviet military administration. Owners of farms or estates of over 247 acres (100 ha) were not only expropriated without compensation but expelled from their place of residence. Out of the 210,000 new peasants, 90,000 were refugees from the territories east of the Oder–Neisse line; the other 120,000 were landless agricultural workers. The outcome for the agrarian structure was a marked reduction in the average size of the agricultural production unit from

27·7 acres (11·2 ha) in 1939 to 20·0 acres (8·1 ha) in 1946. At the same time the number of smallholdings with under 12·4 acres (5 ha) increased by 51,000, and that of farms with between 12·4 and 49·4 acres (5 and 20 ha) by 182,000 or 96 per cent. Farms of between 49·4 and 124 acres (20 and 50 ha) increased slightly from 1939 to 1946, but their number dropped sharply in the following years up to 1951. This clearly reflected the tightening up of agrarian policy directed against the bigger peasant farms. Privately owned farms of between 124 and 247 acres had their numbers reduced by half by 1951, while those of over 247 acres (100 ha) virtually disappeared (Table 2.38).

The land reform of 1945 was perhaps more than just an imitation of the Soviet land legislation of 1918. It was to some extent a natural political response to post-war conditions in Eastern Germany: there were 4 million refugees, a 20 per cent increase in the population from 1939 to 1948 (slightly more even than in West Germany); major industries were being dismantled; agricultural buildings and machinery had been destroyed, vast numbers of livestock had perished, and the supply difficulties were enormous. Under such catastrophic conditions the land reform made economic sense as a means for maintaining production and raising the degree of self-sufficiency. It also provided employment for refugees from predominantly agricultural areas. In its specific form the transformation of 1945 represented a middle course between the Soviet way and the conservative mentality of the German village population.

Modest as standards and expectations were during the immediate post-war years, the fitting out of over 200,000 new peasant farms called for great exertions, all the more so since the expropriated estates had been depleted as a result of war and occupation. The large-scale dismantling carried out by the Soviet occupying power and the priority of reparations impeded the endeavours of the new peasants to procure the means for running their farms. The shortage of building materials, which was particularly acute, held up the construction of dwelling houses and farmbuildings of every kind. In 1946 the amenities available on the expropriated estates for the 210,000 new peasants comprised 47,846 dwelling houses, 50,850 animal houses and 18,956 barns and sheds. In the first seven years, from 1946 to 1953, another 94,668 houses, 104,235 animal houses and 38,406 barns and storage sheds were built, so that in 1953 over 30 per cent of the new settlers were still without a house and over 25 per cent without animal houses. In this situation the new settlers were compelled to look after themselves and barter their products at unofficial markets in order to obtain scarce production equipment. Thus, the reluctance to deliver agricultural products at the official prices and the prolonged duration of the food shortage are readily explained by the shortage of industrial goods urgently needed by the 210,000 new peasants.

Second stage: reorganisation of the agricultural co-operatives. In the subsequent years, agrarian policy concentrated its attention on the reorganisation of the rural co-operatives. The traditional co-operative movement dealt with credit facilities, marketing of agricultural products and purchase of production equipment and materials. The system rested on a decentralised infrastructure of local co-operatives. Economic conditions in post-war Eastern Germany under Soviet military laws called for a tighter organisation. The GDR attempted to meet this need by centralisation. Central machine hire stations (MAS), later renamed machine and tractor stations (MTS) were established. Most small peasants and a high proportion of medium-sized peasant farms were enrolled in the new Peasant Mutual Aid Associations (VdgB). These were subsequently merged with the local rural co-operatives into Peasant Trading Co-operatives (BHG). However, the new organisation retained the old names or at least added them in brackets. But the influence of the better-off farmers on the old co-operatives was broken.

Third stage: agricultural producer co-operatives. The third stage in the transformation of agriculture was proclaimed by Ulbricht at the SED Conference in July 1952. A growing number of peasants, said Ulbricht, desired the setting up of co-operatives embracing all branches of agricultural production. It was up to the Party to meet those wishes by the formation of agricultural producer co-operatives (LPG). Ulbricht's assertions cannot be dismissed as pure fantasy. Questions had been asked in public as to whether the individual peasant farm was rational and viable in the prevailing circumstances. Up to 1952, the official answer was that smaller farms were producing better yields per acre than large ones. In addition, Government and Party seemed apprehensive lest the establishment of large collective farms be interpreted as a step towards the Sovietisation of the GDR, an impression which the Soviet Union and the GDR were at the time determined to avoid at all costs.

Be that as it may, the Government Party decided in 1952 to reorganise agriculture on the basis of large socialist production units and thus to lay the foundations of the socialist society in the village.

The development of the agricultural producer co-operatives over the years is illustrated in Table 2.39 and Figure 2.16, which clearly show the spasmodic character of the development, and the pauses in the process of collectivisation in the years 1953—54 and 1956—58. It was not possible to ignore altogether the resistance of the independent peasants to the en-

Table 2.39

Agricultural producer co-operatives, 1952–1972

Year	Number	AL ('000 ha)	Members	AL (ha)	Members per co-operative	Co-operative land as a percentage of AL
1952 (July)	59	—	—	—	—	—
1952 (20 Nov.)	1,204	99·3	19,902	83	20	1·5
1953 (end)	4,751	714·2	133,775	150	28	11·0
1954 (end)	5,108	920·8	157,767	180	39	14·3
1956 (June)	6,160	1,400·0	207,000	227	34	21·6
1957 (30 June)	6,295	1,562·4	222,177	248	35	24·2
1958 (end)	7,859	1,897·8	299,173	241	38	29·4
1959	9,566	2,586·1	372,906	270	39	40·2
1960	19,313	5,408·1	901,490	281	47	84·2
1962	16,624	5,472·4	973,854	334	59	85·2
1964	15,861	5,458·4	982,219	344	62	85·6
1966	14,216	5,452·7	985,356	383	69	85·8
1968	11,513	5,416·1	957,410	469	83	85·8
1972	7,574	5,405·1	877,600	714	115	85·9

Sources: Friesdorf; *Statistisches Jahrbuch*; author's own calculations.

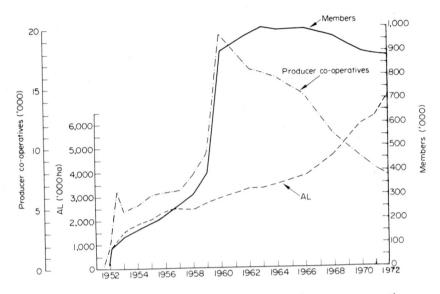

Fig. 2.16   GDR: development of agricultural producer co-operatives

forcement of the decisions of 1952. It may be noted that the periods of respite neatly coincided with the great crises in domestic politics, the first brought on by the East German urban workers' revolt of 16 June 1953, while the second came in the aftermath of the Twentieth CPSU Congress, the ousting of the Stalinist old guard in Poland and the crushing of the Hungarian rising.

Once the enrolment of the peasants was virtually complete, the next step was to reorganise the agricultural producer co-operatives by mergers into larger production units. In 1971 they farmed nearly 86 per cent of the agricultural land. The vast majority of people working in agriculture — 90 per cent — are members of producer co-operatives. Each co-operative has on average 107 members — which means that it comprises less than 107 households — and farms an average of 1,600 acres (648 ha). The size of the production units in terms of area is substantially lower than in the Soviet Union.

The machine and tractor stations were first set up in 1948. Operating on a centralised basis, they were in charge of the use of agricultural machinery at first in the peasant farms, and from 1952 in the agricultural producer co-operatives. Beginning in 1959, they were rapidly wound up and their machines sold off to the agricultural producer co-operatives. A number of them were converted into technical repair stations (RTS) and gradually integrated with the District Enterprises for Agricultural Technology. Thus both the functions and the development of the machine and

106

tractor stations were largely parellel to the fate of the same institution in the Soviet Union (see subsection 2.1.4 (iv) above).

Relatively few data are available on the household plot. In 1971, 5·7 per cent of the agricultural land was farmed privately. Individual live-stock keeping, although it has steadily lost ground, is still of substantial importance for all farm animals. The extent of private animal husbandry is shown in Table 2.43. Beside the socialist sector and the household plots linked with the agricultural producer co-operatives, 11,170 'other agricult-ural enterprises' (evidently private holdings) were recorded in 1968, with an average area of 8·2 acres (3·3 ha). In 1971 the number of self-employed persons and members of their families working in agriculture was put at 9,447. The institution of the household plot is recognised by law and by the statutes of the co-operatives; yet there is hardly a mention of it in recent GDR literature on the subject of agrarian policy.

The publicly owned estates are of limited importance in the agrarian structure of the GDR. As can be seen from Table 2.40, their number barely changed from 1950 to 1972. At first the number rose from 559 to 669, then fell to as few as 500 as a result of mergers. But the agricultural land farmed by them increased from 437,000 to 1,104,000 acres (177,000 to 447,000 ha). Their share in the total agricultural land is only 7·1 per cent. The average area of each unit rose considerably from 783 to 2,206 acres (317 to 893 ha). The number of persons regularly employed in the publicly owned estates is gradually declining.

Table 2.40

The state farms, 1950–1972

Year	Number of estates	AL	Share of total AL	AL per estate (ha)	Permanent labour force[1] less apprentices	Permanent labour force per 100 ha AL
1950	559	177,289	2·7	317	–	–
1955	540	283,243	4·4	525	–	–
1960	669	395,663	6·3	591	78,957	19·9
1964	601	421,757	6·4	702	78,291	18·6
1968	544	433,849	6·9	798	75,998	17·5
1971	500	443,288	7·1	887	73,429	16·6
1972	500	446,700	7·1	893	–	–

[1]   1960: equivalent number of full-time workers.

Source: *Statistisches Jahrbuch der DDR.*

The new forms of inter-co-operative co-ordination, which constitute a further element in the transformation of the agrarian structure, are discussed below in subsection (vi).

(iii) USE OF RESOURCES AND PRODUCTIVE PERFORMANCE

The total area of agricultural land has shown a slight decrease since 1951, from 16·1 to 15·6 million acres (6·5 to 6·3 million ha), or by roughly 4 per cent. There was a slight shift from arable to grassland. Crops and yields are set out in Table 2.41. The cultivation of rye, though still important, shows a long-term decline, while barley has been on the increase. Crops have fluctuated considerably from year to year. Yields have gone up

Table 2.41

Production of selected crops from 1934/38 to 1972

	1934/38	1955	1965	1970	1972
Sown area ('000 ha)					
Wheat	630	400	491	598	690
Rye	1,209	1,074	822	680	646
Barley	437	337	497	640	618
Grain (total)	3,151	2,483	2,304	2,287	2,330
Oil crops	–	196	139	116	119
Potatoes	786	843	725	667	647
Sugar beet	184	215	221	192	222
Gross production ('000 tonnes)					
Wheat	1,547	1,211	1,802	2,132	2,744
Rye	2,070	2,337	1,910	1,483	1,904
Barley	1,024	924	1,651	1,926	2,592
Grain (total)	6,487	6,170	6,730	6,456	8,536
Oil crops	–	245	230	190	243
Potatoes	13,567	11,194	12,857	13,054	12,140
Sugar beet	5,412	5,712	5,804	6,135	7,223
Yields (q per ha)					
Wheat	24·6	30·3	36·7	35·6	39·8
Rye	17·1	21·8	23·2	21·8	29·5
Barley	23·4	27·5	33·2	30·1	42·0
Grain (total)	20·6	24·8	29·2	28·2	36·6
Oil crops	–	12·5	16·6	16·4	20·4
Potatoes	173	133	177	196	188
Sugar beet	291	266	263	320	326

Source: *Statistisches Jahrbuch der DDR.*

Table 2.42

Livestock numbers and animal production, 1938–1972

	1938	1950	1960	1965	1970	1971	1972
Livestock ('000)							
Cows	1,945·2	1,616·4	2,175·1	2,168·6	2,162·9	2,173·4	2,168·8
Cattle (total)	3,653·3	3,614·7	4,675·3	4,762·3	5,190·2	5,292·9	5,379·4
Pigs	5,706·9	5,704·8	8,316·1	8,877·8	9,683·6	9,995·1	10,360·9
Sheep	1,763·4	1,085·3	2,015·4	1,963·0	1,597·5	1,607·2	1,656·8
Poultry	21,690	22,726	36·910	37,988	43,034	43,343	—
Horses	816·0	722·9	446·8	271·6	126·5	105·8	—
Milk yield							
(kg per cow)	—	1,891	2,646	2,982	3,314	3,331	3,500
Production ('000 tonnes)							
Fat stock (total)							
live weight	—	625	1,202	1,578	1,800	1,867	2,000
Pigs	—	402	829	997	1,040	1,090	1,184
Cattle (including							
calves)	—	223	261	440	600	585	612
Poultry	—	—	44	90	114	132	144
Milk (3·5 per cent fat)	—	2,877	4,962	6,371	7,091	7,150	7,515
Eggs (millions)	—	1,209	2,043	3,935	4,442	4,504	4,425

Source: *Statistisches Jahrbuch der DDR.*

Table 2.43

Percentage shares of sectors in livestock keeping and animal production[1]

Livestock	1960	1965	1970	1971
Cows				
Publicly owned estates	4·7	5·2	5·3	5·2
Co-operatives	40·3	53·4	72·7	76·3
Co-ordinating bodies	—	—	0·9	1·0
Household plots	52·0	39·7	20·0	16·5
Cattle (total)				
Publicly owned estates	6·3	6·8	8·6	8·7
Co-operatives	48·1	58·3	72·2	75·1
Co-ordinating bodies	—	—	1·3	1·5
Household plots	43·0	33·4	16·5	13·5
Pigs				
Publicly owned estates	8·1	11·3	12·5	12·7
Co-operatives	42·3	51·9	63·8	66·0
Co-ordinating bodies	—	—	2·0	2·5
Household plots	40·6	30·1	16·7	14·1
Poultry				
Publicly owned estates	3·3	4·4	20·9	24·3
Co-operatives	24·2	21·5	19·1	18·9
Co-ordinating bodies	—	—	5·0	6·9
Household plots	41·7	41·6	29·8	27·3
Animal production				
Fat stock (less poultry)				
Co-operative production	44·7	56·9	71·0	73·2
Household plots	30·1	33·4	15·7	13·1
Pigs for slaughter				
Co-operative production	35·1	46·5	59·7	60·3
Household plots	28·8	27·1	12·5	11·2
Poultry for slaughter				
Co-operative production	48·2	44·4	40·9	39·3
Household plots	14·9	8·1	2·4	2·0
Milk				
Co-operative production	35·0	50·9	72·4	75·9
Household plots	43·8	40·2	19·8	16·4
Eggs				
Co-operative production	19·8	27·7	24·8	22·8
Household plots	18·2	38·5	28·9	26·9

[1] The percentages add up to less than 100, since the livestock held by independent farms and the animal production achieved by publicly owned estates and private farms are not given.

Sources: *Statistisches Jahrbuch der DDR*; author's own calculations.

in respect of most crops and have come closer to the level of West Germany, without closing the gap as yet.

Livestock populations fell as a result of the war, but have gradually been restocked, as Table 2.42 demonstrates. As mechanisation advanced, the number of horses was reduced to a minimum. The livestock industry, notably pig meat and egg production, attracted stronger support than crop farming. Milk yields have reached a high level. The overall trend is similar to that in other industrialised countries: transition to modernised animal husbandry, intensification, increase in yield per animal. Yields are higher than in most socialist countries.

As regards livestock keeping and animal production, the production figures can be broken down according to sectors, as shown in Table 2.43. In the case of cattle, and of cows in particular, the share of co-operatively owned livestock has risen to about 75 per cent, and in the case of pigs to 66 per cent, but in respect of poultry it declined to 19 per cent. By comparison the increase in the share of publicly owned estates is very much smaller, except in the case of poultry. Similar trends are on record in the development of animal production. Thus the level of stock farming activities on the part of the members of agricultural producer co-operatives in their individual capacity has gone down both in relative and in absolute terms since 1960 – that is to say, roughly since the completion of the collectivisation campaign – with the sole exception of egg production. However, the contribution of the household plots to the total agricultural purchases of the state is still substantial. Their contribution to total food supplies is much higher still, since it includes the domestic consumption of the small producers and their families.

Supplies of the most important items of production equipment and materials known to boost output (see Table 2.44) were lower during the immediate post-war phase than they had been before the war, owing to destruction of plant, power shortage, dismantling and reparations deliveries to the Soviet Union. Only in the case of potash fertilisers had supplies not fallen, the GDR being one of the world's leading producers of this commodity. As regards nitrate and phosphate fertilisers, supplies to agriculture were increased only in the 1960s, so that the application of fertilisers is now similar to the standards of Western European industrial countries.

Comparisons are most difficult to draw in the case of tractors and agricultural machinery. Each GDR tractor works on average more than four times the area cultivated by a tractor in, for instance, West Germany, and this is a point operationally and economically in favour of the GDR. Note should be taken here of the greater average tractive power of each

Table 2.44

Use of means of production, 1938–1972

Fertiliser	1938/39	1949/50	1959/60	1969/70	1970/71	1971/72
(kg per ha AL)						
N	32·8	27·8	38·0	78·7	83·7	100·3
P_2O_5	27·3	14·2	32·7	65·3	64·3	65·9
K_2O	48·7	51·1	82·3	101·8	99·1	92·2

Machines		1950	1960	1970	1971	1972
Tractors (number)		36,435	70,566	148,865	148,718	146,914
(ha AL per tractor)		179	84	40	40	43
Combine harvesters		—	6,409	17,911	15,905	14,456
Potato combines		—	6,386	12,000	11,349	11,019
Beet combines		—	3,665	5,276	4,804	4,914
Lorries		—	9,312	27,186	28,222	—

Source: *Statistisches Jahrbuch der DDR.*

unit in the GDR. Large-scale operation and extensive fields enable savings to be made in capital equipment. When comparing the relative effectiveness of the tractor fleets, it must also be noted that in the GDR lorries owned by the co-operatives carry out some of the transport tasks left in West Germany to the tractors. Even so, it is doubtful whether technically the optimum has yet been reached, especially at times of peak activity. It is to be expected that there will be a further slight increase in the number of tractors and that the tractive power per machine will go up.

As regards the availability of the various combines, the optimum from the point of view of work organisation has probably not yet been reached. Ideally, there should be enough machines to cope with the most extreme peaks in work loads and to ensure rapid mobilisation under difficult weather conditions. In the period 1960–1972 the acreage per machine declined for combine harvesters from 840 to 398 acres (340 to 161 ha), for potato combines from 265 to 146 acres (107 to 59 ha), and for beet combines from 163 to 111 acres (66 to 45 ha).

It appears that the process of 'complex mechanisation' has not yet been completed. The agricultural machinery industry, at first built up with some hesitation, now manufactures sets of machines designed for large-scale operation in accordance with conditions in the GDR.

Production and supplies of concentrated feeds still fall considerably short of requirements as regards both quality and quantity. This deficiency is due in part to the shortage of foreign exchange and in part to the neglect of the industries concerned in the economic plans of the GDR. An attempt to tackle this problem was made for the first time in the Seven-Year Plan 1959–65, but the plan targets were not reached. The shortage of concentrated feeds impedes animal production.

(iv) SOCIAL CONDITIONS OF THE LABOUR FORCE

The influx of refugees after the war increased the East German population from 16·7 million to 19·1 million in 1948. The following years, up to 1961, witnessed a massive exodus, especially to West Germany, which reduced the figure again to 17·1 million, at which level it has since been stabilised.

The labour force increased by only a small margin. As shown in Table 2.45, it went up by 498,000 – 6·8 per cent – in the 23 years 1949 to 1972. However, during the same period the agricultural labour force declined by 1·3 million, or 58 per cent. Its share of the total, down to 12·0 per cent in 1972 from 30·7 per cent in 1949, is still higher than in West Germany.

113

Table 2.45

Share of agriculture in number of economically active persons and national product, 1949–1971

Year	Population (middle of year)	Economically active		Agricultural net product	
		Total	Agriculture and forestry ('000)	(percentage of total)	Marks (million)	Percentage of produced national income
1939	16,745	—	—	—	—	—
1949	18,892	7,313	2,242	30·7	7,340	33·0
1950	18,388	7,196	2,005	27·9	8,904	32·7
1955	17,944	7,722	1,721	22·3	10,963	21·8
1960	17,241	7,686	1,304	17·0	11,991	16·9
1965	17,020	7,676	1,179	15·4	12,147	14·4
1970	17,057	7,769	997	12·8	13,188	12·1
1971	17,042	7,804	986	12·6	12,615	11·1
1972	17,043	7,811	936	12·0	13,900	11·6

Source: *Statistisches Jahrbuch der DDR*; author's own calculations.

The large majority of the agricultural labour force is engaged in the agricultural producer co-operatives. Here some interesting sociological trends can be noted (see Table 2.46):

1   The membership has been slowly and steadily declining since 1961, in the ten years up to 1971 by 77,000, or 8 per cent.
2   So long as the machine and tractor stations existed, the labour force of the producer co-operatives exceeded the membership. Since then, the labour force has been substantially below the membership. Evidently the number of old-age pensioners whose membership continues although they have ceased working is increasing.
3   The number of working members as a proportion of all members dropped considerably: from 95 to 79 per cent over the last 11 years. This also points to an increase in the relative strength of the older age groups, comparable to the case in Czechoslovakia.
4   There is a high proportion of female members, showing a moderate

Table 2.46

Members and work force of agricultural producer co-operatives, 1952–1971

Year	Members		Permanent work force	Working members	
	Total	No. females		Total	No. females
1952	37,000	—	—	—	—
1955	196,946	—	—	—	—
1960	901,490	403,044	—	857,630	382,088
1961	964,528	450,976	1,001,667	869,021	404,462
1965	986,622	471,070	910,043	857,869	396,414
1970	890,521	423,886	745,348	710,953	319,942
1971	887,444	421,320	738,102	702,134	313,999
	Female members as percentage of total			Working members as percentage of total	Female members as percentage of total working members
1960	44·7			95·1	44·6
1961	46·8			90·1	46·5
1965	47·7			87·0	46·2
1970	47·6			79·8	45·0
1971	47·5			79·1	44·7

Source: *Statistisches Jahrbuch der DDR*; author's own calculations.

increase from 44·7 to 47·5 per cent in the period 1960 to 1971. The proportion of women among the working members has remained steady at about 45 per cent.

The state of education and training of the agricultural labour force is the subject of Table 2·47. The figures show that a large and growing proportion of the labour force has benefited from specialised training at various levels. The training of women does not entirely do justice to their importance in the agricultural sector. Since the vast majority of the agricultural labour force have undergone training qualifying them as skilled workers, it must be doubted whether such training really covers the whole ground or whether skilled worker status is not rather awarded as a distinction combined with an indirect wage increase.

Table 2.47

Educational qualifications of the permanent work force in socialist agriculture, 1963–1972

	1963	1967	1972
Permanent work force	1,028,927	984,344	839,704
no. females	476,762	443,138	371,024
Training completed at:			
university (or equivalent)	4,095	6,133	9,076
vocational college	16,789	24,424	32,387
Foremen	28,541	36,521	49,726
Skilled workers	136,894	267,709	491,473
No. females:			
university (or equivalent) graduates	335	537	1,036
vocational college graduates	1,905	2,869	6,576
foremen	1,442	2,724	5,417
skilled workers	− 36,714	103,877	219,754

Source: *Statistisches Jahrbuch der DDR.*

When the agricultural producer co-operatives were founded, many agricultural workers became members, thanks to assistance by the state. On 15 November 1955 the total membership of the co-operatives was recorded as 196,946. Out of these 96.146 had been agricultural workers before joining the agricultural producer co-operative; 11,287 were former industrial workers; 77,602 were formerly peasants with small and medium-sized holdings and 2,347 peasants with large holdings. Only about 40 per cent of the members, then, had previously been peasants at all. The agricultural workers were allocated holdings under the land reform out of the land fund, and that was the land they brought into the co-operatives. In this way the agricultural workers were given equality of material as well as social status with the formerly independent peasants. To them the setting up of the agricultural producer co-operatives meant an improvement of their position in every respect.

On agricultural incomes GDR statistics present only fragmentary data. No incomes are stated for the members of the co-operatives. Their remuneration for work was largely based on the methods prevailing in the Soviet Union, although at the beginning the labour norms were different in quantitative terms. On the whole, the GDR followed, with a certain time lag, the changes of the system applied in the Soviet Union. At the end of the 1960s, Blohm estimated the income derived by members from the agricultural producer co-operatives at DM (East) 8,000 a year at the most, leaving out of account any profits from the household plots. This is of the same order as the income of state farm workers, which — as set out in Table 2.48 — rose consistently from 1955 to 1971, without ever catching up with industrial incomes. It must be noted, however, that these average figures are only of limited value as a description of reality, as they

Table 2.48

Average monthly incomes at state farms,
1961–1971 (DM-East)

Year	Workers employed full-time on estates		Full-time manual and clerical workers	
	Manual and clerical workers	Production workers	Industry	All sectors
1955	301	288	460	439
1960	445	434	571	558
1965	574	570	656	640
1970	665	684	770	762
1971	705	724	798	792

Source: *Statistisches Jahrbuch der DDR.*

tell us nothing about the range of variations from the mean and the stratification of incomes.

The social status of co-operative peasants and state farm workers is comparable to that of their colleagues in the Soviet Union.

The level of social security enjoyed by the state farm workers is in line with that of other wage and salary earners. Members of agricultural producer co-operatives were included in the general social insurance scheme on 1 March 1959, earlier than in most socialist countries. In case of sickness and disablement the benefits in kind are the same as those granted to the rest of the population, but co-operative peasants are not eligible for the payment of sickness or unemployment benefit. Old-age insurance is on the same lines as for workers, but is handled by the Deutsche Versicherungsanstalt für Selbständige (German Insurance Institute for the Self-employed). It is a contributory pension scheme, with the member's payment being equalled by the co-operative's. In fixing the contribution, the member's ground rent is taken into account. Early in 1971 the position of the peasants was finally brought into line with that of other sections covered by social insurance by adjusting the rules governing their contributions. Dependants of members of agricultural producer co-operatives are treated in the same way as those of others covered by social insurance.

(v) AGRICULTURE IN THE TWO GERMANYS: A TECHNICAL-QUANTITATIVE COMPARISON

The problems involved in comparing the relative performance of particular sectors in different social systems are discussed in Chapter 7. Comparisons between West Germany and the GDR have been repeatedly attempted by West German agrarian economists. The relevant data, summed up in Tables 2.49 and 2.50, indicate a number of facts and trends.

The GDR has more agricultural land in proportion to the size of its population than West Germany. The livestock population — an indicator of the conversion factor — is lower than in West Germany and showed a slight decline. The drift of manpower away from agriculture proceeded more slowly. Population trends were opposite in the two states: growth in West Germany against decline in the GDR. Use of fertilisers is higher in the GDR, except for phosphate fertilisers which have to be imported. Tractor density is considerably lower. Yields per acre are lower.

In the GDR, food production has risen slowly and steadily, but the increase has always lagged somewhat behind that in West Germany. The net production of foodstuffs per acre — a quantity linked with crop yields per acre — has also followed a rising trend as in West Germany, but has

Table 2.49

Agricultural production in West Germany and the GDR, comparative figures for 1957–61 and 1968

	(1) West Germany		(2) GDR		(2) as a percentage of (1)	
	1957–61	1968	1957–61	1968	1957–61	1968
Agricultural Land (million ha)	14·26	13·87	6·44	6·30	45·2	45·4
Livestock total (million large livestock units)	11·89	12·44	5·06	4·96	42·6	39·9
of which productive livestock	11·02	12·17	4·50	4·77	40·8	39·2
Economically active in agriculture and forestry ('000)	3,794	2,630	1,416	1,068	37·3	40·6
Tractor capacity (million hp)	15·15	30·98	2·30	6·25	15·2	20·2
Fertiliser consumption (pure nutrient, '000 tonnes)						
nitrogen	602	933	239	502	39·7	53·8
phosphate	652	802	209	370	32·1	46·1
potash	1,017	1,046	511	582	50·2	55·6
Gross crop production in million tonnes grain equivalent (GE)	48·05	58·01	19·17	23·35	39·9	40·3
Total animal production million tonnes GE	42·62	52·36	14·57	17·46	34·2	33·3
Food production million tonnes GE	46·21	59·83	16·19	20·10	35·0	33·6
Net food production million tonnes GE	40·82	49·50	13·95	17·86	34·2	36·1
Population (millions)	55·20	59·50	17·26	17·09	31·3	28·7

Source: *Bericht der Bundesregierung…* .

Table 2.50

Indicators for a quantitative comparison of agricultural performance in the GDR and West Germany

		1957–61	1960	1962	1964	1966	1968	1969
Food production (million tonnes GE)	GDR	16·18	17·14	14·59	16·76	18·92	20·10	19·30
	WG	46·21	49·42	49·92	53·62	54·91	59·83	60·79
Index (1957–61=100)	GDR	100	106	90	104	117	124	119
	WG	100	107	108	116	119	129	132
Net food production (quintals GE per ha AL)	GDR	21·6	22·8	19·0	22·5	26·0	28·2	26·8
	WG	28·6	31·3	30·7	32·2	32·2	35·7	36·3
GDR as percentage of WG		76	73	62	70	81	79	74
Labour productivity (quintals GE per worker)	GDR				163	193	220	220
	WG				281	306	360	411
Full-time workers per 100 ha AL	GDR				16·2	15·5	14·5	14·0
	WG				16·5	14·6	13·7	13·2

Sources: Immler; *Bericht zur Lage der Nation.*

again tended to lag a fifth to a quarter behind, depending on the method of calculation. Labour productivity in terms of gross production per member of the agricultural labour force is also substantially higher in West Germany, which recorded a further increase by 46·4 per cent in the six years from 1964 to 1969, as compared with a 38·4 per cent rise in the GDR. However, if labour productivity is measured in terms of size of labour force per 100 acres of agricultural land, the GDR nearly equals the productivity of West German agriculture with its many small production units. This shows that the manpower advantages of large-scale farming are not yet fully exploited in the GDR, either because the equipment capable of supplanting manpower is not available on an adequate scale, or because a portion of the benefits accruing from operating on a large scale is used for the introduction of social improvements.

Quantitative comparisons of this kind presuppose equal ecological starting conditions, which ought to lead to a similar range of crops and pattern of cultivation. In addition, the following factors are disregarded in such comparisons:

(a)   influence of the overall organisation on the individual indices, as regards for instance the distribution of manpower;
(b)   work performed by the co-operative peasant privately on the household plot;
(c)   work load and social norms (regulation of working hours, holidays);
(d)   volume of inputs, limitation of imports owing to use of scarce foreign exchange for other purposes;
(e)   ratio of production achievement to inputs — that is to say, productivity of capital.

Other factors ignored in such comparisons are the macro-economic contributions of agriculture and the targets set for the economy as a whole.

From the outset in 1945, agriculture played a more important part in East than in West Germany. It had higher shares both in the total labour force and in the gross domestic product, as shown in Table 2.45. This difference still remains, even though industrialisation made good progress also in the GDR, which after all has become the leading industrial country in the socialist economic system of Eastern Europe. One of the motives for the different position of agriculture in the GDR lies in the desire to minimise expenditure of foreign exchange on agricultural products and materials and to combine assured food supplies with the smallest possible degree of dependence on the world market. In 1968 the GDR covered 85 per cent of its food consumption from domestic production, as compared with 77 per cent in West Germany.

(vi)   TRENDS OF AGRARIAN POLICY

The agrarian crisis was due to two causes:

(i)   neglect or insufficient consideration of agriculture in the economic plans;
(ii)   resistance of peasants to the rapid transformation of the agrarian structure and the exodus to West Germany.

Both causes now belong to the past.

Current agrarian policy takes the given structure — predominance of the producer co-operatives — as its starting point and seeks to consolidate and modernise it. The aim is no longer to increase the size of the production units in terms of acreage, but rather to achieve economies of scale and the most effective use of modern technology by co-ordinating the activities of independent production units. In the sphere of agriculture, co-ordinating institutions are concerned with the deployment of the largest machines and with breeding, fattening and egg production; and, in the sphere of industry, with the production of mixed feeds, processing of raw materials, and so on. How important the part played by inter-unit co-ordination is in

Table 2.51

Inter-co-operative institutions (ZGE)

	1965	1967	1969	1971
Agriculture				
Number	163	299	622	488
Permanent labour force	749	2,345	39,862	15,317
Forestry				
Number	25	73	296	426
Permanent labour force	181	605	2,191	3,559
Agricultural building industry				
Number	332	404	449	455
Permanent labour force	11,241	16,550	26,442	29,983
Land improvement				
Number	213	218	200	195
Permanent labour force	5,422	7,767	11,398	12,993
All ZGE				
Number	733	994	1,567	1,564
Permanent labour force	17,593	27,267	79,893	61,852

Source: *Statistisches Jahrbuch der DDR.*

actual practice is difficult to estimate. Table 2.51 seems to indicate a decline in its contribution to agrarian production proper since 1969, but it is too early to say whether this is a genuine trend or a temporary consequence of some reorganisation.

The household plot is not a suoject of debate. Planning and administration were reorganised in order to harmonise the production of the household plots with the realities of the economic situation and the needs of the market.

Agricultural production, with special emphasis on animal husbandry, has been boosted by measures in support of the industries manufacturing agricultural production equipment and materials as well as by direct investments in the agrarian sector and by material incentives. Beginning with the 1964 harvest, the dual price system for vegetable products was abolished and superseded by unified prices which were fixed at levels above the average prices previously paid by the Collection and Purchasing Organisation. Compulsory deliveries and purchasing campaigns were largely replaced by delivery contracts designed to ensure a smoother flow of supplies to the market in accordance with market needs. In 1969—1970 the same step was taken in respect of animal products. Since then, differential purchasing prices have been introduced once more, but this time the differentials serve specific agrarian policy aims — encouragement of co-ordination and specialisation — and make allowances for varying ecological conditions.

To ensure substantial increases in labour productivity and productivity per acre, the plan provides for numerous measures, such as plant and animal breeding, introduction of industrial methods and training schemes. The plan index figures for the forecasting period up to 1980 are set high, but are kept in general terms and stated within considerable margins (see Table 2.52). The incomes of the co-operative peasants are to be raised mainly by increasing the prices of agricultural products.

(vii) APPRAISAL

An appraisal of the overall performance of East German agriculture is inevitably bound up with a number of value judgements. It will depend on the importance attached to increases in production, on the evaluation of the social transformation and on the degree to which the political—social and economic aims of GDR policies are accepted.

In quantitative terms, the production figures fell for a long time below those of West Germany. Only in the last few years has the gap been narrowed. The production results were achieved with a lower capital ex-

Table 2.52

Plan indices of agriculture and the food industry for 1980

Aspect	Year	Actual performance	Plan 1980 (forecast)
Productivity and production			
1 One person economically active in agriculture feeds	1967	17	38
Labour productivity to rise at the rate of 9·5 per cent p.a. up to 1980.			
2 Percentage share of materialised labour (machines, implements, buildings, etc.):	1965	55	74
Labour productivity is to be raised by substitution of capital for labour.			
Share of materialised labour in total cost of gross production (per cent)	1965	48	58
Share of living labour power	1965	38	20
3 Increase of labour productivity by use of technological equipment in crop production.			
Grain (man-hours per ha)	1967	34	9–10
Grain (man-hours per q)	1967	1·8	0·4
Potatoes (man-hours per ha)	1967	240	80–90
Potatoes (man-hours per q)	1967	1·6	0·4
Sugar beet (man-hours per ha)	1967	200	45
Sugar beet (man-hours per q)	1967	1·4	0·2
4 Yield per ha sown area (q)			
Grain	1969	29·5	50–60
Wheat	1969	35·5	70
Potatoes	1969	146·2	280–320
Sugar beet	1969	253·2	400–450
Hay	1967	40–50	70–80
5 Increase in animal production			
Meat total	1967	100	140·0
Beef and mutton	1967	100	151·9
Pork	1967	100	120·8
Poultry and rabbits	1967	100	490·0
6 Milk production per cow (kg)	1969	3,363	4,500–5,000

124

Aspect	Year	Actual performance	Plan 1980 (forecast)
7 Maize			
Cultivated area (ha)	1969	1,382	100,000[1]
Production (tonnes)	1969	3,088	500,000[1]
Labour			
8 Economically active in agriculture and forestry (percentage)	1969	13·2	10·0
9 Manpower per 100 ha AL			
Variant I	1965	19·4	7·5
Variant II	1965	19·4	10·0
10 Manpower in crop production per 100 ha AL			3–4
Food consumption			
11 Annual per-capita consumption			
Meat (total) (kg)	1969	65·0	70–80
Beef/veal (kg)	1969	20·7	24–28
Pork (kg)	1969	39·5	38–43
Poultry (kg)	1969	4·8	7–8
Eggs (no.)	1969	226	230–270
Butter (kg)	1969	14·1	12–14
Animal fats (kg)	1969	5·9	5–5·5
Margarine (kg)	1969	10·9	8–10
Milk (kg)	1969	100·5 (2·5% fat)	125–165 (3·5% fat)
Flour and cereal products (kg)	1969	97·5	88–92
Potatoes (kg)	1968	150·0	115–125
Vegetables (kg)	1969	66·5	80–85
Fruit (kg)	1969	51·1	60–65
Chemicals and land improvement			
12 Share of chief nutrients in the form of NPK compound fertiliser (percentage)			40
13 Increase in soil productivity	1969	100	140
14 Land improvement			
New irrigation (million ha)			1·0
New drainage (million ha)			1·2

Aspect	Year	Actual performance	Plan 1980 (forecast)
Training of agricultural labour force (per cent)			
15 Without training	1969	51·8	10
University qualifications	1969	0·8	2–3
Vocational college qual.	1969	2·9	4–6
Foreman's examination	1969	4·7	20–25
Skilled worker's certificate	1969	39·8	50–60
16 Percentage share of science and education in the increase of production			30[1]

[1] 1975.

Source: Immler.

penditure than in West Germany, but with a roughly equal labour force.

West German agrarian economists frequently assume that the starting position in 1945 was the same for both parts of Germany. The lagging behind of production in the GDR can then be attributed to

(a) over-emphasis of the advantages of large production units;
(b) peasants' resistance to the establishment of producer co-operatives;
(c) neglect of agricultural investment.

An observer, on the other hand, who accepts the aims of GDR policies for the purpose of his appraisal, and accordingly takes note of the degree to which these aims are being attained, will argue differently. He will see the deferment of agricultural investments as a necessary and temporary measure within the framework of a general economic strategy. The lower productivity per acre can be rationally explained as the natural consequence of factors such as the lower population density. The transformation of the agrarian structure based on smallholdings and independent peasants into one characterised by large-scale co-operative production units sweeps away the obstacles to a modern agricultural policy and facilitates the most effective use of modern machinery, without bringing about a social polarisation of the agricultural population or creating a capitalist land monopoly. The restructuring of agriculture is also conducive to the application of social norms and the gradual closing of the gap in social and economic status between agricultural and industrial workers, since production relations in agriculture come to resemble those in industry. The establishment of the agricultural producer co-operatives provided a radical solution for a number of problems with which the agricultural policy of the West German Federal Republic and other Common Market countries will have to wrestle for a long time to come.

Yet, the question remains as to whether it was right to apply the Soviet model in carrying out the social transformation, and whether it would not have been possible to avoid the resistance of the peasants, with all its political and economic ill-effects, by using a model designed for the specific conditions of Eastern Germany.

The factors that had compelled collectivisation in the Soviet Union operated only to a limited extent or were altogether absent in East Germany. There was little unused land, and it was unnecessary — certainly in the first years after 1945, with the factories dismantled and industrial production cut back — to recruit additional manpower for industry. The first land reform measures ordered by the Soviet occupying power after 1945 were imitations of the acts of the Russian revolutionary government of 1918 with no regard for the different circumstances. Today, viewed retrospectively, those measures look like unnecessary detours. The fragmentation of the large estates, the destruction of residential buildings and the construction of new settlers' premises are hard to justify in times of an acute shortage of building materials. Perhaps the exceptional political conditions during the years from 1945 to 1948 can explain measures which cannot have been taken on the ground of economic development and which had to be reversed later in order to pave the way for the third stage in the overhaul of the structure of agricultural production, the establishment of the producer co-operatives.

At the outset of its collectivisation campaign in 1928, the Soviet government encountered strong resistance, even on the part of the small peasants. In East Germany, under the conditions of the first ten post-war years, the desire to preserve independent peasant status may not have been quite as overwhelming, particularly when that status meant ownership of smallholdings of less than 20 acres, for which little livestock and no technical equipment was available or likely to be available in the foreseeable future. Some hundreds of thousands of new peasants came to own their land only after 1945. Accordingly the resistance put up against the establishment of the producer co-operatives can hardly have had the support of the smallest and poorest peasants, as had been the case in the Soviet Union. Thousands of peasants, it is true, left the GDR, but the vast majority remained. Moreover, East Germany, as an industrial region, did not have very large manpower reserves hidden in the agrarian sector. Thus the exodus did not benefit the other economic sectors, but the competing economy of West Germany.

Any comparison between the GDR and other countries of the Eastern bloc, or again between the GDR and West Germany, must take account of these fundamental differences in the initial conditions. It is futile to compare the yields per acre of the Netherlands with those of the USA or the Soviet Union, or to juxtapose the number of tractors in East and West Germany. But it was just as futile to attempt launching a land reform in East Germany in 1945 on the model of the agrarian reform effected by the Russian October Revolution of 1917.

3 Countries with a Non-Collectivised Agriculture

There are already three communist states in which agriculture has not been collectivised: Yugoslavia abandoned the attempted collective transformation as long ago as 1951–53; Poland followed suit in 1956; in Cuba the large estates – foreign or Cuban-owned – were nationalised, but holdings of under 160 acres (64 ha) are managed as before.

3.1 Yugoslavia: the first heresy, also in agrarian policy

3.1.1 *Important data of recent history*

1918 (October) After the First World War, the small semi-client state of Serbia is transformed into the multinational state of Yugoslavia; Serbian domination within the new state is opposed above all by Croat nationalists, the Catholic Church and peasant leaders.

1921 Yugoslavia, Romania and Czechoslovakia form the Little Entente under French auspices to defend the post-war status quo against Italian and German revisionist ambitions.

1934 Balkan Treaty concluded by Yugoslavia, Greece, Romania and Turkey, encouraged by Hitler's Germany; Yugoslav rapprochement with Germany and Italy.

1941 (25 March) Yugoslavia joins the Axis Powers, subscribes to Tripartite Treaty.

(27 March) Coup d'état of the 'anti-German' forces in Belgrade.

(5 April) Friendship Treaty with the Soviet Union.

(6 April) German troops cross the frontier, air raid on Belgrade.

(17 April) Surrender of Yugoslav Army.

Yugoslavia is partitioned between Germany, Italy and Hungary, with Croatia set up as an 'independent' state under German–Italian supervision. Two resistance groups are organised; one of them, under communist leadership, fights implacably and gradually assumes the leading role in the resistance struggle.

1943 (November) Formation of National Committee for the Liberation of Yugoslavia under Josip Broz-Tito, Pijade, Kardelj, Kidric and others, who disregard Soviet 'advice' and conduct independent domestic and foreign policies.

1944—45 Victory over Hitler without assistance from the Soviet Army; the few Soviet soldiers are withdrawn in March 1945; Mutual Aid Treaty with the Soviet Union, terminated in 1949; proclamation of Federal People's Republic of Yugoslavia.

1946—47 Land reform, beginning of collectivisation.

1948 Breach with Moscow, expulsion from Cominform.

1949—50 Proclamation of the Yugoslav road to socialism; Moscow replies with a ban on Titoism. Introduction of workers' self-management.

1952 Repeal of forcible collectivisation; US financial and military aid.

1955 Khrushchev and Bulganin visit Belgrade to admit their mistake and improve relations. Since then Yugoslavia has taken an independent course in foreign political and economic policy, and relations with the Soviet Union have been marked by fluctuating tensions (however, the Yugoslavs supported the Soviet Union in its dispute with China in 1962).

1956 Proclamation of a policy of neutralism and peaceful co-existence as a third force; organisation of non-aligned states.

1966 Economic liberalisation entails considerable difficulties of adjustment; mass migration of workers to Western Europe.

1967 Admission of foreign capital under strict supervision.

1968—71 Constitutional amendments to strengthen economic self-government and autonomy of the constituent republics; centrifugal tendencies appear, especially in Croatia.

1970 (September) President Nixon visits Belgrade.

1971 (September) CPSU Secretary Brezhnev visits Belgrade.

3.1.2 *Geography and population trends*

Although Yugoslavia emerged from the Second World War as one of the victorious powers, her territory was increased by only an insignificant margin, from 95,600 square miles in 1920 to 98,800 square miles today.

Regional differences are conspicuous in every respect: climate, topography, population density, economic development, culture, religion. Some areas in the south and south-east find themselves at a disadvantage owing to a combination of natural conditions and circumstances (a long period under Turkish rule). The economic and social disparity between north and south is politically accentuated by cultural and linguistic differences, which contribute to the 'nationalism' of the constituent republics. The

Table 3.1
Area and population of constituent republics and territories

Republic/territory	Area (sq km)	Population ('000)		Inhabitants per sq km	
		1961	1971	1961	1971
Bosnia-Herzegovina	51,129	3,278	4,020	64	79
Croatia	56,538	4,160	4,436	74	78
Macedonia	25,713	1,406	1,670	55	65
Montenegro	13,812	472	556	34	40
Serbia	88,361	7,642	8,391	86	95
Serbia proper	55,968	4,823	–	86	–
Kosovo	10,887	964	–	89	–
Vojvodina	21,506	1,855	–	86	–
Slovenia	20,251	1,592	1,726	79	85
Yugoslavia	255,804	19,507	20,799	73	81

Source: *Länderkurzberichte, Jugoslawien.*

readiness to forgo financial resources for the sake of the development of the backward territories is called in question time after time.

The population has risen by very nearly 75 per cent since 1921, from 11,985,000 to 20,799,000. Over the last decade the population has grown by 1.0 to 1.1 per cent a year. Table 3.1 gives the figures for the constituent republics. Serbia is most densely populated, Montenegro most sparsely. The proportion of the urban population increased from 28·4 per cent in 1961 to close on 50 per cent in 1971. Other salient demographic and economic data are presented in Table 3.2.

As regards employment, the latest complete figures available date back to 1961, when the number of wage and salary earners amounted to no more than 42·3 per cent of the total number of gainfully occupied persons, while the self-employed and members of their families working with them accounted for 55·9 per cent, a clear indication of the predominantly pre-industrial character of the economy. In the same year, 4,748,000 out of the total of 8,340,000 gainfully occupied persons were engaged in agriculture and forestry, or in relative terms 56·9 per cent of the total, a percentage comprising 50·7 per cent of the male and 68·4 per cent of the female gainfully occupied persons. Ten years later, according to the 1971 census, 65 per cent of the population were living in rural areas, but only 39 per cent were engaged in agriculture. The number of gainfully employed persons (excluding the self-employed) rose in the period 1960 to

Table 3.2

Demographic data for republics and territories

Republic/territory	Illiterates 1961 (%)	Net population growth 1967 (%)	Life expectancy 1965/66 Men	Life expectancy 1965/66 Women	Agricultural population as percentage of total, 1969	ha AL per production unit, 1969	Per-capita regional income, 1969 (Dinar)
Bosnia-Herzegovina	32·5	1·35	63·7	67·2	43·2	3·3	3,116
Croatia	12·1	0·95	66·3		35·1	3·3	6,249
Macedonia	24·5	1·45	62·3	70·7	43·1	2·5	3,383
Montenegro	21·7	1·25	66·7	68·4	35·2	4·2	3,235
Serbia	21·9	1·06	64·9	70·4	47·1	4·2	4,821
Serbia proper	23·0	0·90	66·4	62·5	47·7	4·6	5,341
Kosovo	41·1	2·29	61·3	71·1	58·3	3·5	1,564
Vojvodina	10·6	0·90	66·1	72·9	43·4	3·4	5,449
Slovenia	1·8	1·13	66·0		23·8	6·3	9,414
Yugoslavia	19·7	1·15	64·7	69·0	41·7	3·9	5,040

Source: *The Yugoslav village.*

1971 by 26·7 per cent from 3·0 to 3·8 million. This increase includes a rise of 431,000 or 26·6 per cent in the number of persons employed in production. Since industrialisation was able to absorb only part of the population growth and migration from the land, Yugoslavia was the first of the socialist countries freely to permit its workers to seek employment abroad, in capitalist industrial countries. About 1 million Yugoslavs are now believed to be working abroad. In 1960 159,000 persons were registered as unemployed; in 1970 the number was 320,000. Yugoslavia is probably the only socialist country to publish unemployment figures. In 1961, 23·5 per cent of the population over the age of 15 were still illiterate, most of them in the older age groups.

3.1.3 Agrarian reforms and agrarian structure

After the first agrarian reform of 1918 most of the land was in the hands of peasants with small and medium holdings. Many large estates had been expropriated and distributed in the course of the reform of 1918. A number of large-scale enterprises were preserved as breeding and model estates. Thus the land hunger of the peasantry was partially satisfied, and the national problem of foreign — chiefly Hungarian and German — landowners was solved. Altogether, 4,765,600 acres (1,929,344 ha) were distributed among 395,069 families, an average of 12·1 acres (4·9 ha) per family. But the social problems of the countryside remained. In 1931 (see Table 3.3), agricultural holdings averaged 10·6 acres (4·3 ha) of agricultur-

Table 3.3

Agrarian structure: size of production units, 1931

Size in ha	Production units		Agricultural land		Cropland	
	Number	%	'000 ha	%	'000 ha	%
0–2	671,865	33·8	625	7·3	442	7·7
2–5	676,284	34·0	2,002	23·2 .	1,407	24·7
5–10	407,237	20·5	2,432	28·2	1,641	28·8
10–20	174,068	8·8	1,920	22·3	1,240	21·8
20–50	49,314	2·5	1,059	12·3	663	11·6
50–100	5,156	0·3	240	2·7	147	2·6
over 100	1,801	0·1	345	4·0	161	2·8
	1,985,725	100·0	8,625	100·0	5,702	100·0

Source: *Statisticki Godišnjak 1936.*

al land and 7·2 acres (2·9 ha) of arable. Yugoslavia was severely shaken by the agrarian crisis at the end of the 1920s. The holdings distributed under the land reform had been too small, and the overpopulation of the rural areas became more acute.

When the second agrarian reform was introduced in 1945 after the victory of the Communist Party, there were not many privately held estates left to be broken up and distributed. Private holdings were now limited to 74 acres (30 ha), or 112 acres (45 ha) on poor soil. Nearly half the land distributed under the new reform (see Table 3.4) came from peasant owners, most of it from the German-speaking peasants, who lived in villages of their own. They had been singled out as pioneers of the Nazi spirit of conquest and specimens of the master race. Not that they had asked for it — many were not even aware of it — but they willy-nilly became helpers of the Wehrmacht. The Yugoslav reply was drastic. After a large number of the German peasants had fled with the retreating troops, the rest — with the exception of those who had unequivocally opposed Hitler — were deported after the victory of the partisans. In this way the German question was solved as far as Yugoslavia was concerned. The cultural influence of the German settlers was wiped out at the same time. The temporary loss of production was accepted as an inevitable price to pay. Today no uninhabited farmsteads or untilled fields can be seen in the area.

Many thousands of people had been brought by the land reform into fertile territories without knowing anything about their specific climate, soil, vegetation or the appropriate farming methods. It seemed rational, then, to bring them together to work in common. These people, who had received land from the land fund, were not tied to the tradition of private ownership and, as partisans, were particularly receptive to the Communist Party's thinking on agrarian policy. They were to form the nuclei of the new peasants' working co-operatives (seljačka radna zadruga) set up under a law of 1946. The independent peasants were enlisted in a recruiting campaign in which the zeal of the Party workers often got the better of the principle of voluntariness.

In most states of the Eastern bloc there are various types of producer co-operatives differing in the degree to which land and production equipment have been taken into common ownership. In the lower types, profit distribution is governed primarily by the size of the landholdings of the former members. In Yugoslavia, the decision was soon taken to concentrate on a single type of working co-operative. The member brought the greater part of his land and all his equipment into the co-operative, but retained some livestock and a household plot of about 1·25 acres (about

Table 3.4

The agrarian reform of 1945: sources of the land fund and its distribution

Source	Expropriated owners (no.)	Expropriated land ('000 ha)	Recipients	ha	%
Landed property	2,653	235	Peasants	797,357	51·0
Banks, business firms	837	78	State farms	287,715	18·3
Churches, monasteries	2,625	164	Collective farms	41,000	2·6
Holdings in excess of upper limit	8,636	122	State enterprises	39,650	2·5
Non-agriculturalists	14,131	109	Health institutions	20,052	1·3
Germans	96,874	637	Forests	380,256	24·3
Others	36,415	221			
	162,171	1,566		1,566,030	100·0

Source: Priručnik, vol. 1, after Osteuropa-Handbuch Jugoslawien.

0.5 ha) surrounding his house. A part of the income of the co-operative was distributed in proportion to the amount of land brought in by each member.

Up to 1951, in the course of four years, 6,797 agricultural producer co-operatives were set up, farming 18·6 per cent of the agricultural land. Another 17·5 per cent was held by the state farms, which gave the socialist sector 36·1 per cent of the total agricultural land. The remaining 64 per cent remained in the hands of small and medium peasants. Thus the reorganisation of agriculture was from the outset much less thoroughgoing than it had been in the Soviet Union. The bulk of the new co-operatives were in Serbia (with 2,080), Croatia (1,496) and Bosnia-Herzegovina (1,381). There were only a few in Slovenia, Macedonia and Montenegro.

The conditions under which the co-operatives started to operate were made harder by Yugoslavia's conflict with the Soviet Union, which affected economic life as a whole and slowed down the pace of industrialisation. The result of the general and special difficulties was that the new co-operatives were undersupplied with production equipment and materials and that there was an insufficient number of new vacancies for employment in industry. The machinery available for the 8,500 agricultural co-operatives of all types which existed at the end of 1953 comprised 4,707 tractors, 4,881 tractor ploughs, 5,000 seed drills, 2,876 mowing machines, 3,347 reaper-binders, 4,203 motor sprayers, and 3,742 threshing machines. Therefore, as far as the former independent peasant was concerned, his change of status to that of a co-operative peasant was not accompanied by any compensatory change in working methods that might have reconciled him to the loss of his position as master over his land.

When international tensions abated in the years 1951 to 1953 and Yugoslavia extended the period for the attainment of her economic plan targets, the reins were slackened in the rural areas as well. The 'Decree on Property Relations and the Reorganisation of the Peasants' Working Co-operatives', issued on 28 March 1953, reaffirmed the hitherto more or less theoretical freedom of movement of the members of co-operatives, and laid down the conditions under which they could secede. Under this law, if individual members resigned and the co-operative continued to exist, the seceding peasant had no right to his original fields, but was to be given land at the periphery of the co-operative fields, so as not to interfere with the cultivation of the co-operative fields. He would be *pro rata* liable for any debts of the co-operative. At the same time, the 'Law on the Fund of Agricultural Land within the Framework of Public Ownership and on the Allocation of Land to the Agricultural Organisations', issued on 22 May 1953, reduced the upper limit of private landholdings to 25 acres (10 ha), or 37 acres (15 ha) where the soil is poor, from the previous figures of 74 and 112 acres (30 and 45 ha) respectively. The intention was to make sure that, if a communist organisation of agriculture were not feasible, at least there should be no return to the capitalist exploitation of man by man in agriculture, and limits should be set to the formation of capitalist fortunes. The land netted by this new law was bound to be inconsiderable. A total of 672,000 acres (272,000 ha) was obtained, of which agricultural producer co-operatives received 230,000 acres (93,000 ha) and independent peasants 301,000 acres (122,000 ha), while the remainder of 141,000 acres (57,000 ha) had not been distributed by 1954.

As Table 3.5 shows, the principle of voluntariness had now become a reality that was eagerly made use of by the members. The total number of

Table 3.5

Development of producer co-operatives, 1946–1962

End of year	Co-operatives	Members ('000)	Agricultural land ('000 ha)
1946	454	75·2	122
1947	779	174·5	211
1948	1,318	286·2	324
1949	6,626	1,707·1	1,839
1950	6,964	2,028·9	2,595
1951	6,797	2,083·6	2,329
1952	4,679	1,504·9	1,665
1953	1,258	244·2	327
1954	924	116·4	281
1955	704		233
1956	578		
1957	507		216
1958	390		206
1959	229		183
1960	150		132
1961			127
1962			94

Sources: *Bulletin of Information and Documentation* no. 2, 1954; and others.

producer co-operatives fell in two years from 6,797 to 1,258 and declined further to 924 by the end of 1954. Those 924 co-operatives comprised 47,645 members with their families, a figure that cannot be equated with the number of formerly independent peasant farms on the same land. The number of members dropped even more sharply. Serbia alone accounted now for two-thirds of all co-operatives, most of them concentrated in the Vojvodina region, where resettlers from the south of Yugoslavia had been given land. Unfamiliar with local conditions, they found collective work in a co-operative advantageous. The agricultural land farmed by the co-operatives fell from 4,113,000 acres (1,665,000 ha) at the end of 1952 to 697,000 acres (282,000 ha) by the end of 1954. Of the latter figure, one-third was former peasant land, and two-thirds had come from the state's land fund (see Fig. 3.1).

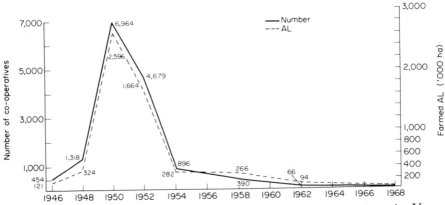

Fig. 3.1   Development of agricultural producer co-operatives in Yugoslavia, 1946–1968

In the following years the decline continued, and eventually only an insignificant number of co-operatives remained. Some of them were reorganised and transformed into multi-purpose co-operatives pursuing farming merely as one of a number of activities. These are now counted in the statistics among the socialist enterprises.

The government took no action against the exodus from the co-operatives, the exact volume of which could not have been foreseen, but is unlikely to have come as a surprise. After the dissolution of the majority of the producer co-operatives — which even in their heyday had farmed no more than 16·4 per cent of the total agricultural land — the agrarian structure is purely one of small peasant proprietors.

The official data on the number and size of peasant farms are incomplete; nor do they indicate how often peasants with capital resources

138

Table 3.6

Peasant farms according to size and social type (in thousands)

Size (ha)	1960			1969		
	Holdings	'Part-time' enterprises[1] included in (1)	(2) as a percentage of (1)	Holdings	'Part-time' enterprises[1] included in (4)	(5) as a percentage of (4)
	(1)	(2)	(3)	(4)	(5)	(6)
−2	915·8	485·6	53·0	1,013	558	55·1
2—3	392·8	154·9	39·4	400	171	42·8
3—5	552·3	181·0	32·3	526	191	36·3
5—8	421·3	113·6	27·0	384	117	30·5
8—10	141·8	33·7	23·2	129	35	27·1
10—	187·4	48·5	25·9	147	46	31·3
All holdings	2,618·1	1,017·3	38·9	2,599	1,118	43·0

[1] This term is not clearly defined, but appears to cover auxiliary and sideline enterprises.

Source: *The Yugoslav Village.*

exceed the legal limit for the size of private holdings. In the picture presented by Table 3.6, the smallest production units predominate. In terms of statistics, their total number has remained almost unchanged since 1949. In 1964 they farmed 86 per cent of the agricultural land. Small-holdings are tied up to a considerable degree with non-agricultural sources of income. Table 3.6 shows that in the period 1960 to 1969 the proportion of private agricultural holdings with such incomes rose from 39 to 43 per cent, while for the category of the smallest holdings (under 5 acres) the figure is as high as 55 per cent. This means that in 43 per cent of all private agricultural holdings one or more persons were permanently employed on work outside the holding. If those working abroad were counted realistically as permanently employed — official statistics consider them

Table 3.7

Development of social production units

	1950	1960	1970
Number of production units			
State and factory-owned farms	858	475	270
Peasant work co-operatives	6,913	147	–
General agricultural co-operatives	8,004	4,086	1,102
Total[1]	26,130	5,121	1,929
Cultivated areas ('000 ha)			
State and factory-owned farms	276	477	975
Peasant work co-operatives	1,589	120	–
General agricultural co-operatives	13	373	321
Total[2]	2,326	1,033	1,489
Average size of production unit (ha)			
State and factory-owned farms	320	1,001	3,611
Peasant work co-operatives	220	830	–
General agricultural co-operatives	2	91	291
Total	9	202	772

[1]   Total includes farms owned by schools, universities, institutes, the army, etc.

[2]   Total includes 116,416 ha of land that is socially owned but not used for social production.

Source: *The Yugoslav village.*

140

to be 'temporarily' employed — the proportion of agricultural holdings supplemented by non-agricultural sources of income would be much higher still. The conclusion to be drawn from these facts is not that agricultural incomes are low, but rather that the families are large and that there is accordingly a manpower surplus, while the limited employment prospects, as well as the housing shortage in the towns, act as disincentives to leaving the land altogether.

Beside the peasant farms there exists a small socialist sector in which the state farms predominate, as shown in Table 3.7. From 1950 to 1970, the area farmed by them increased by nearly 1,730,000 acres (700,000 ha) to 5,189,000 acres (2,100,000 ha), or 14 per cent of the entire agricultural land. The number of production units, however, was reduced through mergers to 2,155 (a fall of about 60 per cent). Half of them farmed under 250 acres, while the 88 largest state farms, each of more than 12,300 acres (5,000 ha) accounted for about half the 5,189,000 acres managed by all the state farms. After 1954 additional land was acquired only by renting, purchase or wasteland cultivation. In 1971 the socialised agricultural production units — including some major agro-industrial kombinats — held 15 per cent of the agricultural land; employed 5 per cent of the agricultural labour force; produced 24 per cent of the total output of the agricultural sector in terms of value; and supplied 47 per cent of the produce sold in the official markets (leaving the local peasant markets out of account). Thus, as set out in Table 3.8, they made

Table 3.8

Overall structure of agrarian sector, 1971

	Social		Private		Total
	No.	%	No.	%	
Production units ('000)	2·1	0·1	2,600	99·9	2,602
Work force ('000)	186	5	3,749	95	3,935
Agricultural land ('000 ha)	1,484	15	8,641	85	10,125
Cattle ('000 large livestock units)	455	9	4,683	91	5,138
Tractors	25,747	40	39,046	60	64,793
Market sales[1] (million Dinar)	8,439	47	9,412	53	17,851
Gross production value (million Dinar)	8,392	24	26,896	76	35,288

[1] Officially organised markets only; does not include sales at peasant markets and between enterprises.

Source: *Statisticki Godišnjak.*

a vital contribution to the needs of the market and food supplies, especially in the big towns. The socialised sector, then, acts as a safeguard against any possible reluctance to deliver on the part of the individual small producers.

The tasks of the agro-kombinats are as follows:

(a) to contribute to agricultural production and to food supplies for the non-agricultural population;
(b) to make products for use in agricultural production and conversion: breeding and growing of seed crops, animal breeding;
(c) to try out new production methods;
(d) to build up modern animal husbandry enterprises;
(e) to organise delivery contracts with small agricultural producers to ensure supplies for high-grade animal husbandry enterprises.

It is not intended that the example of the kombinats should be a direct influence on the production methods of peasant farms in the area. Such local response is not to be expected.

The principle of workers' self-management applies in agriculture as it does in other sectors of Yugoslav life. The workers and salaried employees elect a workers' council and management committee annually, by direct ballot. Two-thirds of the members of these bodies have to be changed at every election. No one may be elected more than twice running. Work in the elected bodies is honorary. Everyone has to continue his or her normal job. The director is elected by the self-management bodies and can be deposed. Workers' self-management discharges the following functions:

(a) discussion of enterprise plans for investments and production;
(b) checking on director's activities and, if the appropriate need arises, voting him out of office;
(c) working discipline;
(d) social welfare and sanitary facilities;
(e) determination of wages and distribution of profits.

For each of these tasks, especially the last, guide-lines are laid down and the decisions taken by the self-management bodies must meet certain conditions. It is the dual function of self-management to, on the one hand, educate the elected members, fostering a sense of responsibility and appreciation of their role, and, on the other, participate in management and check on the bureaucracy. The two functions are to some extent conflicting, yet they also complement one another.

142

3.1.5 General agricultural co-operatives

Apart from the more-or-less negligible producer co-operatives, there is a much larger number of other agricultural co-operatives operating similarly to the typical corresponding bodies in, say, Western Europe, where they perform an auxiliary economic role in organising the supplies needed by the members to run their farms and their households. These bodies are called 'general agricultural co-operatives' (obšta zemljoradnička zadruga). They handle the procurement and sale of production equipment and materials, purchase and marketing of products, joint processing enterprises, paid contract work with agricultural machinery for the members, and so on. In some places they run bakeries, abattoirs, flour mills and wine presses, and also some establishments for bulk buying of food, since the private trade was nationalised or turned over to co-operatives in 1945 and some villages have no consumer co-operatives. Moreover, some general co-operatives run cinemas and restaurants. Even banking facilities are offered by a few.

The general agricultural co-operatives are spread evenly over the whole country, with the exception of the constituent republic of Montenegro, where agriculture as a whole is weak. In Croatia in particular the general co-operatives represent an important factor. The decline in their number, indicated in Table 3.9, does not reflect a decline in strength, but rather a concentration and consolidation, an interpretation borne out by the virtually constant level of membership.

The most important tasks of the service co-operatives are:

(a)   hiring out of machines,
(b)   sale of fertilisers at reduced rates,
(c)   advice,
(d)   contract production.

Table 3.9

General agricultural co-operatives

1945	4,825	1950	8,004
1946	8,011	1951	7,581
1947	6,632	1952	6,973
1948	8,662	1953	7,114
1949	9,060	1954	6,538

Source: Bergmann, 1957; Kardelj, 1958; Markert, 1954; *Statisticki Godišnjak*, 1965.

Membership and active participation in the general peasant co-operatives remains voluntary. Nevertheless, the general function of co-operatives and the effect of their work are not identical in a socialist system and in a Western capitalist society. In the socialist system peasant co-operation is dominated by the influence of socialist aids to production, which are the fruits of socialised industry:

> This joint effort, based on linking the socialised means of production with the land of private production units, we call socialist co-operation, and it enables us to organise and develop the socialist mode of labour within the framework of large-scale agricultural production. (Kardelj, pp. 136 f.)

In the system of flexible planning, it is the task of the co-operatives to establish a link between the individual producer and the market, to ensure a regular flow of supplies to the market by means of delivery contracts, to integrate the peasantry into the plan, to popularise agro-technical progress, to organise optimum utilisation of the scant technical equipment and to take charge of untilled areas. In connection with their work of pioneering the use of novel technical equipment, they may be said to be organising the first steps towards co-operative production; moreover, they actually farm such land as was assigned to them or came to them by default.

The high-grade animal husbandry enterprises of the agro-kombinats and the co-operatives endeavour to integrate the small peasants into the market by way of production under contract. No political pressure can be applied to induce the peasants to conclude such contracts with the animal husbandry enterprises.

3.1.5 Agricultural production: inputs and performance

The climate and topography of the country show wide variations, which are naturally reflected in a number of widely different systems of tillage and farm management. In addition to the crops customary in Germany or Britain, maize and tobacco are grown, wine is produced on a large scale, and most of the trees native to the Mediterranean zone grow there. In hilly Slovenia small farms predominate, with much grassland and livestock. Arable farming is the main line in the lowland plains of Serbia, especially in the Vojvodina region. In the bare karst mountains of Bosnia, Montenegro and Macedonia, agriculture is reduced to the keeping of sheep and goats, and in the poorest tracts to nomad grazing. Accordingly, there is little or no scope for modern mechanised large-scale cultivation – large-scale in terms of operation rather than ownership — except in the broad riverain plains of the Danube, the Tisa and the Sava.

In keeping with the country's agrarian structure up to 1945 — when over 80 per cent of the population derived its livelihood from agriculture — there was little technical equipment and the use of commercial fertilisers was rare. Beside the low level of education of the peasantry, the balance of foreign trade and the sparseness of communications militated against the use of fertilisers and machinery. In 1945, then, 38 per cent of all agricultural production units had no plough, 18 per cent used wooden ploughs, 4·5 per cent had seed drills, and barely 50 per cent had draught animals of their own.

The total area of agricultural land declined in the period 1960 to 1969 by 1,853,000 acres (750,000 ha), or 5·5 per cent, to 35·1 million acres (14·2 million ha). Grassland was most affected by the decline (see Table 3.10).

Land utilisation is dictated by soil quality and the type of terrain. The black earth areas have for a long time been important maize growing regions. On higher ground, cattle farming is practised on an extensive scale. Vine and fruit growing are widespread at the foot of the mountains and in the plains. In the szik regions the high salinity and heaviness of the soils put a limit to some forms of arable farming. In the regions where loess and pulverised loam predominate soil erosion constitutes a problem that should not be underrated.

As regards arable farming, maize and wheat are the most important

Table 3.10

Agricultural land (thousand hectares)

	1960	1969
Cropland	8,352	8,241
fruit-growing	410	442
vine-growing	272	256
Meadows and pastures	6,640	5,994
Irrigated area	117	113[1]
AL total	14,992	14,235
Forest	8,831	8,867[1]

[1]   1968

Source: *Länderkurzberichte.*

Table 3.11

Production and yields of main crops; use of machines and fertilisers

	Average 1930–39	1950	1960	1970	1971
Cultivation ('000 ha)					
Maize	2,600	2,210	2,570	2,354	2,357
Wheat	2,140	1,790	2,060	1,833	1,930
Barley	423	325	363	280	280
Oats	366	389	334	283	265
Potatoes	275	241	288	329	330
Sugar beet	35	98	78	95	85
Sunflower	6	110	74	194	180
Production ('000 tonnes)					
Maize	4,300	2,090	6,160	6,928	7,179
Wheat	2,430	1,830	3,570	3,792	5,604
Barley	410	266	529	402	463
Oats	310	195	373	309	312
Potatoes	1,650	1,050	3,270	2,930	3,000
Sugar beet	616	851	2,290	3,636	2,948
Sunflower	9	69	98	264	347
Yields (q per ha)					
Maize	16·4	9·4	23·9	29·4	30·5
Wheat	11·4	10·3	17·3	20·7	29·0
Barley	9·7	8·2	14·6	14·4	16·5
Oats	8·5	5·0	11·2	10·9	11·8
Potatoes	60	43	112	89	91
Sugar beet	176	86	294	381	346
Sunflower	15·2	6·3	13·3	13·6	16·7
Machine stocks ('000)					
Tractors	2·5	6·3[1]	31·7	68·2	–
Combine harvesters	–	–	3·1	11·9	–

	1948–52	1961–65	1970/71
Fertiliser consumption ('000 tonnes nutrient)			
Nitrogen	6·0	145·6	293·6
Phosphate	8·4	122·9	182·7
Potash	3·2	121·0	155·5

[1] 1953.

Sources: *Länderberichte; Länderkurzberichte;* FAO, *Production Yearbook.*

crops, while sugar beet plays only a minor part (see Table 3.11). Sunflower is the most important oil crop. Growing conditions are determined by the dry continental climate with warm summers. Root crops are relatively unimportant. Harvests have tended to increase in the long term, but setbacks due to climatic variations from year to year have been frequent. Yields per acre have also gone up, although for some crops they are still substantially below those attained in the highly industrialised countries of Western Europe. Crop and stock farming yields are higher on the state farms run by modern intensive methods than on the peasant farms.

The use of fertilisers indicates a gradual change to more intensive methods of farming. Mechanisation, on the other hand, makes only slow progress, owing partly to the agricultural structure based on small production units and partly to the slow pace of industrialisation.

In animal husbandry the following trends can be noted:

(a)   the number of horses declines only slowly;
(b)   the numbers of cattle in general and cows in particular have gone up;
(c)   owing to intensified use of land, the number of sheep is gradually going down, while goats are on the point of vanishing altogether;
(d)   pig and poultry populations, now independent of landholdings, are rapidly increasing. (See Table 3.12, p. 151).

As a result of war-time devastation, the pre-war level of production had not been restored by 1950 in respect of the most important animal products. By 1971, however, pre-war levels had been considerably exceeded, except in the case of mutton and wool.

3.1.6   *Current agrarian policy and trends*

In the immediate post-war years the Soviet economic policy model was imitated in Yugoslavia, prompted partly by a desire for rapid industrialisation, and partly by Soviet pressure and advice. After Yugoslavia's political breakaway from the Soviet Union in 1948, the country evolved an economic policy model of its own, setting out from the realisation that a different starting position calls for a different economic policy. Yugoslavia was not industrialised, and a crash programme of industrialisation was neither necessary nor even possible. However, without the prior development of industry, a flow of manpower away from agriculture was bound to lead to unemployment. Thus the new agrarian policy was in part a pragmatic response, a retreat in face of the small peasant producers' reluctance to deliver their products.

Yugoslavia's agrarian policy, being general economic policy applied in a particular sector, must be seen within the framework of the specific Yugoslav model of a socialist society. The most important characteristics of this model are:

(a)   central planning is confined to the most important sectors and tasks, the remaining planning decisions being transferred to the lower echelons;
(b)   administrative controls are kept to a minimum;
(c)   workers' self-management is designed to facilitate the participation of producers in planning and management and helps to counteract alienation;
(d)   the federal constitutional structure provides a further counterpoise against bureaucracy and centralism;
(e)   the market — as the sum total of the needs of the consumers and their social institutions — is intended to play a part in regulating production;
(f)   whereas socialist enterprises dominate the secondary and tertiary sectors, they have only a supervisory function in the primary agricultural sector, so that the economic system as a whole is a mixed economy in which the sector subject to socialised supervision is dominant;
(g)   the pace of economic growth and industrialisation is slow, hence it is not possible to offer a sufficient number of non-agricultural work places: there is a manifest causal link between the retention of the old agrarian structure, the low factor contribution of agriculture and the low rate of economic growth;
(h)   Yugoslavia is the first socialist country to have allowed its unemployed to work in foreign capitalist countries — thus taking politics out of the migration of labour — to have made its currency convertible into the currencies of Western countries, and to have countenanced project cooperation with foreign capitalists. (Similar measures, however, were adopted by the Soviet Union during the NEP period in the early 1920s.)

Yugoslavia's agrarian policy was restated by Kardelj at the end of the 1950s. He pointed out the lessons to be learnt from the failure of collectivisation in Yugoslavia and analysed the reasons for the resistance of the peasants in many countries. He did not see this simply as a romantic clinging to tradition, nor as a violation of the principle of voluntary participation. What mattered most, according to Kardelj, was the fact that all those co-operative farms had brought the peasants together yet without supplying them with new aids to production, that is to say machines, tractors and fertilisers. Had they been available, and only then, it would have been possible to raise labour productivity, to make jointly the transition to new working methods in keeping with large-scale production, to achieve higher yields and thus give the members a convincing demonstration of the advantages of large-scale production units. But the industrial basis was missing and so that policy had been impossible. In other words, collectivisation in Yugoslavia had led to large-scale ownership without large-scale operation, and had created 'co-operatives of have-nots'. To Kardelj, this was pointless, and he argued that socialism makes sense only if, so far from being a sum total of poverty in the land, it effects a rapid modernisation and the raising of standards on a broad front for society as a whole. Accordingly he made a point of refusing to measure the success of socialism in the countryside by the percentage of collectivised agricultural land, a yardstick still applied in most countries of the Eastern bloc.

The peasant, says Kardelj, has a long way to go before he will take part in modern production. This transition is a very protracted process, and — a point he never tires of stressing, so as to impress it on his Party comrades — it must take its course entirely on the basis of voluntary participation. In capitalist countries with abundant industry this can be done — slowly — by increasing the production units and/or injecting large capital investments into each unit. That capitalist way is rejected by Kardelj, who pleads emphatically for the retention of the upper limit of 25 acres (10 ha) introduced under the land reform for private holdings. In a poor and hitherto backward country, he says, the integration of the farming population into the economic construction effort can be accomplished only through the co-operatives, in which the small peasants must be active of their own free will. The co-operatives must not only provide the peasants with the new aids to agricultural production, such as tractors, ploughs, seeds, fertilisers and pedigree stock, but also give advice on plant protection and artificial insemination, and assistance in marketing products or further converting them into animal products.

In a country where tens of thousands of so-called peasants have neither draught animals nor plough, and therefore are in reality no more than allotment holders, such tasks and many others can be solved only on a co-operative basis. Efficient technical advice, higher yields, better production through collective work in a co-operative and higher incomes for the peasant proprietors would carry far more conviction than any amount of political propaganda, let alone official coercion. The new aids to agrarian production — Kardelj argued — were too big for the small production unit and still too complex for the small peasant who was contributing his land and his labour to a mode of production that would increasingly acquire co-operative features. In this development, the importance of privately owned land as a production factor must gradually decrease, while that of labour and the new, co-operatively owned means of production increases. There was no getting round the need to pay the land-owner a ground-rent that must be included in his share of the proceeds. This, of course, runs counter to one of the basic theses of communist economic policy, but it is accepted by Kardelj as a necessary concession to the peasants. (It may be recalled here, however, that in the other communist states, too — the Soviet Union excepted — some types of producer co-operatives pay ground-rent to their members.) As the other factors of production gain in importance, the part played by ground-rent is bound to decline in comparison to other components of the co-operative peasant's income.

On the strength of his analysis of Soviet collectivisation, Kardelj arrives at a scheme in which the order of the stages is reversed. He points out that socialist production in agriculture requires not only the nationalisation and consolidation of the land, but also modern socialised means of production. Whereas the Soviet Union, in its compulsory collectivisation drive, put the main stress on the land, because the modern production equipment and materials were not available, the Yugoslavs intend to follow the opposite course by bringing the modern means of production into the village. In this way they will also be in a position to honour the principle of voluntary participation. Undoubtedly it will take a long time before the peasants find their way into the co-operatives, for first the machines must be produced and the peasants must satisfy themselves of the superiority of the new system. The process of transformation is prolonged in this way, but its harshness is eliminated.

This new line was adopted in its essentials in 1957; but its working out in detail needs time. It is also evident that Yugoslav policy proceeds with unhurried deliberation, and Kardelj warns time after time against blind zeal. He believes that the drastic changes in the national economy — industrialisation, the drift from the land, mechanisation of agricultural production — will alter the relative weight of individual problems. Once the peasants are a minority of the population, their issues dwindle in importance.

To avoid complete dependence on the small peasant, state farms were established and extended on lands which had not been in use before, or which had belonged to expelled German or Hungarian peasants or landowners. Interference with the property titles of Yugoslav peasants was avoided wherever possible. However, some peasants voluntarily gave up land to the state farms, and that was the only peasant land to which operations were extended. The output of the big estates, the agro-kombinats, is to help in safeguarding the food supplies of the urban population and thus lessen their dependence on the mood of the small producers and their readiness to deliver. On the strength of their contribution, the agro-kombinats are in a position to keep a check on the quality and prices of the products supplied by the private sector, all the more so as the urban population is growing at a relatively slow rate and the size of the market is limited.

The forcible collectivisation of the first phase was self-critically recognised as an unnecessary and, under Yugoslav conditions, harmful imitation of the Soviet model. It is not likely that the government will repeat the same mistake.

However, all these measures leave one problem unsolved: it is the problem of how it can be possible for a developing country like Yugoslavia, in which agriculture still represents the largest economic sector, to develop industry and agriculture simultaneously and mobilise the state's resources so as to support them even-handedly. In a country with a limited output of steel and tractors, a level of mechanisation comparable to, say, West Germany's — where in 1971 1·2 million tractors served 424,000 agricul-

Table 3.12

Livestock numbers and animal production

	1931	1950	1960	1970	1971
Animals ('000)					
Horses	1,333	1,097	1,272	1,076	1,230
Cattle (total)	4,718	5,248	5,295	5,029	5,138
cows	2,345[1]	2,340	2,522	2,865	2,786
Pigs	4,457	4,295	6,208	5,544	6,567
Sheep	10,934	10,046	11,460	8,974	8,703
Goats	2,316	789	—	160	158
Poultry	19,939	20,207	30,288	36,566	40,104
Production ('000 tonnes)[2]					
Beef	100	133	138	258	234
Pork	171	145	291	287	338
Mutton and goat	57	30	59	51	48
Cow's milk	1,480	1,380	2,214	2,626	2,500
Wool (in the grease)	14·9	15·1	13·5	7·3	7·2
Eggs (millions)	1,286	800	1,533	2,866	3,021

[1]   Including heifers over one year old.

[2]   Carcase weight; production in abattoirs and households, first column refers to average production 1930–39.

Sources: *Länderberichte*; FAO, *Production Yearbook.*

tural enterprises — seems wasteful over-investment. For the time being, and until there are sufficient steel-making and tractor-manufacturing capacities, it is just not possible to offer a tractor for sale to every peasant.

At the present stage in the development of Yugoslavia, the mass of the peasants cannot be given more assistance out of state resources than they are already contributing through taxation. If anything, they may have to get less. But it is not easy to levy taxes on small independent producers who sell directly to the market. Thus the lack or paucity of state support for the peasants can be interpreted either in political terms as a government policy designed to hamstring the independent peasants economically, or in economic terms as a simple consequence of poverty and the priority of other social tasks, such as education, social insurance, industry and transport.

Endeavours to raise production and productivity per acre and to integrate the independent peasant into the market continue to be given priority over measures aimed at a radical transformation of the rural social structure.

3.2   Poland: small peasants in a communist economy and society

3.2.1   *History*

1918–19 Poland restored as a state, having endured three partitions at the hands of the neighbouring powers; the Soviet Union, Germany and Austria cede their Polish territories to the new state.

1925 Pilsudski establishes his military dictatorship; persecution of left-wing parties.

1933 After Hitler's accession to power in Germany, the Polish military regime loosens its ties with France and looks to Hitler's Germany for support.

1938 Poland participates in the dismemberment of Czechoslovakia.

1939 Hitler brings pressure to bear to regain former German territories lost to Poland after the First World War; Britain and France give Poland a guarantee and open negotiations with the Soviet Union.

1939 (27 August) Stalin–Hitler Pact.

(1 September) Outbreak of the Second World War: the German armies invade Poland. The country is provisionally partitioned between the Soviet Union and Germany; the Polish Army smashed after three weeks' resistance; oppression, terror, expulsion of Polish peasants, to be replaced by German farmers; mass killing of Jews in vast death camps,

rising in the Warsaw ghetto and elsewhere; complete destruction of the capital by the Wehrmacht and SS.

1944 Poland rises again; rival efforts by East and West to gain influence over the new state and to determine its definitive frontiers.

1945 Potsdam Conference ends with acceptance of the Soviet Union's proposals; the new borders signal a westward shift of the Polish state and entail large-scale resettlement of Germans and Poles.

1948 Internal struggles and Stalinisation; Wladyslaw Gomulka is removed from the Party leadership and arrested, one of the chief points at issue being collectivisation, which Gomulka opposes.

1949 Start of collectivisation.

1956 Twentieth CPSU Congress and de-Stalinisation.
(June) Disturbances and strikes by Polish workers in Poznan and other industrial towns.
(October) Gomulka re-elected General Secretary of the Party; de-collectivisation within three months.

1970 (December) Turbulent demonstrations by Polish workers in Gdansk, Szczecin and other industrial towns on the Baltic coast; Gomulka finally dismissed and replaced by Edward Gierek; the harsh economic policy is abandoned.

3.2.2 *Agrarian structure*

Poland is in a state of transition from an agrarian to an industrial state: in 1931 60 per cent of the population were engaged in agriculture, but by 1950 the figure had dropped to 47 per cent and by 1970 to 30 per cent. This percentage is slowly but steadily declining, owing to the combined effect of the overall growth of the population and the reduction in the number of people engaged in agriculture. As Table 3.13 shows, the first trend predominated between 1950 and 1960, when the percentage of the agricultural population dropped from 47 to 38 per cent while in absolute figures it declined only slightly, from 11,597,000 to 11,244,000; between 1960 and 1970, however, the percentage drop from 38 to 30 per cent was accompanied by a marked fall in the absolute figure (to 9,732,000). The rate of population growth was very high after the war. The annual increase was 19·5 per thousand in 1953, but had dropped by 1969 to less than half that figure; that is, 8·3 per thousand. One population forecast predicted an increase of the population from 31·3 million in 1964 to 34·4 million in 1975. More recent estimates envisage a somewhat slower population growth. The non-agricultural population increased at a substantially higher rate than the general population.

Table 3.13
Polish population trends, 1931–2000 (in thousands)

End of year			Agricultural population		Non-agricultural population	
			No.	%	No.	%
1931		32,107	19,134	60	12,781·5	40
1938		34,849		–		–
1946 (14 Feb.)		23,930		–		–
1950		25,035	11,597	47	13,016·2	53
1960		29,893	11,244	38	18,124·6	62
1965		31,496		–		–
1968		32,426	10,701	33	21,725	67
1970		32,807	9,732	30	19,530	70
1972		33,068				
Forecasts						
1975	Alt. I	34,425				
	Alt. II	34,354				
2000	Alt. I	40,166				
	Alt. II	38,856				

Source: *Rocznik...* .

Table 3.14
Agrarian structure in terms of size of production units, 1950–1960

Size (ha)	Agricultural production units				Agricultural land	
	1950	1960	1950	1960	1950	1960
	('000)		(%)		(%)	
0·1– 0·5	199·7	347·7	6·3	9·7	0·3	0·5
0·5– 2	621·6	829·9	19·6	23·1	4·5	5·8
2 – 5	991·8	1,091·9	31·3	30·4	20·1	21·7
5 – 7	477·5	475·7	15·1	13·2	17·0	16·7
7 –10	499·0	462·0	15·7	12·9	25·0	22·8
10 –20	339·0	350·2	10·7	9·7	26·2	26·8
over 20	39·9	34·5	1·3	1·0	6·9	5·7
over 0·5	2,968·8	3,244·2	93·7	90·3	99·7	99·5
Total	3,168·5	3,591·9	100·0	100·0	100·0	100·0

Source: *Rocznik...* .

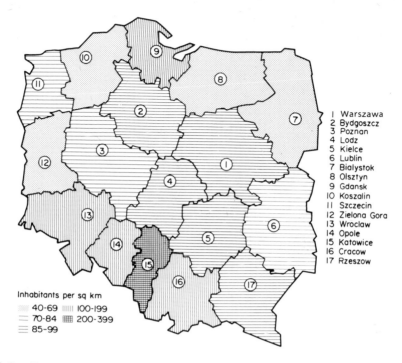

Fig. 3.2   Poland: population density, December 1969

The agrarian structure is characterised by small peasant proprietors. Between 1950 and 1960 the number of agricultural enterprises increased from 3,168,500 to 3,591,900 (see Table 3.14). Since the total area of agricultural land remained virtually unchanged, the increase in numbers meant that the average size of peasant farms was reduced to 11·9 acres (4·8 ha). This compares with the maximum size set by the land reform at 124 acres (50 ha) or, on poor soils, as much as 248 acres (100 ha). With landholdings of that size, even a highly industrialised state would not be able to provide every small farmer with up-to-date technical equipment.

The economic trend illustrated by Table 3.14 — showing that during the decade in question the number of farms with up to 12·4 acres (5 ha) rose by 457,000, while those with more than 12·4 acres fell by 34,000 — is the outcome of a set of circumstances which, in that combination, are not present either in the Soviet Union or in any Western industrial state. The development of Polish heavy industry made good headway on the whole, but did not in the earlier stages provide enough work-places to absorb the additional manpower available as a result of population growth. Thus, in the absence of the suction effect of industry, the pres-

155

sure on the countryside increased. There was no need for collectivisation to promote the building up of industry.

The growth of the state farms, set out in Table 3.15, is characterised by a steady increase in their total holdings of agricultural land, from 4,533,000 acres in 1950 to 7,182,000 acres in 1971 (1,828,000 to 2,896,000 ha); in 1969 they managed 15 per cent of the agricultural land in Poland. The number of state farms increased steadily from 5,679 in 1950 to 6,110 in 1969, then dropped sharply to 4,941 in 1971, a development reflected in the marked rise of the area of agricultural land per state farm from 799 acres in 1950 to 1,091 acres in 1969 and 1,453 acres in 1971 (322 to 440 to 586 ha). The labour force belonging to the state farms increased roughly in proportion to their holdings of agricultural land, while cattle and pig stocks registered dramatic increases. The state farms engage in seed growing, livestock breeding and technological experiments, as well as in market production. Their contribution to market supplies acts as a price regulator and as a safeguard against shortages that might arise from any reluctance on the part of the independent peasants to deliver their produce. The management of the state farm has been decentralised and functions nowadays with little interference from the central planning authorities. Besides the state farms administered by the Ministry of Agriculture, there is a considerable number of agricultural enterprises under the management of other institutions and apparently

Table 3.15

State farms under the Ministry of Agriculture, 1950—1971

	1950	1960	1969	1971
State farms	5,679	5,734	6,110	4,941
AL ('000 ha)	1,828	2,353	2,688	2,896
Full-time personnel ('000)	276	309	368	392
Horses ('000)	107	149	77	?
Cattle ('000)	260	755	1,523	1,879
Pigs ('000)	347	550	751	1,202
AL per state farm (ha)	322	410	440	586
Full-time workers per state farm	49	54	60	79
Full-time workers per 100 ha AL	15	13	14	14

Source: *Kleines statistisches Jahrbuch*; author's own calculations.

156

catering for their needs. There were 2,266 of them in 1969, with a total of 211,000 acres (85,000 ha) of agricultural land.

In 1949 a start was made with the formation of agricultural producer co-operatives on the Soviet model, in spite of the warnings uttered by Gomulka and his supporters. In the course of seven years up to 30 September 1956, the establishment of 10,510 such co-operatives is recorded in the statistics. They had some 192,000 members and held over 4,851,000 acres (1,963,000 ha) of agricultural land. This — as Table 3.16 shows — marked the height of the development of the agricultural producer co-operatives in Poland, and even then they held no more than 9·6 per cent of the country's agricultural land, 76·6 per cent being farmed by independent peasants and the remaining 13·8 per cent by the state farms. Perhaps one in 15 of all the families of peasants and agricultural workers, not counting workers employed by the state farms, had joined the producer co-operatives. In central Poland the share of the agricultural producer co-operatives in the agricultural land was far below the figure for the country as a whole: in Kielce Province, for instance, the proportion was no more than 1 per cent, in Cracow Province 1·6 per cent. In some of the newly gained Western Territories, on the other hand, the co-operative share was substantially higher than 20 per cent, for instance in Szczecin and Wroclaw Provinces, with 26·5 and 31·7 per cent respectively (see Table 3.17).

Table 3.16

Agricultural producer co-operatives, 1949–1972

End of year (or date stated)	Number	Area	Member households ('000)	Area (ha) per co-operative	Households
1949	243	41,700	6·1	171	25
1950	2,199	190,300	60·4	212	27
1955	9,790	1,866,900	188·5	193	19
1956 (30 Sept.)	10,510	1,963,000	191·6	187	18
1956 (31 Dec.)	1,534	260,100	–	170	–
1957 (31 March)	1,752	210,600	26·4	146	15
1960	2,072	267,000	25·6	110	13
1965	1,251	229,000	21·6	183	17
1970	1,096	280,000	25·3	256	23
1972	1,081	293,000	28·4	271	26

Source: *Rocznik....*

Table 3.17

Regional distribution of producer co-operatives

Province	Share of producer co-operatives in Agricultural land (percentages)		AL (ha)	Number of co-operatives
	1956	1963	1963	1963
Warszawa	2·0	0·6	12,375	108
Bydgoszcz	15·6	1·8	23,484	142
Poznan	15·4	4·3	81,858	354
Lodz	2·5	0·7	9,428	85
Kielce	1·0	0·3	4,773	58
Lublin	3·0	0·8	13,280	113
Bialystok	3·4	0·2	3,178	16
Olsztyn	7·8	0·4	5,775	26
Gdansk	14·3	1·5	9,255	43
Koszalin	13·6	0·3	2,669	15
Szczecin	26·5	1·2	9,251	36
Zielona Gora	16·6	0·6	4,289	23
Wroclaw	31·7	0·9	10,308	67
Opole	21·6	1·4	8,560	52
Katowice	2·4	1·1	6,411	53
Cracow	1·6	0·2	2,836	40
Rzeszow	5·0	0·7	8,647	64
Poland (total)	9·6	1·1	216,377	1,295

Source: *Rocznik... .*

These figures cast light on several aspects of the collectivisation drive.

(a)   In the areas of small peasant farms in central Poland the agrarian structure remained virtually unchanged.

(b)   Collectivisation affected chiefly the new Polish Western Territories and the regions characterised by large-scale farming.

(c)   Neither as regards speed of execution nor as regards comprehensiveness is the Polish campaign at all comparable to the forcible collectivisation drive in the Soviet Union. The modest results achieved after seven years of the campaign indicate that there can have been little coercion.

Industry had not made the preparations required to supply the new co-operative large-scale production enterprises on an adequate scale with modern production equipment and materials. Thus, membership of the producer co-operative did not entail the benefits of technological progress and an easing of the burden of work. Had new agricultural machines been available, they would have come to co-operative farms as jointly acquired capital. Their presence would have tied the members to the co-operative; for one thing, it would have been difficult to distribute them among the members in the event of a break-up, in contrast to the equipment brought by the members into the co-operative. But the machines were not available, and so the agricultural producer co-operatives merely presented the outward form of a potential large-scale production enterprise. Without the new technology they did not get beyond the stage of pre-industrial manufacture, and the specific advantages of large-scale production — economies of scale — did not materialise.

Moreover, the formerly independent peasants looked askance at the co-operative, which in their eyes appeared to be levelling down their social status and curtailing their roles as decision-makers and managers. The position was reversed in the case of the members who had formerly worked on the big estates, property-less, and deprived of most human rights. To them, membership of the co-operative held out prospects of social advancement: they could look forward to participating on equal terms in the processes of decision-making and to sharing in the collective ownership. Thus, the lack of technological aid, combined with the traditional spirit of independence, confirmed the resistance of the peasants to the collectivisation campaign, which was on the whole conducted with comparative moderation. The peasant opposition was one of the factors that led to the turning point of October 1956.

At the decisive October Plenum of the Central Committee of the Polish United Workers' Party in 1956, Gomulka was once again elected General Secretary of the Party. Membership of the agricultural producer co-operatives became truly voluntary. This led to the winding up of the majority of co-operatives within three months: the former peasants preferred to return to the ways of farming they were used to. In practice it was mostly the former agricultural workers and the destitute new settlers who stayed behind in the resettlement co-operatives on land assigned by the state under the land reform. To this group the co-operative spelt progress, something they were ready to accept voluntarily. Since 1957 the remaining agricultural producer co-operatives have become consolidated. They have been equipped with new machines and buildings, and their organisation has become more effective. Yet, with a total of 751,000 acres

Table 3.18

Structure of agricultural producer co-operatives in terms of size, 1963

Size of holding of AL (ha)	Percentage of all producer co-operatives
−100	34·4
100−200	36·5
200−300	17·3
300−500	7·5
over 500	4·3

Source: *Rocznik....*

I Warszawa
2 Bydgoszcz
3 Poznan
4 Lodz
5 Kielce
6 Lublin
7 Bialystok
8 Olsztyn
9 Gdansk
I0 Koszalin
II Szczecin
I2 Zielona Gora
I3 Wroclaw
I4 Opole
I5 Katowice
I6 Cracow
I7 Rzeszow

ha :
2·2-3·9   6·0-7·9
4·0-4·9   8·0-9·1
5·0-5·9

Fig. 3.3   Poland: average size of independent farms in the provinces, December 1963

(304,000 ha) of agricultural land and a total membership of 30,700 families, they are not of major significance for agriculture as a whole. Only in a few provinces do they hold an appreciable proportion of the agricultural land. Such is the case for instance in Poznan Province, where there were 354 producer co-operatives in 1963, over one-quarter of the number in the whole country; they were farming nearly two-fifths of the total agricultural land held by producer co-operatives in Poland, 4·3 per cent of the agricultural land in the Province. Table 3.18 shows that the agricultural producer co-operatives are predominantly medium-sized enterprises rather than giants. In 1963 some 71 per cent had less than 494 acres (200 ha) of agricultural land, and only one co-operative in 23 − 4·3 per cent of the total − had over 1,235 acres (500 ha).

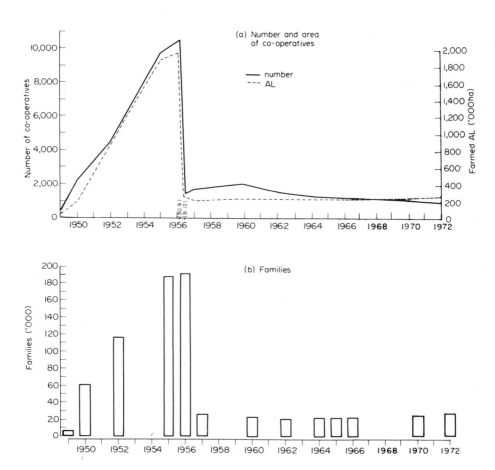

Fig. 3.4   Development of agricultural producer co-operatives in Poland, 1949−1972

More important than the producer co-operatives are other types of agricultural co-operatives, which were resuscitated after 1956. The planners had no choice but to accept the structural development of agriculture and the fragmentation of the food producers. The task of advising them and encouraging production and delivery called for new methods and institutions working in harmony with the market. Accordingly, official support was extended once again to the traditional forms of rural co-operatives, which have a long history in Poland, as the most effective way of linking the millions of small producers with, on the one hand, the market organised by the state or the consumer co-operatives, and, on the other, the few suppliers of production equipment and materials.

The most common form of rural co-operative is the agricultural circle. The circles purchase the larger machines, above all tractors and the whole range of attachments as well as reaping and threshing machines. They collect contracts for work which is subsequently carried out by the machine stations on the private fields of the members. They also advise their members on all production problems. From 1957 to 1972 the number of agricultural circles increased more than threefold; they are established in 88 per cent of all villages and cover one-third of all peasant farms. Membership rose from 325,000 to 1,500,000, a clear indication of the

Table 3.19

Agricultural circles and rural women's associations, 1957–1972

	1957	1960	1965	1969	1970	1972
Agricultural circles ('000)	11·6	23·1	32·6	34·5	35·1	35·4
Communes with circles (percentage of total)	28·5	56·8	80·1	86·5	87·8	88·5
Rural women's associations ('000)	3·6	10·5	24·8	33·0	34·9	35·6
Membership of circles ('000)	390·6	803·5	1,680·4	2,420·0	2,605·0	2,700·0
Members of circles also belonging to women's associations ('000)	64·1	203·1	582·9	1,000·0	1,088·2	1,200·0
Machine bases[1] managed by agricultural circles				1,820	2,091	2,398
State machine stations				730		748
Personnel[2] ('000) of agricultural circles			{ 114·0 }	99·0	95·2	99·8
of machine bases				56·0	64·4	75·2

[1]   Owned jointly by several agricultural circles.
[2]   Number of full and part-time workers (no conversion factor for latter).

Source: *Kleines statistisches Jahrbuch.*

voluntary character of the circles (see Table 3.19). The membership spans all sizes of farms from the smallest to the largest, as set out in Table 3.20; 78 per cent farmed less than 24·7 acres (10 ha). Comparison with Table 3.14 shows that the membership comprises proportionately more farms at the upper end of the range (above 24·7 acres, 10 ha) and fewer smallholdings (under 4·9 acres, 2 ha) than the national average; the proportion of dwarf holdings (under 1·2 acres, 0·5 ha) in particular is less than one-fifth of the corresponding figure for the country as a whole. The membership of individual agricultural circles is not very high – 71 on average.

Table 3.20

Landholdings of members of agricultural circles, 1969

Agricultural land (ha)	Percentage of members
– 0·5	1·8
0·5– 2	14·0
2 – 5	28·7
5 –10	33·6
10 –15	14·8
over 15	7·1

Source: *Rocznik...*

Even the agricultural circle, however, is too small a unit to warrant complete and economical mechanisation under present-day conditions. Accordingly, the machinery is kept at machine bases shared by a number of circles (usually five or six). The machine base keeps as a rule ten to 12 tractors as well as other agricultural machines and is responsible for their operation, servicing and repair. With this arrangement it is possible to ensure the employment of sufficient numbers of skilled staff without overstraining the financial resources of the agricultural circles. In the early stages of mechanisation a station with several tractors offers a better chance of spreading the risks, and thus enables its clients to carry out the appropriate modifications of their production organisation and work schedules. It has not so far been possible to ascertain the amount of work actually carried out by the agricultural circles and their machine bases. It is of course on the volume of such work that the usefulness of the agricultural circles to their members depends. The members are running their own farms without any outside interference. There is no provision in the

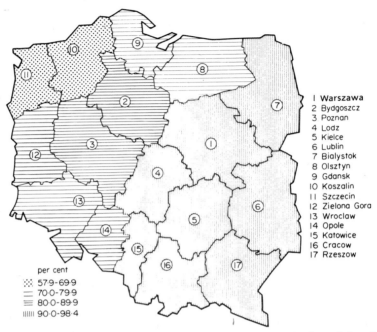

Fig. 3.5   Poland: independent peasants' share of agricultural land, December 1963

statutes ' for transferring any privately owned holdings to co-operative ownership, nor has any suggestion or recommendation been made to that effect.

Difficulties were encountered at first in raising the capital required to enable the agricultural circles to cope with their increased tasks: smallholders have very limited resources, while the big farmers hold back on political grounds. For that reason the government set up an agricultural development fund, into which it pays the difference between free market prices and the prices paid for quota deliveries. Out of this fund each local commune is allocated a sum representing the quantity of quota deliveries multiplied by the price differential. This money, however, may be claimed only by co-operative institutions such as the agricultural circles, not by individual peasants. Three-quarters of the money accruing to the agricultural circles from the development fund is tied for the purpose of machine purchases; the remaining quarter can freely be used for other village amenities. But the village only gets the money once an agricultural circle has been founded thanks to the initiative of some active local peasants or to the persuasion of an official agricultural adviser. There is a material incentive, then, for the formation of an agricultural circle and for joining

164

it, but there is no administrative coercion of any kind. This form of indirect guidance is comparable with the specific subsidies used as an instrument of agricultural policy in Western Europe.

As explained above, the agricultural circles do not exercise any authority over the landholdings of their members. Nevertheless, by June 1964 there were 4,300 circles, which engaged in co-operative farming on a limited scale. The state land fund had handed to them for long-term exploitation 303,000 acres (122,600 ha) of land earmarked for distribution under the land reform; in addition 4,400 head of cattle, 600 pigs, 3,300 sheep and 100 horses were held co-operatively. In this way the state contributed to the financing of the work of the agricultural circles and ensured the cultivation of land that had been expropriated in the course of the land reform but had not been given to independent peasants.

The building housing an inter-circle machine base often serves simultaneously as an advice centre (Polish: 'agronomowka'), where as a rule an academically qualified consultant has his office.

Many building materials enterprises have been set up on similar lines to the co-operative machine bases, serving a number of agricultural circles and other co-operatives. These enterprises manufacture building components for the construction or modernisation of outbuildings and farmhouses; they supply all the materials and to a limited extent advise the peasants through their architects in the planning and execution of building work.

General agricultural co-operatives – comparable with the German Raiffeisen co-operatives – are concerned with the purchase and marketing of goods. There were 2,513 of these in 1964, with a total membership of 4 million registered members. In 1966 each co-operative share cost 250 Zloty, about £5 sterling. The head organisation of these co-operatives is the Association for Peasant Self-help (Samopomoc Chlopska). The foremost functions of the general co-operatives are the purchase of all produce offered for sale by the peasants, with the exception of sugar beet and milk; the sale of all products needed for farming and for the peasant households; and the provision of services of many kinds. The co-operatives sell fertilisers, plant-protection agents, agricultural machinery and coal; they undertake repairs of electrical implements; and they run workshops, retail shops and restaurants. They act as agents of the government in purchasing quota deliveries, but they also buy up any other quantities and goods the producers are willing to supply. Engaging as they do in many not purely agricultural functions for the whole village population, the general co-operatives give the impression of excessively multifarious organisations lacking in specialisation. To increase their turnover, they trade with members and non-members alike. Sales of foodstuffs and industrial consumer goods amounted in 1963 to Z 69,810 million (about £ 1,300 million sterling), a figure that indicates the important role played by the general co-operatives in supplying goods to the rural population. The functions of the Association for Peasant Self-help and the co-operatives affiliated to it have changed over the years and it is likely that they have not yet reached their definitive form.

Table 3.21

Agricultural production, 1934–1972

	1934–38	1949	1955	1965	1970	1972
Production index (1950–52=100)						
Gross production at						
comparable prices	106·3	97·2	109·9	151·7	166	186
vegetable products	112·7	104·6	107·4	150·0	166	180
animal products	96·0	85·6	113·9	154·5	167	195
market production	–	81·8	117·7	181·9	211	242
Crop production (million ha)						
Sown area	17·6	14·8	15·4	15·1	15·0	14·7
Production (million tonnes)						
Grain	12·5	11·9	12·7	13·5	15·4	19·4
Potatoes	35·0	30·9	27·0	42·7	50·3	48·7
Sugar beet	2·8	4·8	7·3	12·3	12·7	14·3
Yields (q per ha)						
Wheat	11·2	12·3	14·9	20·6	23·2	25·4
Potatoes	121	122	100	154	184	184
Sugar beet	216	184	186	259	312	327
Livestock numbers and animal production						
Cattle (million head)	10·6	7·1	7·9	9·9	10·8	11·5
Cows (million)	7·2	4·8	5·5	5·9	6·1	6·0
Pigs (million)	7·5	6·1	10·9	13·8	13·4	17·3
Horses (million)	3·9	2·7	2·6	2·6	2·6	2·4
Meat ('000 tonnes)	967	843	1,378	2,015	2,207	2,477
Milk (million tonnes)	10·0	7·1	9·6	12·9	14·5	15·3
Milk yield (kg per cow)	1,382	1,648	1,763	2,186	2,458	2,550
Means of production						
Fertiliser (N+P+K) kg per ha AL[1]	7·1	17·7	26·7	56·4	123·6	149·1
Tractors ('000)	–	22·5	48·3	124·1	224·5	278·1
Cropland, ha per tractor	–	658	319	124	54	53

[1]   Pure nutrient.

Source: *Rocznik*; *Kleines statistisches Jahrbuch*; FAO, *Production Year-book*.

3.2.3 Yields and efficiency

The salient figures, illustrating the development of agricultural production in Poland from 1934 to 1972, are set out in Table 3.21. They show a slow increase in production and a gradual rise in yields, starting from a low initial level. High-grade animal husbandry involving a high conversion factor could be greatly extended if the large stock of horses were severely reduced. But mechanisation cannot go ahead fast enough, owing to both the agrarian structure with its multitude of small peasant farms and the attitude hitherto adopted by the planners.

3.2.4 Means of production

The production of fertilisers has only been intensified in the last few years. The few tractors there are belong predominantly to state farms and agricultural circles. Supplies of building materials are ample for all, including the independent peasants.

An economic policy review after October 1956 led to changes in planning. The standard of living of the people was to be raised in the long term; the consumer goods industries and agriculture received priority in the allocation of investments. In the current expansion of the chemical industry special attention is given to the production of fertilisers and plant-protection agents. The output of horse-drawn agricultural implements has been increased, but the mechanisation has so far been very slow. In the second half of the 1960s about 25,000 to 26,000 tractors a year were supplied to agriculture. Some of these were manufactured under an industrial co-operation scheme with Czechoslovak enterprises. But Poland also exports tractors. The stock of tractors increased from 28,400 units in 1950 to 189,500 in 1969. Out of the latter figure, 65,100 or 34·4 per cent were kept by the state farms, 81,900 or 43·2 per cent by the agricultural circles, 3·1 per cent by the producer co-operatives,

Table 3.22

Compulsory deliveries, 1955–1969

| | Quota deliveries as a percentage of total state purchases | | |
	1955	1965	1969
Grain	70	40·7	26·7
Potatoes	84	37	44
Livestock	43	23	19
Milk	37	—	—

Source: *Rocznik...* .

3·5 per cent by the remaining state machine stations, and 15·8 per cent by the larger peasant farms, where the use of those rare and hence costly machines is a reasonably sound economic proposition.

3.2.5 *Marketing*

Compulsory delivery quotas of agricultural produce have been progres-

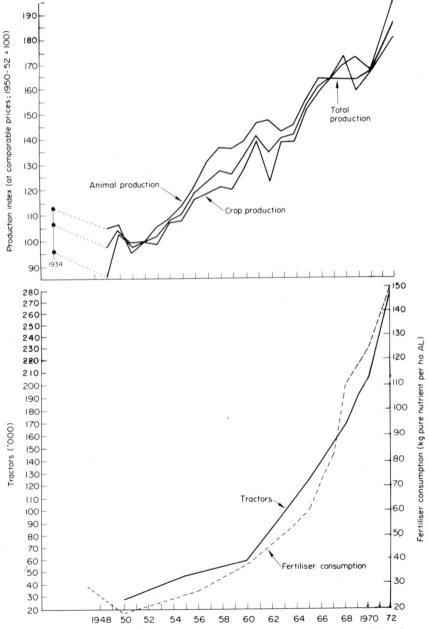

Fig. 3.6   Poland: agricultural production and input of production factors

sively reduced over the years and are due eventually to be abolished altogether. The decline in the relative importance of quota deliveries is illustrated in Table 3.22. Quota deliveries of grain, for instance, accounted for 70 per cent of state purchases of grain in 1955, but for no more than 26·7 per cent in 1969. Once a producer has met his quota, he can freely dispose of the rest of his produce. Price policy is aiming at a gradual unification of prices. Accordingly the gap between quota delivery and free market prices has been consistently narrowed by increasing the producer prices for quota deliveries. Eventually the gap is to disappear.

Beside co-operative marketing, contract deliveries have come to play an increasingly important part in recent years. Such delivery contracts may be concluded by the producers with sugar refineries, slaughter houses, meat processing factories, co-operatives, and so on. Most of them, it is true, are run by the state or by co-operatives, but the producer can now deal with them on a quite different footing from that he had at the time when quota deliveries predominated. He is now in a position to negotiate the terms of the contract: quantities, quality, delivery dates, to some extent even prices. If the terms offered are not to his liking, he looks round for another partner. Finally, the peasant has the option of taking his produce himself to the urban markets, an option still taken by many.

Thus, the marketing channels of agriculture have increased in number, giving the peasant producers more freedom of movement. The relative proportions of the four main channels are shifting: while quota deliveries are about to come to an end, co-operatives and contract purchasers are coming to the fore. As for free market sales, their volume is difficult to estimate, but they are undoubtedly important both in helping to assure varied food supplies for the population and in buttressing the bargaining position of the producers.

The trend of agricultural production has been rising, but even so supply difficulties have occurred on some occasions since 1956 and were dealt with by importing foodstuffs or by raising producer prices. This clearly shows that collectivisation — which in any case never reached quantitatively significant proportions — cannot have been the sole factor responsible for the earlier shortages. The real reason for the various supply shortages is probably to be sought above all in the circumstances of the transition from an agrarian to an industrial state. The difficulties are bound to be increased if there is a marked population growth during the crucial stage, and they are further aggravated if the speed of the transition is stepped up. But in essence they are characteristic concomitants of the stage of transition. Not until industry supplies the production equipment and materials needed by agriculture to intensify production and replace manpower will it be possible for a shrinking agricultural population to satisfy the rising demands of an expanding national population.

It was necessary temporarily to import coarse and bread grains. Great efforts are being made to export foodstuffs, in particular to the EEC countries. Large quantities of livestock on the hoof have been sold to Italy. Temporary shortages are caused by increased consumption combined with the independent peasants' lack of interest in the marketing of their produce.

3.2.6 *Agrarian policy*

Polish economic policy is based on centralised planning, from which, however, some sectors are largely exempt. This applies in the first place to agriculture as well as to some of the artisan trades. In pursuing its specific aims, agrarian policy makes use of the following instruments:

(a)   expansion of state farms through intensification and the reclamation of wasteland;
(b)   imports of foodstuffs and coarse grains;
(c)   price policy;
(d)   contracts between individual producers, co-operatives and state purchasing enterprises;
(e)   preferential supply of production equipment and materials to specific institutions, such as co-operatives or agricultural circles formed by independent peasants;
(f)   official support of co-operatives;
(g)   land cession annuities for small peasants giving up their farms.

3.2.7 *Outlook*

What conclusions can be drawn for the future in the light of Polish agrarian policy and the Polish government's experience to date?

The Polish example shows above all that it is perfectly feasible for a communist state to pursue an agrarian policy without collectivisation. In other words, the automatic association — equally prevalent in east and west — of 'communism' and 'collectivisation' as twin concepts must be abandoned. On the other hand, there is little likelihood of the Polish policy of de-collectivisation being imitated in other communist countries, least of all in the Soviet Union.

Polish agrarian policy is the subject of fierce and open debate within the country. The dividing line in this controversy, however, does not run between communists and bourgeois elements, but cuts across the customary groupings, with the Workers' Party exercising restraint and not committing itself to any definite position. The following points have to be considered.

Both the economic development and the political situation have been and are vastly different in Poland from those in the Soviet Union. Hence the requirements of structural policy were different in the two countries. As soon as the Soviet Union had ceased to bring pressure to bear, there was then no further reason to comply with the Soviet scheme. The application of Stalinist notions in Poland's agrarian policy was sharply criticised by Mieszczankowski:

> The Polish debate of 1956–1959 subjected Stalin's concept of the transformation of the countryside to wide-ranging criticism and revealed its serious errors. Lenin's concept, in its basic outline, says: the development of production, accompanied by changes in production relations, leads step by step to the socialist transformation of the countryside, with the principle of voluntariness being fully upheld and agricultural production being constantly increased. A general review of the findings of Marxist ideology in respect of the socialisation of agriculture must arrive at the conclusion that there can be no universally valid scheme of socialisation. While it is possible to formulate the general principle, the specific mechanisms and forms are bound to appear in a number of practical and theoretical variants ... .

Poland's agrarian policy is now based on the assumption that independent peasant farms will continue to exist for a considerable period. Their productive capacity is to be expanded. To further this aim, state subsidies have been made available since 1967 for the renewal of farm buildings. By 1980, Polish agriculture is to have 450,000 tractors, instead of the 110,000 operating in 1964. Misiuna cites other, even more ambitious targets set by the Planning Commission; according to him, Poland is to have more than 334,000 medium-weight tractors by 1970 and 564,000 by 1980. (This compares with the figure of 214,000 actually achieved in 1970.) The medium types to be produced are predominantly below 20 hp. In 1961 there was one tractor per 477 acres (193 ha) of agricultural land; by 1980 the figure is to be reduced to 94 acres (38 ha). It must be borne in mind, however, that with the present structure dominated by smallholdings, even that great production effort would make available no more than one tractor for every nine farms.

The plan targets for tractor production do not point to a design for collectivisation. On the other hand, the model computation associated with the plan figures indicates that a mechanisation of agriculture after the fashion of West European industrial nations cannot be contemplated for the time being. The output of tractors is small, the number of farms great, and the agricultural land of the individual production unit is just not extensive enough to warrant the use of this costly machine. Szewczyk has calculated that under current conditions individual ownership and utilisation of agricultural machinery is three times as expensive as collective utilisation. Okuniewski, Under-Secretary of State for Agriculture, said:

> The main task in the transformation of the agrarian structure will fall to the producer co-operatives and the agricultural circles, which should step by step develop the forms of collective work in agricultural production.

The bitter experience with collectivisation in Poland is likely to have confirmed Gomulka as well as his successors in their original rejection of this road. It does not seem probable, therefore, that the experiment will be repeated. However, the continued existence of 3,600,000 small farms and dwarf holdings has posed rather than solved the problem of the country's agrarian structure. Perhaps, indeed, there is no definitive solution, but only a continuing process in the course of which agriculture must time after time adjust to changed circumstances and redefine its place in society. Many Polish politicians concerned with agriculture consider an expansion of the state farms possible; others are inclined to set more store by co-operative forms of agriculture. As for government experts, they probably attach most importance to modern production methods and means of production as instruments bound to promote co-operation in the long run.

All these arguments lay the greatest stress on pragmatic considerations. Other observers, in particular a number of West German and North American agrarian economists, tend to look upon collectivisation rather as a politically motivated measure. They hold that communist policy will never be able to come to terms with the existence of independent peasants, but is driven by the inherent laws of communist rule to seek to liquidate this stratum and to degrade the peasants to the status of agricultural labourers paid by the state. It is a fact, however, that since 1956 Poland has not pursued this path and is thus one of the three communist states — the other two being Yugoslavia and Cuba — where producer co-operatives play only an insignificant part in agriculture and a multitude of small peasant farms determines the agrarian structure. Agrarian policy in these states is confronted with the problem, so far unsolved, of integrating into a planned economy an agrarian sector dominated by small production units.

3.2.8 *Causes of the divergencies in agrarian policy*

In the Soviet Union rapid industrialisation was a necessity, hence intensive capital formation and mobilisation and transfer of capital from agriculture were the order of the day. In the 1920s Russia stood alone, politically isolated and economically ostracised. A strong domestic basic and heavy industry was the foundation for establishing a modern agriculture and an independent state as well as for victory in the Second World War. In Yugoslavia and Poland it was both possible and necessary to industrialise at a slower pace, because intensified police pressure would have placed the state in jeopardy. Neither country was isolated. To some extent both were able to play on the rivalry between the aid-giving countries. Rapid population shifts to the towns would have led to visible unemployment. Hence collectivisation was not dictated by economic circumstances. Moreover the two countries' industries were not in a position to supply the production equipment and materials which alone could have made collectivisation palatable to the peasants.

4 Models of Socialist Agrarian Policy in Developing Countries

4.1 China: agrarian revolution without modern technology

4.1.1 *History*

1840 Irruption of the European powers; the Opium War; the Peace of Nanking; unequal treaties. China's weakness leads to a scramble for privileges on the part of the powers.

1850 First attempts at anti-colonialist risings, followed by punitive expeditions and colonial wars, ending with Chinese defeat and new concessions.

1850—64 Taiping rising, accompanied by an attempt at a land reform.

1860 Treaty of Peking: establishment of European legations; removal of restrictions on trade and missionary activities.

1864—78 Muslim rising.

1900 Boxer rising; punitive expedition under German command. Rivalry between the colonial powers preserves China from partition, hence policy of the open door.

As a result of the forcible entry of Western capitalism, China's trade, customs duties and taxes pass into foreign hands; imports of cheap industrial goods destroy Chinese crafts and artisan trades; in the densely populated rural areas standards of living fall; the traditional social order decays; a proletariat and a revolutionary intelligentsia emerge in the growing ports. The Empire declines.

1905—12 Foundation of Kuomintang.

1911 Revolution of the Young Chinese; abdication of last Manchu Emperor.

1912 Establishment of Republic.

1916—26 Internal wars between the war lords.

1921 Foundation of the Communist Party of China.

1925—49 Civil war and peasant risings.

1927 Chiang Kai-shek defeats workers in Canton and other towns and quells peasant risings; expulsion of the Soviet military advisers; beginning of the confrontation between Kuomintang and communists.

1928 Foundation of the Red Army; establishment of peasant associations;

expropriation of large estate owners; redistribution of land; reduction of farm rents.

1931 Central government formed in Peking; Japan invades Manchuria.

1937–45 Sino-Japanese War; parts of China occupied by Japan.

1949 Chiang Kai-shek defeated; establishment of communist central government.

1950 Occupation of Tibet.

1950–56 Land reform in four stages: distribution of land, mutual aid, formation of co-operatives, collective farms.

1953 First Five Year Plan.

1957 Unsuccessful offensive against Formosa (Taiwan).

1958 Setting up of people's communes and launching of the Great Leap Forward, which ends in failure.

1960 Beginning of the ideological conflict with Moscow.

1961–63 Famines, unrest.

1962 Open breach with CPSU; border conflict with India.

1964 China's first atomic bomb.

1969 Armed clashes with Soviet troops over a border island in the Ussuri river.

1971 China returns to the UN on her own terms and takes over a Security Council seat as a recognised world power.

1972 President Nixon visits Peking.

4.1.2 *Natural conditions and population*

China extends from longitude 73° to 135° east, and from latitude 22° to 54° north. The country covers an area of 3,692,000 square miles. In the west there are high mountain ranges, in the east vast lowland plains; in the north and in Shantung there are forest soils, in the north-west steppe soils, and in the south red earths.

There are marked climatic differences between the regions: in the north areas with a raw temperate climate; in the south tropical areas; in the west a continental climate; in the east maritime influences. Precipitation is affected by the rainy south-west monsoons in spring and summer. The winters are mostly dry. In the south precipitation is more evenly distributed over the seasons, and the total volume is higher. Peking has an annual rainfall of only 11·8 inches (300 mm), the bulk of it between June and August. In the south the figure reaches up to 66·9 inches (1,700 mm), and the bigger volume — as stated before — is more evenly distributed. Large areas in the interior of the country are arid or even approaching desert-character. Inundations in the great river valleys necessitate flood protec-

Table 4.1

Population and rural population, 1912–1969

Year	Total (million)	Increase over preceding year (%)	Inhabitants per sq km	Urban population	Rural population	Economically active (million)		Those economically active in agriculture as a percentage of total
				(percentage of total)		Total	Agriculture	
1912	430·0	–	45·0	8·5	91·5	–	–	–
1933	500·0	–	52·3	9·3	90·7	–	–	–
1950	546·8	1·7	57·2	10·9	89·1	–	–	–
1952	568·9	2·0	59·5	12·1	87·9	270·4	237·8	87·9
1960	683·0	1·8	71·4	15·5	84·5	361·0	284·6	78·8
1969	798·6	2·0	83·5	14·6	85·4	387·2	329·1	85·0

Source: Rochlin and Hagemann.

tion measures, in particular the construction of dykes and reservoirs.

Up to 1949, no comprehensive agricultural statistics were issued, and the computations based on the existing regional investigations and analyses bore little relation to reality. After 1949 statistics were organised on a central basis. But since the setback following the Great Leap Forward no further statistics or statistical year-books have been published by the government. Accordingly all numerical data concerning the population, agriculture and industry are highly uncertain and controversial. They are mostly taken from calculations by Japanese, Soviet and American research workers.

Population estimates diverge widely. It is reasonable to assume that at the end of the 1960s, China had a population of the order of 700 million people. The 1953 census resulted in a figure of 582·6 million; an FAO estimate put the figure at 780·5 million in 1966; while German research workers came out with a figure of 740 to 800 million. The figures of Table 4.1 — derived largely from extrapolation on the assumption of certain rates of growth — indicate that the population has nearly doubled since 1912. The growth rate is estimated at about 2·0 per cent per year. The relative proportion of the rural population shows a very gradual decline, while in absolute figures it has constantly increased. The same applies to the number of people working in agriculture, who still represent 85 per cent of the country's labour force. The development of the secondary and tertiary sectors is still too weak to absorb even the annual increment of people of working age.

Population density is very uneven, as illustrated in Table 4.2 and Fig. 4.1. The population is crowded into the coastal regions and the lower reaches of the river valleys, while vast tracts are almost uninhabited or only used by nomads. The Tibetan plateau, at an altitude of 13,000 feet above sea level, does not for the time being lend itself to settlement at increased densities. Other regions still await internal colonisation. Over 20 per cent of the world's population are Chinese, but China has only 8 per cent of the world's agricultural land, 0·4 acres (1,600 sq m) per inhabitant. Agricultural raw materials and goods processed from them account for 60 to 70 per cent of all export goods.

4.1.3 Agricultural production

In the south and east rice predominates as bread grain; in the north wheat and sorghum are the preferred crops. The form of agriculture practised is mostly digging or spade husbandry and is concentrated in the densely populated river valleys and coastal marshes. The production units are very

Table 4.2
Area and population of the People's Republic of China, 1957 and 1967

Administrative unit	Capital	Area ('000 sq km)	Population ('000)		Inhabitants per sq km	
			1957	1967	1957	1967
Provinces						
North-East China						
Heilungkiang	Harbin	464	14,860	21,000	32	45
Kirin	Ch'ang-ch'un	187	12,550	17,000	67	91
Liaoning	Shen-yang	151	24,090	28,000	160	185
Northern China						
Hopeh	Tientsin	213	41,500	43,000	195	202
Shansi	T'ai-yüan	157	15,960	18,000	102	115
Eastern China						
Anhwei	Ho-fei	140	33,560	35,000	240	250
Chekiang	Hang-chou	102	25,280	31,000	248	304
Kiangsu	Nanking	107	45,230	47,000	422	439
Fukien	Fu-chou	123	14,650	17,000	119	138
Shantung	Chi-nan	153	54,030	56,000	352	366
Central and Southern China						
Kiangsi	Nan-Ch'ang	165	18,610	22,000	113	133
Honan	Cheng-chou	167	48,670	50,000	291	299
Hunan	Ch'an-sha	211	36,220	38,000	172	180
Hupeh	Wu-han	188	30,790	32,000	164	170
Kwangtung	Canton	231	37,960	40,000	164	173
South-West China						
Kweichou	Kuei-yang	174	16,890	17,000	97	98
Szechwan	Ch'eng-tu	569	72,160	70,000	127	123
Yunnan	K'un-ming	436	19,100	23,000	44	53
North-West China						
Tsinghai	Hsi-ning	721	2,050	2,000	3	3
Kansu	Lan-chou	367	12,800	13,000	35	35
Shensi	Hsi-an	196	18,130	21,000	93	107
Autonomous Regions						
Inner Mongolia	Huhehot	1,178	9,200	13,000	8	11
Kwangsi	Nan-ning	220	19,390	24,000	88	109
Ninghsia	Yinch'uan	66	1,810	2,000	27	30
Sinkiang	Urumchi	1,647	5,640	8,000	3	5
Tibet	Lhasa	1,222	1,270	1,400	1	1
Urban Areas						
Peking		4·7	4,010	7,800	853	1,660
Shanghai		0·7	6,900	11,000	9,857	15,714
Tientsin		2·3	3,220	4,000	1,400	1,739
Total		9,569·4	656,220	725,500	68	76

Sources: *China-Informationen...;* and others.

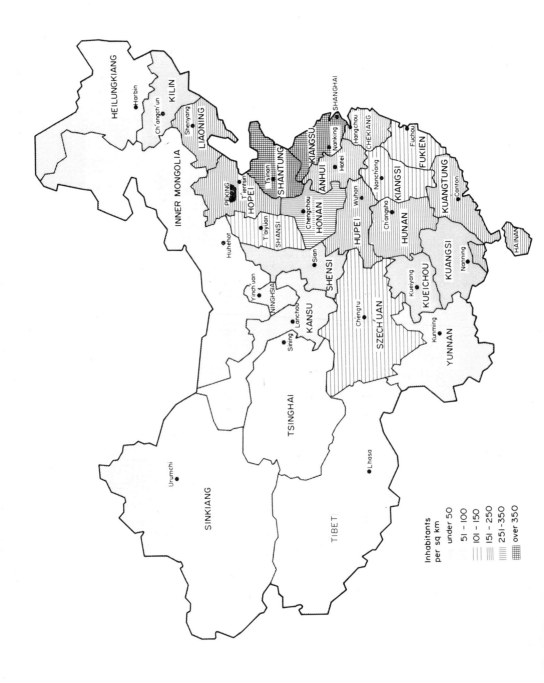

Fig. 4.1   Population density in Chinese provinces, 1961

180

small; the land is used intensively. Draught animals are rare. The interior of the country is scarcely utilised for agriculture owing to the arid climate and the absence of tractive power. It will need irrigation and tractors to accelerate the colonisation of the interior.

Regional differences are substantial. Skibbe distinguishes the following nine zones:

(i)   extensive pastoral economy in the west and north;
(ii)   spring wheat zone;
(iii)   sorghum—soy bean zone in the north-east and Manchuria;
(iv)   winter wheat—millet zone;
(v)   winter wheat—sorghum zone;
(vi)   Yangtse rice—wheat zone;
(vii)   south-western rice zone;
(viii) rice—tea zone;
(ix)   two-crop rice zone.

In 1969 agricultural land totalled 724 million acres (293 million ha), of which 277 million acres (112 million ha) is cropland. Two crops were harvested on 124 million acres (50 million ha) or 45 per cent of the entire cropland. Accordingly the land utilisation index works out at 145 per cent or 1·45. Table 4.3 shows the increase of the irrigated area from 52·6 million acres (21·3 million ha) in 1952 to 85·7 million acres (34·7 million ha) in 1957 and 197·7 million acres (80 million ha) in 1969. But the table also shows that despite the increase in the acreage of cropland and intensified cultivation by means of irrigation and multiple harvests, the utilised area

Table 4.3

China's agricultural land

	1949	1960	1969
Cropland (million ha)	97·8	105·5	112·0
Permanent grass (million ha)	175·0	178·1	181·0
AL total (million ha)	272·8	283·6	293·0
Sown area[1] (million ha)	135·0	145·8	162·4
Multiple cropping factor[1] (%)	138·1	138·2	145·0
Irrigated area (million ha)	16·0	66·3	80·0
Cropland ⎫ ha per head of ⎧	0·20	0·18	0·16
Sown area ⎭ rural population ⎩	0·28	0·25	0·24

[1]   Sown area is cropland multiplied by multiple cropping factor.

Source: Rochlin and Hagemann.

181

per head of the rural population has constantly declined. It must be feared that the worsening of the man—land ratio renders an increase in labour productivity difficult or impossible. This highlights a grave problem of economic policy.

Table 4.4

Crop production, 1932–1969

	Average 1932–36	1949	1958	1960	1969
Cultivated area (million ha)					
Rice	26·8	25·8	32·9	30·5	34·0
Wheat	28·7	21·6	26·8	24·0	24·5
Other cereals	54·3	47·4	45·7	48·5	54·8
Grain total	109·8	94·8	105·4	103·0	113·3
Potatoes	4·6	7·0	16·3	12·0	13·5
Soy beans	8·7	8·3	9·3	9·5	10·5
Cotton	3·0	3·0	5·7	5·2	5·2
Production (million tonnes)					
Rice	67·8	48·7	113·7	77·5	113·8
Wheat	30·6	13·8	29·0	20·0	25·9
Other cereals	63·2	35·8	61·9	43·6	59·2
Grain total	161·6	98·3	204·6	141·1	198·9
Potatoes	34·8	39·4	181·6	88·0	124·2
Soy beans	9·9	5·1	10·5	7·8	11·3
Cotton	0·7	0·4	2·1	1·6	2·2
Yields (q per ha)					
Rice	25·3	18·8	34·5	25·4	33·5
Wheat	10·7	6·4	10·8	8·3	10·6
Other cereals	11·6	7·6	13·6	9·0	10·8
Grain total	14·7	10·3	19·4	13·7	17·6
Potatoes	76	56	112	73	92
Soy beans	11·5	6·1	11·3	8·2	10·8
Cotton	2·3	1·7	3·6	3·1	4·1
Per-capita production (kg)					
Rice		90	173	113	143
Wheat		26	44	29	32
Grain total		183	312	207	249
Potatoes		74	277	129	156
Soy beans		9	16	11	14

Source: Rochlin and Hagemann.

As regards particular crops, the most notable increases in acreage have been for rice, potatoes, soy beans and cotton, as shown in Table 4.4. Rice has shown the most substantial increases in production and yields over the years. It should be noted that the figures for 1958, the year of the Great Leap Forward, are most probably exaggerated. Nevertheless, the harvests of most of the basic crops can be seen to have gradually increased up to 1969. Yields are considerably above those in India or Pakistan, but lower than in Japan. China has reached the highest level attainable on the basis of traditional technology.

The use of chemical fertilisers was initiated only after 1950 and was effectively promoted both by domestic production and by imports (see Table 4.5). Although considerable progress has been made in this respect, the application of fertilisers still lags far behind the level customary in modern, densely populated industrial countries. However, considering the rates of growth to date and those that might be achieved in the future, it is perfectly feasible for China to catch up with the industrial nations in this respect within the foreseeable future.

Table 4.5

Production, importation and consumption of fertilisers[1]

Year	Production ('000 tonnes)	Imports ('000 tonnes)	Total ('000 tonnes)		Consumption per ha	
			Gross	Pure nutrient	Cropland	Sown area
1949	27	–	–	–	–	–
1952	181	137	318	67	0·6	0·5
1960	2,000	1,134	3,134	665	6·3	4·6
1965	5,677	2,250	7,927	1,683	15·7	10·6
1969	12,150	4,250	16,400	4,050	36·2	24·9

[1]   All fertilisers combined.

Source: Rochlin and Hagemann.

Electrification and the introduction of tractors are still in their early stages. According to figures published by the Soviet Union, the output of tractors was 45,000 in 1966 and 40,000 in 1967. A different set of figures – presented in Table 4.6 – was given by Rochlin and Hagemann. Their estimate is substantially below the Soviet figures. They put the increase in Chinese tractor stocks, measured in 15 hp units, at 85,000 during the four years from 1965 to 1969, an average of some 21,000 a year.

The supply of staple foods seems on the whole assured.

Table 4.6

Stock of modern agricultural machines, 1940–1969

Year	Tractors[1]	Combine harvesters ('000)	Cropland per tractor[2] (ha)
1940	0·4	—	—
1950	1·3	—	550,300
1955	8·0	—	38,050
1960	68·0	5·7	4,250
1965	118·0	13·3	2,050
1969	203·0	23·4	850

[1] 15 hp units.
[2] Physical units.

Source: Rochlin and Hagemann.

Table 4.7

Livestock numbers, 1949–1969 (million)

Year	Cattle		Pigs	Sheep and goats	Horses	Donkeys and mules
	Total	Water buffaloes				
1949	43·9	10·2	57·7	42·3	4·9	11·0
1952	56·6	11·6	89·8	61·8	6·1	13·4
1955	66·0	12·5	87·9	84·2	7·3	14·1
1959	65·4	13·5	180·8	112·5	7·6	12·3
1960	56·5	11·8	130·0	118·0	7·6	11·8
1961	44·0	11·8	90·0	96·0	5·4	11·2
1965	50·3	13·8	185·0	113·0	6·3	18·0
1969	63·0	15·3	226·0	122·0	7·6	25·0

Source: Rochlin and Hagemann.

Livestock trends are shown in Table 4.7, and graphically represented in Fig. 4.4 (p. 217). There are only 7·6 million horses, which is not enough for tillage work. Since 1949 the numbers of horses, donkeys and mules have been greatly increased, though the upward trend was temporarily interrupted by a decline at the beginning of the 1960s. Virgin lands cannot be brought under the plough for lack of draught animals. Cattle stocks are low in relation to the size of the population, at any rate in terms of European levels of demand for milk and meat. Cattle stocks declined after collectivisation and the Great Leap Forward from 65·4 to 44·0 million head; that is by almost one-third. By 1969 the former level had almost been reached once again. The setback resembled the consequences of collectivisation in the Soviet Union, but on a smaller scale. The pig population has been increased substantially. Traditionally, pig and poultry keeping is of greater importance than dairy farming. The keeping of sheep and goats has also expanded.

For the purposes of price policy, agricultural products are divided into three categories by the government. The first category comprises food grains, cotton, oil crops, important industrial crops and a number of animal products. All these products have to be delivered at fixed prices to the state trading corporations. The second category comprises 'export products', of which a fixed quota is to be delivered to the same corporations at prices fixed in the course of negotiations between the government and the producers. The third category comprises all other agricultural products, which may be freely sold at the village markets.

4.1.4 *Agrarian structure, agrarian revolution and the people's communes*

China's agrarian structure and the social set-up in the villages provided a unique starting position for subsequent developments. Owing to the highly intensive spade husbandry, landholdings in most areas were much smal-

Table 4.8

Class structure of rural population, 1934

Class	Land owned per household (ha)	Percentage of rural house-holds	Percentage of total arable land
Landlords	11·5	3	26
Rich peasants	5·1	7	27
Medium peasants	2·2	22	25
Poor peasants and workers	0·5	68	22

Source: Mao Tse-tung.

Fig. 4.2   Inhabitants and area of Chinese provinces, 1961

ler than in Europe or America. In one of his early works Mao Tse-tung defined the social groupings in the village and estimated their relative numerical strength (see also Table 4.8).

1 Landowners: they do not work, but let their land to peasants, administer real property, and levy ground-rent. Their holdings averaged 28·4 acres (11·5 ha). Usurers are classified together with landowners.
2 Big peasants: they own and/or rent land in order to farm it themselves. They take part in the work, but also employ paid labourers, and they may let some of their land to peasants. They derived a large proportion of their income from the exploitation of the labourers employed by them. Average landholding 12·6 acres (5·1 ha).
3 Medium peasants: they own and rent land. The main source of their livelihood is their own labour. They have their own stock and working capital. Average holding 5·4 acres (2·2 ha).
4 The village poor: they own little or no land as well as little stock. They rent land, need loans, and work part of the time for others as wage labourers. Average holding 1·2 acres (0·5 ha).
5 Workers.

The polarisation of landholdings before the communist take-over was not very far-reaching. The ratio of population to land is unfavourable. The village and the agricultural land are overpopulated, with no opportunity for migration: hence the growing exploitation of tenant farmers and agricultural labourers by the landowners. The Chinese revolution and the Red Army derived their support from the peasants. Even before 1945, cautious measures of agrarian reform were introduced in the territories under communist rule: reduction of rents, limitation of landholdings, expropriation of landowners who had collaborated with the Japanese, partial redistribution of the land. During 20 years of civil war the peasants had time to adjust to the social transformation carried out step by step.

From 1950 on, these successive steps led systematically in the direction of collectivisation. Here, the first stage was the setting up of mutual-aid labour teams which worked together for a season or for a whole year. From then on both the size and the scope of the co-operative units were increased progressively by the formation first of 'lower-level', then of fully socialist, co-operatives and finally of people's communes. This development is set out in numerical terms in Table 4.9, while Table 4.10 illustrates the organisational structure of the people's communes. It appears from these tables that the number of people's communes declined, as a result of amalgamations, from 26,400 in 1958 to 24,000 in 1960, after which the trend was drastically reversed, the large units being divided and

Table 4.9

Stages of collectivisation, 1950—1958

Mode of collective	1950	1952	1954	1956 (May)	1957 (June)	1958 (30 Sept.)	1960 (Estimate)
Peasant households ('000)							
Total	105,536	113,683	117,331	120,761	122,500	125,500	
No. in mutual aid working							
groups	11,313	45,364	68,478	*	*	†	
seasonal	–	33,916	37,765	*	*	†	
all year	–	11,448	30,713	*	*	†	
No. in producer co-operatives							
total	0·2	59	2,297	110,134	118,800	†	
elementary type	0·2	57	2,285	35,414	4,500	†	
fully socialist type	0·0	2	12	74,720	114,300	†	
No. in people's communes	–	–	–	–	–	121,936	
Producer co-operatives ('000)	19	3,644	114,366	1,003,657	752,113	†	
Elementary type	18	3,634	114,165	700,901	72,032	†	
Fully socialist type	1	10	201	302,756	680,081	†	
People's communes	–	–	–	–	–	26,425	24,000‡
State farms	1,215	2,336	2,415	–	–	–	2,500

* All, apart from a few, absorbed into producer co-operatives.
† All, apart from a few, absorbed into people's communes.
‡ Reduced by fusion to 24,000 by the end of 1959, subsequently increased by division to 74,000 in 1963.

Sources: Chao Kuo-Chün; Lichnowsky.

Table 4.10
Structure of rural people's communes, 1959

	Number	Average size	
		Cropland (ha)	Households
People's communes	24,000	4,500	5,500
Production brigades	500,000	220	264
Production teams	3,000,000	35	42

Source: Lichnowsky.

the figure rising sharply to 74,000 in 1963. In 1959 each commune comprised on average 5,500 households (other estimates have put this figure at 5,000 or 5,250) and 11,100 acres (4,500 ha) of arable land. They were subdivided into production brigades and production teams.

The collective farmers' income is supplemented by the proceeds of their household plots. These are small, taking up 5 to 8 per cent of the co-operatively farmed agricultural land. There are marked regional variations in the average size of household plots, depending on the intensity of land use. About 9 to 30 per cent of family incomes is derived from the private plots. Reflecting the general conditions of Chinese agriculture, the household sector is confined to the keeping of pigs and poultry and the maintenance of a vegetable plot, without dairy cattle or pasture land.

The functions of the various types of co-operative organisation characterising the successive stages of collectivisation are summed up in Chart 4.1.

In an eight-point programme the communes were assigned the following tasks:

(i)   construction of water storage projects, using manpower reserves not needed for agricultural work;
(ii)   increased and more judicious use of chemical fertilisers;
(iii)   introduction of scientific crop rotation;
(iv)   instruction of the peasants in the techniques of deep ploughing and soil preservation;
(v)   raising yields by closer planting of crops;
(vi)   protection of crops by plant-protection agents;
(vii)   increased use of improved implements;

Chart 4.1

Stages of collectivisation: changes in organisational set-up

Period	Type of organisation	Ownership (land, draught animals, machines)	Average size (households, agricultural land)	Type of work	Members' income
1950–55	mutual aid (seasonal or permanent)	private	6–15 households; no estimate of acreage	agricultural work	to each the produce of his land, occasionally plus bonus for extra work
1952–56	lower-level producer co-operatives	private and co-operative	32 households; 91 acres (37 ha)	agricultural work; some subsidiary occupations	dividends from shares in co-operative (incl. ground-rent) plus pay for work
1953–58	higher-level producer co-operatives	collective	160 households; 370 acres (150 ha) (June 1958)	agricultural work; subsidiary occupations and major agrotechnical projects	chiefly remuneration for work; little or no pay-out for land brought in
1958–	people's communes	collective	5,500 households; 11,278 acres (4,564 ha) (1959)	agriculture, forestry, fishing, livestock, subsidiary occupations, local industries, etc.	20–30 per cent of income paid in kind (foodstuffs, sometimes also clothing); remainder in cash as wages (1960)

Source: Lichnowsky.

190

(viii)   better leadership and improved management of production equipment and products.

The character of the people's communes is a controversial issue. It
is difficult to organise work schedules for tens of thousands of people
labouring in the fields, and economies of scale cease to accrue above a
certain limit. Mass mobilisation of labour cannot serve any useful purpose
except for vast building projects for which modern earth-moving and construction plant is not available. The reports of commune members living,
or having lived, in mass dormitories segregated according to sex are certainly unfounded. Perhaps the people's communes are administrative units
operating at a level above that of the agricultural production enterprises
and charged with the task of establishing local industries. In some places
canteens supplying staple foods have been installed as a substitute for
government rationing schemes.

In describing the organisation and tasks of the people's communes, Biehl
notes the passage in the Central Committee resolution of September 1958
on the establishment of people's communes, which said: 'The people
themselves are demanding the opportunity to organise themselves in military fashion for work and to lead a collective life'. The people's commune
(Biehl continues) covers not only all the branches of the rural economy; it
embraces in addition all walks of life: the peasant, the artisan, the industrial worker, the militia man. It absorbs the lowest unit of the state
administration, the district or 'hsiang' as well as the local branches of the
state banking and trade organisation and of the health and education
services. During the initial period, the structure of the lower echelons, as
taken over with the agricultural producer co-operatives, was to be left
intact, changes to be introduced only in cases of proven urgency, in order
to avoid any interference with production. In Biehl's view, the time has
not yet come when it would be appropriate to take the step from group
ownership (collective) to ownership by the whole people (nationalisation).
Even if that step were to be taken at some time in the future, the people's
commune would still be a socialist rather than communist institution, that
is to say, it would still be based on the principle of 'from each according
to his ability, to each according to his contribution'. Even though the
system of distribution (remuneration for work) does not give to each
according to his needs, Biehl is convinced that the people's commune is
none the less the form of organisation best suited to the attainment of
socialism and the gradual advance to communism.

Liu Shao-ch'i, who at that time was a leading politician, stated:

Many people's communes operate a supply system which assures all members free food supplies at an appropriate level. Generally, such free allocations make up 20 to 30 per cent of the members' income. The main purpose of this method is to safeguard the sustenance of the physically disabled and the children. This is an excellent way of establishing a form of social insurance in our rural areas ... .

At the beginning of 1959, supplementary guide-lines were issued for the reorganisation of the people's communes, which settled the question of the ownership of the means of production. According to these guide-lines, the ownership of the assets brought into the commune is vested in the production brigades – the successors to the producer co-operatives out of which the commune was formed – while the property vested in the commune is to be built up gradually from newly created and newly acquired assets such as irrigation plant and stocks of agricultural machinery, which represent the fruit of the members' common effort. In work organisation, too, the production brigade remains the fundamental unit.

The institutions of 'collective life' – canteens, crèches, children's nurseries, old-age homes – served the practical task of enabling the women to devote as nearly as possible their entire working time to the collective.

According to the new guide-lines, 'existing old dwelling houses must be replaced step by step' – that is to say, not precipitately – 'by new ones ... . In the construction of new living quarters, care must be taken to ensure that the houses are suitable for the accommodation of man and wife, the aged and the children of each family living together'.

It had been common practice in the past for the village community to entrust the farming of a portion of the village fields for a whole year to a fairly small work team under conditions laid down in a contract (one of the rules providing that the members of the team should not all be drawn from the same lineage). Under the new regulations such annual contracts for the farming of small areas may be concluded even with single families belonging to the village community.

The establishment of the people's communes has ushered in an institutional reform. But there are few agricultural machines and tractors. Work goes on predominantly with the old technology. Modern equipment is usually allocated to the new state farms set up in previously underpopulated regions, often on the state frontier: an arrangement meeting the demands of both agrarian and national policy. The development of the centrally administered state farms during the period 1949 to 1964 is illustrated in Table 4.11. It appears that their acreage reached a peak in 1960 with 12,924,000 acres (5,230,000 ha); by 1964 it had dropped again to 10,205,000 acres (4,130,000 ha). The labour force reached 990,000 in

Table 4.11

Area and equipment of state farms[1] , 1949–1964

Year	State farms (no.)	Agricultural land ('000 ha)	Cropland ('000 ha)	Labour force ('000)	Tractors[2] (no.)	Combine harvesters (no.)	Virgin land reclaimed ('000 ha)	Grain crop ('000 tonnes)
1949	18	31	31	4	401	13	–	–
1952	404	565	255	390	1,792	283	149	193
1957	710	1,199	1,025	500	10,177	1,537	271	595
1958	1,442	2,655	2,272	990	16,955	1,982	829	–
1960	2,490	5,230	–	–	28,000	–	–	2,500
1964	–	4,130	–	–	–	–	–	2,035

[1] Only the state farms under the Ministry for the Reclamation of Virgin Lands (including livestock farms) included; the smaller experimental farms administered by the regional governments are not.
[2] In 15 hp units.

Source: *Länderberichte.*

1958 – the last year for which this figure is available – when the total acreage amounted to 6,561,000 acres (2,655,000 ha) and the arable to 5,614,000 acres (2,272,000 ha). Another institution is that of the state machine stations, of which there were 2,263 in 1965. No data concerning their equipment have been published.

4.1.5 *The Chinese model of development*

(i) ECONOMIC STRUCTURE AND ECONOMIC POLICY

What little industry existed prior to 1949 was concentrated in the large ports and the Manchurian heavy-industry region of Anshan-Harbin. After 1949 a planned build-up of industry was launched with Soviet assistance. Plant was built for the production of basic materials, heavy machinery, public transport vehicles, lorries and the most important basic consumer goods. Soviet aid was withdrawn at the end of the 1950s. China does not now receive any financial aid from abroad, but she is buying technological industrial processes, chiefly from Japan, West Germany, France and Britain. Thus the starting speed of China's industrial development is slow, but then, her foreign indebtedness is slight and the burden of interest small. All the capital must be formed on the internal capital market. Thus China is politically independent, yet at the same time politically and technologically isolated.

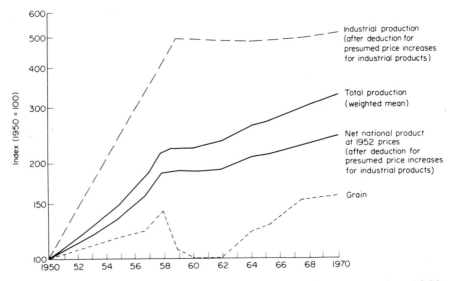

Fig. 4.3   China: production and net national product per capita, 1950–1970

Within the development programme, the main stress was laid at first on the primary sector, and subsequently shifted to the secondary and tertiary sectors, with equal emphasis on each. In view of the vast quantitative preponderance of the agrarian sector, the Soviet model based on a long-term neglect of agriculture was impracticable, as much on economic as on political grounds. 'Agriculture is the foundation of the economy. Industry is the leading force.' Agriculture receives large quantities of chemical fertilisers, but so far few agricultural machines or tractors. Owing to the slow pace of industrial growth and the low demand for manpower, the replacement of men by machines in agriculture is at the present stage neither necessary nor possible.

The Great Leap Forward was launched in 1959 simultaneously with the setting up of the people's communes. It was an attempt to force the pace of industrialisation through the operation of small, decentralised units, pocket-size blast furnaces, etc. Deficiencies in quality, uneconomic work and spurious statistics led to a setback. In modern industry, technological factors dictate certain minimum sizes of production units, which cannot be ignored with impunity. Spurious statistics and false victory claims in the end harm their authors. In 1962, candid action was initiated in order to rectify the mistakes. There were food shortages in the large cities. Large quantities of wheat had to be imported. A systematic drive was launched to send townspeople and Party officials into the countryside.

As Table 4.12 shows, agricultural production did recover from the setback and registered a long-term increase of over one-quarter during the period 1952 to 1969. However, non-agricultural gross production increased nearly fivefold during the same period, so that the share of agricul-

Table 4.12

Structure of agricultural production, 1952–1969

	1952	1955	1960	1965	1969
Gross production ('000 million Yüan)	102·8	142·8	129·7	196·7	324·3
Agricultural gross production (AGP)	48·4	55·5	38·9	48·7	62·2
Percentage share of agriculture in total production	47·1	38·9	29·9	24·8	19·2
Crop production (as a percentage of AGP)[1]	64·7	67·7	59·6	67·5	66·4
Animal production (as a percentage of AGP)[1]	14·9	11·0	20·5	11·6	14·6

[1] Not including domestic consumption by people's communes.

Source: Rochlin and Hagemann.

ture in the national gross output dropped from 47·1 to 19·2 per cent. The share of high-grade animal husbandry has remained virtually unchanged at a low level.

Chinese foreign trade at the present stage is still relatively unimportant. Exports always exceed imports. Foodstuffs account for about 30 per cent of all exports, but the figure dropped to a low of 18 per cent in 1961. In most years more food is exported than imported in terms of value. However, in respect of grain a negative trade balance of 2·6 to 6·1 million tonnes has been on record every year since 1961.

China is still in the early stages of the economic reorganisation linked with her emergence as a modern state. The transition from an agrarian to an industrial society in a land of over 700 million people is a venture without parallel in the history of mankind. It is an undertaking that calls for a new economic model and for new technological forms.

(ii)   AGRARIAN POLICY

For a considerable time to come, agriculture is bound to remain the key sector on which the progress of industrial development will depend. Agriculture supplies raw material and, on the basis of terms of trade loaded against it (price scissors), also supplies capital: low producer prices of foodstuffs contrast with high prices of agricultural production equipment and materials and consumer goods. The main points of current agrarian policy are as follows:

(a)   fostering of agricultural production, expansion of fertiliser industry, construction of dykes as flood protection, irrigation;
(b)   supplementing domestic production by imports in case of need;
(c)   gradual expansion of the cultivated area, in particular by state farms in the interior of the country;
(d)   maintenance of collectivisation combined with toleration of private production on the household plots;
(e)   there is no need for measures designed to force migration from the land, nor could they succeed, if attempted;
(f)   mechanisation of agriculture to be accomplished gradually rather than throug a crash programme.

The problem of collectivisation and mechanisation constituted one of the main issues in the ideological conflict in which Mao Tse-tung and Liu Shao-ch'i were the principal protagonists. Mao wanted to ensure the formation of communes — the transformation of production relations — as a first step, even though it was not yet possible to provide new means of production. It should be left to the communes partly to make them, partly to pay for their acquisition. In Liu's view, however, mechanisation should have been the first step, involving the supply of pumping engines and tractors, the building up of machine and tractor stations, etc. The creation of new productive forces was to have raised production and to have helped the peasants both materially and psychologically to accomplish the transition to new production relations. This dispute can be traced back to 1958, the year in which the Great Leap Forward was launched, the leap that failed.

4.2 North Vietnam: agrarian transformation as part of the revolutionary liberation struggle*

4.2.1 *Geography, terrain, climate*

The Democratic Republic of Vietnam (DRV) has an area of 61,294 square miles, about two-thirds of the area of the United Kingdom. The country extends from latitude 17° north (Ben-Hai river) to 24° north, and from longitude 102° to 108° east. In the north the DRV borders on the Chinese People's Republic (common frontier 435 miles), in the west on Laos (common frontier 620 miles), in the south on the Republic of (South) Vietnam (common frontier 34 miles), and in the east, along a coastline of 435 miles, on the Gulf of Tongking.

Topographically, North Vietnam can be divided into three zones:

1 The Plain of Tongking with the delta of the Red River (Song-koi) and its two northern tributaries, the White River (Song-kai) and the Black River (Song-bo), covers about one-tenth of the country's total area. The alluvial soil of the delta is exceptionally fertile and highly suitable for the cultivation of paddy rice.
(2) The Tongking Plain is framed by the horseshoe of the Tongking Highlands, which constitute about two-thirds of the area of the DRV. They are built of magmatic rock as well as sandstone and limestone sediments, and form, between Cao-bang in the east and Lai-chao in the west, three successive stepped plateaus, 2,000, 3,300 and 4,000 feet high respectively. The highest peak is Fan-Si-Pan (11,195 feet). The highlands have a

---

* This section is a revised and amplified version of a paper by Onno-Hans Poppinga, first published in *Zeitschrift für auslandische Landwirtschaft* vol. 11, no. 2, 1972, pp. 175–94.

southern spur in the range of the Annamite Cordillera, which extends as far as the Mekong delta. Large tracts of the highlands are wooded.

3   The coastal belt stretching from the Gulf of Tongking to the Annamite Cordillera.

The DRV has a subtropical climate. The annual mean temperature at Bac Bô (Tongking) is 23° C, the mean temperature of the coldest month (January) 16° C and of the hottest months (June/July) around 30° C. In the highlands the temperatures are somewhat lower, depending on altitude. Snow is unknown.

The seasons are not distinguished by contrasting temperatures, as they are in Europe, but by changes in the direction of the wind. The summer monsoon (April to October) blows from the south-west (South China Sea) and brings heavy rains; the winter monsoon (November to March), however, Blows from the north-east (Southern China) and brings little rain. This leaves Nam Bô (Cochinchina) extremely dry, whereas in Bac Bô some moderate precipitation is maintained in winter in the form of a fine drizzle.

The coastal belt exhibits transitions to the tropical climate of Nam Bô; the rainy period shifts from summer to autumn. The marked contrasts in rainfall are not only seasonal; there are equally striking fluctuations from year to year. The town of Vinh, for instance, has an annual average of 70·4 inches (1,788 mm), which however includes dry years with only 38·9 inches (987 mm) as well as wet years with 105·2 inches (2,671 mm) of rain, almost three times the minimum figure.

The changing monsoons also cause large fluctuations in the volume of water carried by the rivers; thus the flow of the Song-kai varies from 25,000 cubic feet per second in the dry season to over 1 million cubic feet when in full spate.

For the agricultural utilisation of the land these extreme contrasts in precipitation entail two principal problems:

(i)   large dykes are needed to prevent cropland from being flooded regularly — this applies above all to river dykes, but also to sea dykes as a protection against typhoons;

(ii)   intensive farming presupposes a wide-ranging irrigation network.

It is appropriate in this context to recall the proposition that where production depends on irrigation the producers are required, and enabled, to reach relatively high standards of proficiency, since planning on an extensive scale is essential.

4.2.2 *Population*

The population of the DRV (shown in Table 4.13) increased from some 13 million in 1955 to well over 20 million in 1968. The annual growth rate is higher than 3 per cent. Population density is characterised by marked regional variations between extremes of 34 and 2,258 inhabitants per square mile. The highlands are thinly populated, while in the delta the density is very high. Urban concentrations are not responsible for the wide variation in densities. Although the proportion of the urban population

Table 4.13

Population trend, 1955–1968

	1955	1960	1965	1968
Population ('000)	13,574	15,917 (18,373)	19,000 (19,340)	20,700
Inhabitants per sq km.	86	100	120	130
Annual growth rate of population (per cent)	–	3·6	3·3	–

Figures in brackets according to FAO.

Sources: *Länderkurzberichte; Statistisches Jahrbuch der DDR.*

Table 4.14

Age structure of population in DRV and West Germany
(in per cent)

Age group	DRV (1 March 1960)	West Germany (31 Dec. 1959)
Under 1	4·2	1·7
1– 7	21·4	9·1
7–16	18·7	12·1
16–56	47·5	56·1
over 56	8·2	21·0
Total	100	100

Source: *Länderberichte.*

has been rising, it is still low; the figure was about 10 per cent in 1960. There are only 18 towns in the whole country with more than 10,000 inhabitants.

The age structure of the population (Table 4.14) clearly reflects the dynamic demographic trend: 44 per cent are under 16, 8 per cent over 56 years of age.

Nearly 15 per cent of the population are ethnically not Vietnamese but belong to national minorities which had for centuries lived in a state of tension with their Vietnamese neighbours. The integration of these minorities into the society of the DRV was one of the vital tasks of the Vietnamese revolution. A large part of the minorities lives in the two autonomous regions of Tay Bac and Viet Bac.

Vigorous efforts have been made to combat illiteracy, a serious legacy of the French colonial regime (which in 1900 had banned instruction by Vietnamese teachers). By 1960 the illiteracy rate was down to 30 per cent. Apart from the over-50s and the inhabitants of the most remote villages, illiteracy has largely been overcome.

4.2.3 *Economic structure*

According to the census of 1 March 1960, there were 8,119,000 gainfully employed persons in the DRV, about 51 per cent of the population. Their distribution over the various branches of the economy (shown in Table 4.15) indicates that North Vietnam is still a peasant country, with 78·5 per cent of the employed working in agriculture and forestry. Nevertheless, the trend of gross production figures (set out in Table 4.16) clear-

Table 4.15

Occupations, 1960

Economic sector	Percentage of economically active persons
Agriculture and forestry	78·5
Industry and artisan trades	8·2
Trade and transport	4·1
Others	9·2
Total	100

Source: *Länderberichte.*

200

Table 4.16

Value of gross production of agriculture, industry and artisan trades
at 1956 prices

Year	Total (million Dong)	Agriculture (%)	Industry and artisan trades (%)
1955	1,881·1	83·1	16·9
1957	2,758·6	68·6	31·4
1959	3,695·3	64·5	35·5
1961	—	57·1	42·9
1963	—	50·5	49·5
1965	—	46·3	53·7

Sources: *Länderberichte*; Vietnam (WUS) Freyberg and Steinhaus.

ly reflects the advance of industrialisation. The share of industry and artisan trades in the national gross product rose from 16·9 per cent in 1955 to 53·7 per cent in 1965. Moreover, within that sector industry drew ahead of artisan production, beginning in 1958. The index of industrial production rose from 100 in 1955 to 923 in 1965.

Natural conditions are favourable for industrialisation. The country is rich in mineral deposits — coal, phosphates, iron ore, copper, tin, lead, wolfram, bauxite, mercury, gold — and has ample reserves of timber and water-power. On the other hand, the social, technological and economic conditions were anything but favourable for industrialisation at the time it became possible to embark on the work of socialist construction; that is, after the Geneva conference on Indochina. The population was exhausted after a five-year war against the Japanese, followed by a war of independence lasting eight years. Standards of nutrition were poor. Widespread destruction had been caused by the war, and even more by the French in the course of their withdrawal. Most roads, railways and bridges were damaged, factories destroyed, mines flooded. A large proportion of the technicians and skilled workers, who had spearheaded the resistance, had been killed. The complete and precipitate withdrawal of French capital and Diem's decision to sever South Vietnamese economic relations with the DRV added to the strain.

Before setting out to build anew, it was at first necessary to repair the damage. This phase of reconstruction began in 1955 and was completed in

1957. Agricultural production, with the exception of soy beans, already had reached the pre-war levels (1939) in 1955. The following period of the Three-Year Plan (1958–1960) is described as the period of socialist transformation. In agriculture, industry and the artisan trades, private ownership of the means of production was replaced to a substantial degree by co-operative and state ownership.

In the development of production, priority was given to consumer goods, so as to ensure a marked improvement in the supply of goods to the population. That is why in 1955 about 73 per cent of the country's artisan production, and in 1959 still about 68 per cent, was made up of consumer goods.

The first Five-Year Plan (1961–1966) initiated the development of the light and heavy industries. The mining of the valuable anthracite deposits of Hong-gay was greatly extended. A modern iron and steel works with an annual capacity of 200,000 tons of raw steel was erected at Thai-nguyen. The Hanoi machine tool factory and the shipyards of Vinh were extended, and new factories were built for the manufacture of superphosphates, nitrate fertilisers and plant protection agents.

This period also witnessed the expansion of the system of social insurance, which became a comprehensive service providing old-age, disablement, sickness and industrial accident insurance, as well as social security during pregnancy, for all public service employees and the labour force of the state enterprises. No information is available on the question of the inclusion of the peasants in this system of social insurance.

Some of the achievements of the construction effort were destroyed in the US bombing raids on the DRV, which were first launched in 1964 and continued for many years. Most of the plant, however, was preserved by evacuation. The economic upsurge of the DRV was helped by aid from the socialist countries.

It is a fact of great political and economic importance that material incentives play a very minor part in the social system of North Vietnam. Werner Holzer, a German correspondent visiting the DRV, wrote on this point:

> North Vietnam is in the process of evolving a most peculiar social structure where, at any rate, the income differentials between a worker and a highly qualified technician, between a small artisan and a government minister are slight ... (*Frankfurter Rundschau*, 9 December 1970).

Naturally, the improvement of the people's material conditions is one of the most important goals of the DRV. However, the intention is not to grant improved standards to individuals in a fashion that would foster subjective feelings of rivalry, but to raise standards equally for all.

4.2.4   *Agrarian reform and the agrarian structure*

In a country where 80 per cent of the gainfully employed work in agriculture, the conditions of land ownership are of the highest importance. During the French regime, a substantial part of the agricultural land in North Vietnam, and even more in South Vietnam, was in the hands of big landowners. It appears from Table 4.17 that in 1940, in what was then the Indochinese state of Tongking and is now the DRV Province of Bac Bô, 46,000 peasant proprietors with holdings of up to 12·4 acres (5 ha) held 40 per cent of the agricultural land, while 180 owners of farms and estates of over 124 acres (50 ha) held 20 per cent. Yet, the picture given by these figures is still incomplete, because the ta-dien (agricultural workers) are left out of account. In Bac Bô the ta-dien constituted 13 per cent of the rural population. Moreover the village commons, making up another 20 per cent of the agricultural land in Bac Bô, had in actual fact passed into private ownership. By 1930 at the latest, the commons had been divided among big landowners and French colonists. The distribution of landownership in North Vietnam in 1945 is set out in Table 4.18. These

Table 4.17

Vietnam agrarian structure, ca 1940

	Bac Bô (Tongking)		Trung Bô (Annam)	
	no.	%	no.	%
Landowners	964,180	100·00	655,650	100·00
Small owners (under 5 ha)	946,500	98·20	646,700	98·64
Medium owners (5–50 ha)	17,500	1·78	8,900	1·35
Large owners (over 50 ha)	180	0·02	50	0·01
Total land holdings (ha)	1,200,000	100	800,000	100
Small holdings (ha)	480,000	40	400,000	50
Medium holdings (ha)	240,000	20	120,000	15
Large holdings (ha)	240,000	20	80,000	10
Common lands (ha)	240,000	20	200,000	25

Source: Kôi, *3000 Jahre Vietnam.*

203

Table 4.18

North Vietnam agrarian structure, 1945

Class of owner	Area	
	ha	%
Non-peasants	829,506	52·0
French colonists	15,952	1·0
Catholic missions	23,928	1·5
Landlords	390,825	24·5
Village communes	398,801	25·0
Peasants	735,390	46·1
Large peasant farms	113,260	7·1
Medium peasant farms	462,609	29·0
Small peasant farms	159,521	10·0
Rural workers	30,309	1·9
Agricultural workers	17,547	1·1
Other workers		
(artisans, traders, etc.)	12,762	0·8
Total	1,595,205	100·0

Source: *Länderberichte.*

figures — which cover 3,591 of the 3,653 communes in the DRV — reveal that half the cropland was held by non-peasants.

The rent exacted from the tenant farmers — quite apart from the obligatory 'presents' due to the landlord — varied between 40 and 75 per cent of total harvest yields, so that every poor harvest or any other untoward event forced the tenant to borrow money at a rate of interest of about 20 per cent a month. Widespread pauperisation resulted. The struggle against the French was still in progress when the first steps towards an agrarian reform were taken. However, a genuine solution of the agrarian question had to wait till independence had been won. The principles of the Agrarian Reform Act of 19 December 1953 were utterly simple. As Government Decree 239 put it:

Much will be given to those who suffer much privation; little will be given to those who suffer little privation; nothing will be given to

those who suffer no privation. We shall take where there is super-
fluity, in order to give where poverty reigns.

The Decree divides the rural population into five categories:

1 Big landowners: proprietors who acquire the major part of their income through the exploitation of agricultural labour, irrespective of
whether they farm their own land or lease it to tenants. In addition to
landowners, this category includes plantation managers and officials, intermediate tenants living on sub-tenancies, and money lenders.
2 Big peasants: peasants owning both land and production equipment,
which is operated either by themselves or by paid labour.
3 Medium peasants: peasants owning as a rule an adequate holding of
arable or paddy, or who supplement a smallish holding by renting more
land, which they cultivate themselves. This category also includes peasants
who own no land, but rent their entire holding from a big landowner.
4 Small peasants: peasants owning very little arable or paddy and very
little or no production equipment. They make their living chiefly by
selling their labour. They live mostly on rented land, are as a rule heavily
in debt or take employment as agricultural labourers.
5 Agricultural labourers and the village poor: mostly persons who own
nothing at all, neither land nor implements, and who must sell their labour
to keep alive.

The reform was intended above all to improve the material condition of
the poor peasants and agricultural labourers. Table 4.19 shows that out of

Table 4.19

Results of land reform at the end of 1957

Recipients	Distributed		Recipient households ('000)	Land allotted per household (ha)
	Area ('000 ha)	Buffaloes ('000)		
Agricultural workers	170·4	38·8	416·0	0·41
Small peasants	440·4	31·0	1,059·8	0·42
Medium peasants	179·0	2·5	539·6	0·33
Landless	8·5	1·4	35·8	0·23
Others	11·7	0·3	52·9	0·22
Total	810·0	74·0	2,104·1	0·38

Source: *Länderberichte.*

2 million acres distributed under the land reform by 1957 about three-quarters went to some 400,000 agricultural labourers and over 1 million small peasant households, each recipient getting 1 acre on average.

According to Chesneaux, certain distinctions were made in the mode of expropriation:

(a)   the property of French colonists was seized without compensation;
(b)   land and other assets of Vietnamese collaborators were expropriated, but they were compensated on a scale depending on the extent of their guilt, as judged by the people's court;
(c)   as regards 'democratic individuals and ordinary big landowners', they were compensated for the expropriation of their land, livestock and agricultural implements; they were left in possession of the remainder of their assets.

By the end of 1957 the land reform was by and large completed. About 45 per cent of the country's arable land was distributed; 77 per cent of rural households benefited.

During the execution of the agrarian reform a number of grave mistakes and excesses occurred, in spite of Ho Chi Minh's emphatic warnings that 'under no circumstances is a policy of total and ruthless expropriation to be applied by us'. Yet, even big landowners who had actually supported the Vietminh were sentenced. In Nghe An disturbances broke out among the peasants. The leadership of the Dai Lao Dong (Workers' Party) and the government were obliged to engage at length in self-criticism. Vo Nguyen Giap described the agrarian reform as a 'patchwork full of errors'. Truongh Chinh, General Secretary of the Party's Central Committee, who had been responsible for the execution of the agrarian reform, was relieved of his position, although he had fought alongside Mao Tse-tung and was one of the few survivors of the Long March. The Party's leadership was once again entrusted to Ho Chi Minh. Even so, in spite of all the mistakes, the radical reform has decisive achievements to its credit:

(a)   the traditional submissiveness of the peasants towards the notables and landowners, an attitude that in the past had stood in the way of comprehensive reform, was overcome;
(b)   agricultural production increased. In an exploited agrarian country in which tenancy is the chief mode of land tenure and where small and dwarf holdings predominate, distribution of land to the erstwhile tenants· is a first step towards raising agricultural production.

On the other hand, the agrarian reform at the stage reached in 1957 had not brought about any basic change in the structure of the agricultural production units in the DRV.

The need of manpower for the reconstruction of the economy, the scarcity of agricultural machines and draught animals and the even greater shortage of qualified personnel in agriculture all pointed to collectivisation as a possible way out. This notion was further supported by the circumstance that a great deal of work in agriculture had traditionally been carried out on a collective basis: work such as the construction and maintenance of dykes cannot be performed by individuals acting in isolation. In addition, the common struggle against the colonial power and the feudal overlords was conducive to organised joint production. Beginnings of a collective mode of production had already emerged during the war of resistance: there were the labour pooling groups and the mutual aid groups, to which half the peasants belonged by 1956.

Collectivisation proper, however, began only with the Three-Year Plan of 1958. Whereas the labour pooling groups had left the individual ownership of the means of production intact, the agricultural producer co-operatives are characterised by collective ownership and collective planning. Four different types of producer co-operative were introduced. They are, in order of the extent of collectivisation, elementary, semi-socialist, advanced, and socialist. Their progress is illustrated in Tables 4.20 and 4.21. For the sake of simplicity Table 4.20 brackets the first two and the last two of the four types, and so distinguishes only between 'semi-socialist' and 'socialist' co-operatives. This table shows clearly that collectivisation was not carried out at one fell swoop but step by step. Only in

Table 4.20

Production relations in agriculture, 1957—1967

	1957	1958	1960	1964	1967
Agricultural producer co-operatives	45	4,820	41,400	31,900	23,550
semi-socialist	42	4,800	37,000	16,390	5,511
socialist	3	20	4,400	15,510	18,039
Collectivisation ratio (percentage of peasants)	0·03	4·7	85·8	86·7	93·7
Co-operatives' share in cropland (per cent)	–	–	76	–	90

Sources: Chesneaux; Freyberg and Steinhaus; Honly.

the last two types is all the agricultural land pooled and the member's income determined almost exclusively by the amount of work he has performed. The number of agricultural producer co-operatives declined from its peak of 41,400 in 1960 to 23,500 in 1967, while their share in the sown acreage increased from 76 to 90 per cent. During the same period the number of the two most thoroughly collectivised types rose from 4,400 to 18,000. Transition to a higher type, then, is accompanied by mergers. The average number of households (Table 4.21) increased from 14 per co-operative in 1957 to 126 in 1967. The average arable acreage of an agricultural producer co-operative rose from 62 acres (25 ha) in 1959 to 183 acres (74 ha) in 1967. According to the agrarian policy of the DRV this increase in size is necessary,

(a) because scarce production equipment can be used more effectively;
(b) because the expansion of the production unit clears the way for a division of labour;
(c) because it facilitates the development of local small-scale industry.

Table 4.21

Development of agricultural producer co-operatives, 1957–1967
(year end figures)

	1957	1958	1959	1960	1964	1966	1967
Agricultural producer co-operatives ('000)	–	4·4[1]	28·6	41·4	31·9	–	23·6
Peasant households in co-operatives (million)	–	0·1	1·2	2·5	–	–	–
Percentage of all peasant households in co-operatives	–	4·5	45·0	95·0	–	–	–
Households per producer co-operative	14	25	40	60	–	108	126

[1] The discrepancy with Table 4.20 is unexplained.

Sources: Freyberg and Steinhaus; Honly; Kaye.

The social construction effort in North Vietnam, which derives its force from the mobilisation of the country's natural resources and its manpower, has already led to a shortage of labour in agriculture. By 1966 the agricultural producer co-operatives had lost about 650,000 workers to industry and the artisan trades. The tasks of defence further aggravated the shortage. In 1968 no less than 60 per cent of the agricultural labour force were women.

The structure of the agricultural producer co-operatives is laid down in the Statutes of 28 April 1969. These define the producer co-operative as 'a socialist collective economic organisation set up by the working people in agriculture. It is based on the principles of voluntariness, mutual advantage and democratic leadership. It enjoys the support of the leading Party and of the state. All the means of production of the agricultural producer co-operative are vested in the community'. The highest organ is the Congress of Members or, in the case of very large co-operatives, the Congress of Delegates. Every member is entitled to take part in the election of the management of the co-operative and to be elected. The management is a collective body and is bound by the decision of the Congress. It has to draw up plans governing production, work organisation, finance and distribution. Each agricultural producer co-operative must direct special attention to the task of increasing its accumulation fund.

A characteristic feature of the agricultural producer co-operatives in the DRV is the way in which collective farming is combined with the private household plot. Each member is entitled to use for his own purposes 5 per cent of his share in the land. This works out at roughly 240 to 360 square yards (2 to 3 are) per family.

The complete mobilisation of manpower to deal with the effects of attacks by the US Air Force and Navy tended to accelerate the changeover to producer co-operatives of higher types. In the two most severely hit provinces, Vin Linh and Quang Binh, the membership of the agricultural producer co-operatives comprises respectively 97 and 100 per cent of all the peasants, and the share of the producer co-operatives of the socialist type in the arable land reaches close on 80 per cent in both provinces. In the mountainous provinces the degree of collectivisation is lower.

The collectivisation of agriculture in the DRV went hand in hand with the setting up of state farms. They are almost invariably established by army personnel. After the demobilisation of their units the peasant soldiers revert to the role of peasants pure and simple. It is the predominant function of the state farms to carry out pioneering work. They play an important part in the opening up of virgin lands. During the first Five-Year Plan, covering the period 1961–1966, the Ministry for State Farms planned to bring close on half a million acres (200,000 ha) under cultivation. The best known example is that of the state farm of Dien Bien Phu. Nearly all the experiments with new crops are made on the state farms. Rubber and coffee plantations – which in 1962 covered areas respectively of about 9,000 and about 15,000 acres (3,600 and 6,000 ha) – were

Table 4.22

State farms

Year	No.	AL (ha)	Percentage of total AL
1955	10	1,200	1
1962	50	50,000	3
1970	–	ca 200,000	10

Sources: Burchett; Holzer.

started almost exclusively by the state farms. Those in the highlands are of great importance for the development of cattle keeping. Table 4.22 illustrates the growth of their total acreage from 3,000 acres in 1955 to about half a million acres in 1970.

The supply of producer co-operatives and state farms with manufactured production equipment and materials has so far been accomplished only on a limited scale. In keeping with the general principle governing the development of society and the economy in the DRV, the available resources are not concentrated on a few key points, but spread over all production units. In 1967, more than 5,000 agricultural producer co-operatives had small mechanical workshops of their own, equipped with generators, fodder and chaff cutters, grinding and threshing machines, decorticators and pumps. One year later, 6,500 co-operatives had been provided with such machine stations. There were 2,070 tractors in operation in 1963. The construction of a tractor works was started in 1965.

4.2.5 Agricultural production and marketing

(i) CROP PRODUCTION

Only a relatively small proportion of the total area of the DRV has so far been found suitable for agricultural utilisation on a permanent basis. The recent extension of the agricultural land by 124,000 acres (50,000 ha) was achieved by bringing virgin lands in the highlands under the plough. Since the areas potentially suitable for cultivation appear to be limited, the extension of the irrigated area is of the utmost importance. The proportion of the irrigated areas in relation to the agricultural land as a whole rose from 35 per cent in 1955 to 79 per cent in 1961. An ever-increasing part of the irrigated areas yields two crops a year. As far back as 1958,

Table 4.23

Land use in the DRV (thousand hectares)

	1958	1966
Total area	15,875	15,875
Agricultural land[1]	1,951	2,018
percentage of total area	12	13
Irrigated sown area[2]	1,588	2,400[3]
Forest land[4]	7,900	7,900
Other areas	6,024	5,957

[1] Not including pasture land.
[2] Including multiple cropping factor.
[3] 1964.
[4] Including forest pastures.

Source: *Länderberichte.*

Table 4.24

Percentage shares of main crops in total acreage

Crop	1955	1963
Rice	82·0	72·2
Other food crops	14·7	19·6
Industrial crops	2·7	6·0
Vegetables	0·5	1·9
Fruit	0·1	0·3
Total	100	100

Source: Freyberg and Steinhaus.

this proportion was 40 per cent. The irrigated cropping area (with double-cropping areas counted twice) increased from 3,924,000 acres in 1958 to 5,931,000 acres in 1964, as shown in Table 4.23.

Rice is by far the most important crop: 82 per cent of the arable land was planted with rice in 1955, 72·2 per cent in 1963 (Table 4·24).

Table 4.25

Rice cultivation, production and yield in the DRV, 1939–1972

Year	Cultivated area ('000 ha)	Production ('000 tonnes)	Yield (q per ha)	Production per capita (kg)
1939	1,841	2,407	13·0	–
1955	2,176	3,523	16·2	260
1956	2,284	4,136	18·2	295
1957[1]	2,192	3,948	18·0	272
1959	2,274	5,193	22·8	334
1961	2,409	4,651	19·3	274
1963	1,959	4,296	21·9	240
1965	2,500	5,000	20·0	–
1967	2,500	4,700	18·8	234
1969	2,500	4,900	19·6	229
1971	2,400	4,600	19·2	213
1972	2,300	4,600	20·0	–

[1] Agricultural crisis caused by mistakes in carrying out of land reform.

Sources: Chau; FAO, *Production Yearbook*; *Länderberichte*; *Statistisches Jahrbuch der DDR*.

According to a different set of figures, however, cited by the FAO and other sources (Table 4.25), the acreage under rice actually increased from 5,377,000 acres in 1955 to 6,302,000 acres in 1967 (2·176 to 2·55 million ha). Since these figures are substantially above those for the total area of the country's agricultural land (see Table 4.23), they evidently refer to the 'sown area' in the sense of Table 4.3, with the double-cropping areas counted twice; that is, the actual acreage multiplied by the land utilisation or multiple cropping coefficient (see subsection 4.1.3). The yields per unit area given in Table 4.25 fluctuate slightly between 14·4 and 14·9 cwt per acre (18·0 to 18·6 q per ha) during the period 1956 to 1967. But this represents yield per unit area per harvest, and the figure has to be multiplied by the above factor to get the yield per physical unit area per year. Since the notional 'sown acreage' increased while the physical acreage declined, the land utilisation coefficient rose substantially, and the same applies to the annual yield per acre of agricultural land. The total rice crop increased by 34 per cent from 1955 to 1967, yet per-capita production declined owing to the fast growth of the population.

The following chief targets have been set for the increase in agricultural production:

(a)   annual yield of 2 tonnes of paddy per acre;

(b)   one member of the labour force for every 2·5 acres of arable;

(c)   two pigs per 2·5 acres agricultural land.

The first of these targets was reached in 1965 by about 700 producer co-operatives, in 1967 by no less than 2,500, including the whole province of Thai Binh with about 210,000 acres of agricultural land. In this year, average yields of 2 tonnes were obtained on about 395,000 acres (5 tonnes per ha on 160,000 ha). It appears from the official report, *Economic Progress in 1970*, that the '5 tonnes of rice per hectare' movement is being followed by a '7 tonnes of rice per hectare' movement. According to the report, 100 producer co-operatives reached the higher target in 1970. The increase in rice production has been largely due to the introduction of a new strain, 'spring rice', which takes only three months from planting to harvest as compared with five to six months for the traditional winter–spring rice. The new strain is said to produce average yields of 22·2 cwt per acre (2·77 tonnes per ha); moreover, the harvests are more conveniently spaced and enable the labour force to be more efficiently utilised.

Among the other crops — the share of which in the total area of agricultural land increased from 18 per cent in 1955 to 27·8 per cent in 1963 (Table 4.24) — maize leads in terms of acreage, while sweet pota-

Table 4.26

Production and yields of selected crops, 1961–1972

	Area ('000 ha)		Production ('000 tonnes)		Yield (q per ha)	
	1961–65	1972	1961–65	1972	1961–65	1972
Maize[1]	232	200	290	220	12·5	11·0
Sweet potatoes	185	195	860	860	46·6	44·1
Manioc	107	110	823	780	76·8	70·9
Dry beans	60	60	16	15	2·6	2·5
Soy-beans	27	38	10	19	3·8	5·0
Cotton	18	20	6	6	3·3	3·0
Sugar-cane	19	19	704	600	362	316
Jute	6	6	6	6	10·0	10·0
Tea	11·8	13·0	3	3	2·8	2·3
Sesame	7	7	3	3	4·0	4·3
Castor oil	5	4	2	2	4·9	5·0
Tobacco	4·2	4·3	4	4	9·7	9·3
Coffee	13·4	10·0	1	2	0·8	2·0

[1]   1961 instead of 1961–65.

Source: FAO, *Production Yearbook.*

213

toes and yam (taken together), manioc and sugar-cane produce the heaviest crops, as shown in Table 4.26. Special attention is given to the expansion of the acreage of industrial crops.

The use of mineral fertilisers was increased from about 7,000 tonnes in 1955 to about 114,000 tonnes in 1960, but is still very low in relation to the extent of the agricultural land. The construction of factories producing superphosphates and nitrogenous fertilisers has led to further substantial increases in the use of fertilisers, but no numerical data are as yet available on this point. Since 1960, attempts have been made to improve nitrogen supplies by applying a species of water fern (*Azolla pinnata*) as green manure.

(ii) ANIMAL PRODUCTION

The protein intake of the population has so far come mainly from fish. Catches of fresh and saltwater fish rose from 94,000 tonnes in 1958 to 289,000 tonnes in 1962.

The livestock industry is still relatively little developed. However, considerable efforts are being made to improve the supplies of animal proteins, as can be seen from Table 4.27. Since conditions of reproduction are particularly favourable in the case of pigs and poultry, efforts have been concentrated on these. The pig population nearly trebled from 1956 to 1968. The breeding of hybrid pigs (F 1) has advanced well beyond the experimental stage. The structure of the agricultural production units — i.e. producer co-operatives and state farms — lends itself to modern pig

Table 4.27

Livestock numbers (thousands)

	1958	1960	1965	1966	1970	1972
Horses	21[1]	39	48	51	58	60
Cattle	756[1]	950	796	820	865	880
Water buffaloes[2]	1,084	1,451	1,535	1,550	1,700	1,700
Pigs	2,137[1]	3,629	4,208	4,230	6,600	6,900
Chickens and ducks	–	47,469	57,684	–	–	56,000

[1]   1956.
[2]   Figure for October.

Sources: *Länderberichte*; *Statistisches Jahrbuch der DDR*; FAO *Production Yearbook*.

214

farming with its pronounced division of labour.

Water buffalo — whose number increased by nearly half from 1958 to 1966 — play an important part as draught animals. They are particularly suited to working in the flooded paddy fields. They are likely to retain their position for a considerable time, as the mechanisation of agricultural work makes only slow progress.

(iii) MARKETING OF AGRICULTURAL PRODUCE

The first nationalisation measures in the sector of distribution were taken during the very first stage of reconstruction (1955—57). By 1960 state enterprises accounted for 93·5 per cent of the total wholesale turnover. In the retail sector during the same year 40 per cent of the turnover was handled by state enterprises, 27 per cent by trade co-operatives, 22 per cent by mixed enterprises and 11 per cent by private traders. In 1959 the state trading organisations ran 571 shops in towns and 856 in rural areas, while maintaining 153 stations for the purchase of agricultural produce as well as 98 purchase-and-sales groups. In the same year there were 238 predominantly rural co-operatives engaged in buying and selling, which had 3,835 shops, 45 mobile or fixed sales groups, as well as 234 stations and 194 groups for the purchase of agricultural produce.

The state trading organisations and the co-operatives engaging in trade have the exclusive right to purchase the most important agricultural products. Thus, they also control prices. Beside the state sector, a limited 'free market' is allowed to operate. This is where the co-operative farmers offer some of the produce grown on their private plots. This market is still of some importance, especially as regards supplies of vegetables, fruit, poultry, eggs, potatoes and manioc. The part played by this sector, however, has been much reduced by rationing measures necessitated by the war.

Table 4.28 lists state purchases of a number of important products in 1959, including over 850,000 tonnes of rice, followed by 52,000 tonnes of maize. The proportion of the total crop purchased by the state ranged from nearly four-fifths for jute to about one-ninth for cotton.

4.2.6   *Summary*

After the phase of reconstruction, ending in 1958, came the stage of socialist transformation, which in 1961 was followed by the first Five-Year Plan. The renewed outbreak of hostilities, involving the country in war with South Vietnam and the USA, caused great difficulties but did not stop the upward trend.

Table 4.28

State purchase of important agricultural products, 1959

Product	Quantity ('000 tonnes)	Quantity (percentage of crop)
Rice	852·7	16·4
Maize	52·1	21·1
Sugar and honey	19·3	—
Groundnuts	14·5	41·9
Soy-beans	4·5	38·4
Cotton	0·7	11·4
Hemp	0·3	60·0
Jute	6·2	79·2
Sesame	1·6	64·5
Castor oil	1·4	64·9
Tea	1·6	65·1
Tobacco	0·4	50·0
Meat	70·8	—

Source: *Länderberichte.*

The agrarian reform, which put an end to the concentration of land ownership in the hands of a few families, led at first to the distribution of land to the peasants, and at a second stage, to the formation of agricultural producer co-operatives. The third stage brought the enlargement of the producer co-operatives. In addition, state farms were established, primarily for research and experimental purposes.

Rice continues to be the main crop. Annual yields per unit area were substantially increased by the extension of irrigation and by the introduction of new strains. A process of diversification is going on at the same time, in the course of which crops other than rice are gaining in importance. The volume of animal production is still relatively low. In view of the favourable conditions governing reproduction, special efforts are being made to extend pig farming. Water buffaloes are as important as ever as draught animals. Mechanisation makes slow but steady progress.

The marketing of agricultural products and the procurement of consumer goods and production equipment and materials is in the hands of state trading organisations and agricultural trading co-operatives.

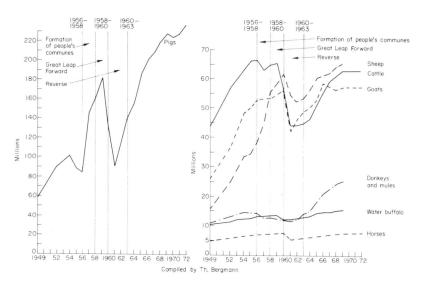

Compiled by Th. Bergmann

Fig. 4.4   China: livestock 1949–1972

4.3   Cuba: social revolution without collectivisation of agriculture

4.3.1   *History*

1492 Columbus lands in Cuba.

1511–13 Cuba conquered; becomes Spanish colony.

1522 First consignment of negro slaves arrives.

1886 Final abolition of slavery; the negroes become plantation workers or urban proletarians.

1895 Second uprising against Spain leads to

1898 US intervention and Spanish defeat.

1899–1902 US military rule.

1901 Cuban republican constitution grants USA Guantánamo naval base and special powers of intervention.

1933–44 ⎫
1952–59 ⎭ Military dictatorship by Fulgencio Batistá.

1934 USA waives its privileges in Cuba: Roosevelt's 'good neighbour policy'.

1956–59 Guerrilla war against Batistá.

1959 Victory of revolutionaries under Castro; expropriation of the foreign-owned sugar industry.

217

1960 USA annuls import quota for Cuban sugar and starts trade blockade; USSR buys Cuban sugar and extends economic aid.

1961 USA breaks off diplomatic relations with Cuba. Fiasco of Bay of Pigs landing attempted by Cuban émigrés with US support.

1962 (January) Cuba 'excluded' from the Organisation of American States; Mexico the only Latin American country to maintain full diplomatic relations.

(October) US–Soviet missile crisis ends in compromise; Cuban government gradually adopts a more detached attitude towards the Soviet Union within the communist camp, and holds a middle position in disputes between communist states.

1970 A number of Latin American states lift the political–economic blockade and resume relations with Cuba.

Growing of sugar-cane was introduced under Spanish rule. Large plantations were set up; Negro slaves were imported from Africa. After the Spanish influence was broken, the same economic policy was continued by the USA, leading to a growing concentration of capital, which came to exert a strong influence on domestic policies. Cuba became the world's largest producer of cane sugar.

4.3.2 Geography, demography and economic structure

Cuba covers an area of 44,216 square miles, predominantly lowland plains not more than 300 feet above sea level. In the region's subtropical climate these plains are well suited to agriculture, in particular sugar-cane plantations. The lesser mountains, up to 3,100 feet high, and the highlands, ranging up to 8,400 feet, are suitable for extensive pastoral farming. Precipitation fluctuates between 43 and 63 inches (1,100 and 1,600 mm). The population grows very fast. In 1972 there were 8·86 million inhabitants, 200 per square mile. In 1960, 55 per cent of the population lived in the towns. With a per-capita income of 460 US dollars, Cuba is one of the richest countries in Latin America.

In 1965, out of 7,631,000 inhabitants, 2,530,000, that is one in three, were gainfully employed, 990,000 of them – 39 per cent of the total employed – in agriculture. By 1970 that proportion had fallen to 33 per cent. Industry is weak and mostly processes materials supplied by agriculture. The service sector is very strong. Of 4,870,000 acres (1,970,000 ha) of cropland, 4,200,000 acres (1,700,000 ha), that is to say 86 per cent, were growing sugar-cane in 1966. Sugar and tobacco make up 80 to 85 per cent of all exports. Cuba is a typical agrarian country dependent on a monoculture. A few North American firms exercised an export monopoly. The bulk of the exports used to go to the USA. As a result of the monoculture, which meant a generally one-sided economic system, there was high seasonal unemployment. Under normal conditions, the geographical position dictated economic links with the USA. The cost of transport to more distant markets militates against a diversification of foreign trade.

Up to 1959 Cuba played a dominant role in world sugar production, with 18·6 per cent of the world's sugar-cane acreage and 17·9 per cent of the production of raw sugar, including beet sugar. The island's share in the world market was bigger still. In the period 1945—49, Cuba accounted on average for half the world's sugar exports; in 1958 her share was still one-third of the total.

Out of the 829,668 persons who were working in agriculture in 1945, 352,700 (according to Gutelman) were peasants and members of their families, while wage-earners numbered 477,400. Of these, however, only

Table 4.29

Production and yields of main crops, 1948—1971

	Area ('000 ha)		Production ('000 tonnes)		Yields (q per ha)	
	1948—52	1971	1948—52	1971	1948—52	1971
Maize	275	120	243	115	8·8	9·6
Millet	15	13	13	15	8·5	11·5
Rice	61	180	106	452	17·4	25·1
Sugar-cane	1,204	1,160	50,466	49,000	419	422
Raw sugar			5,786	4,500		
Potatoes	10	9	84	120	86	133
Sweet potatoes						
and yams	99	62	290	250	29	40
Manioc	55	33	179	220	33	67
Dry beans	60	35	32	23	5·3	6·6
Oranges and						
tangerines			46	140		
Other citrus fruit			2	12		
Bananas	4	3	39	30	93	100
Pineapples			120	20		
Groundnuts	16		14		9·0	10·0
Cotton	13[1]	4	3[1]	1	2·1[1]	2·9
Coffee	89	?	31·2	33·0	—	—
Tobacco	52	50	32·4	40·0	6·2	8·0
Agave	12	10	14·7	10·5	—	—

[1] 1961—65

Source: FAO, *Production Yearbook.*

54,000 were permanently employed, the remaining 424,000 being temporary workers.

4.3.3 Agriculture

The most recent Cuban figures concerning land use date from 1962. They put cropland at 4,870,000 acres (1,970,000 ha), irrigated areas (1952) at 148,000 acres (60,000 ha), meadows and pasture 9,630,000 acres (3,897,000 ha), forests 7,379,000 acres (2,986,000 ha).

Agriculture is divided into a plantation sector and a peasant-farm sector, within which arable and livestock farming are largely separated. Acreages, crop weights and yields of the most important crops are set out in Table 4.29.

Sugar-cane, of course, is the most important crop. Maize has been displaced by rice as the most important cereal crop. Over the 20 years up to 1971 covered by Table 4.29, the maize crop fell from 243,000 to 115,000 tonnes, while the rice crop rose from 106,000 to 452,000 tonnes. Independent peasant farming plays a secondary part in terms of total production. The chief crops cultivated on peasant farms are maize, beans, tubers, coffee and tobacco (see subsection 4.3.5 below and Table 4.35). There used to be substantial exports of tropical fruits to the USA, especially pineapples, bananas, citrus fruit, and avocado pears. Field crops are not sufficient to meet domestic needs. Yields, with the exception of tobacco and sugar-cane, are generally mediocre, although Table 4.29 shows appreciable increases over the 20 years covered. Fertiliser supplies are low, but slowly increasing. The use of tractors is gradually expanding (Table 4.30): under 9,000 were operating in 1953, as compared with 38,000 in 1971.

There is a clear division of functions between the plantation sector and the peasant sector; the use of tractors is on the whole probably confined to the commercial sector.

There has been a substantial expansion of livestock keeping and animal production in recent years, as shown in Table 4.31. The cattle population in particular increased by more than 60 per cent and the production of cow's milk by over 160 per cent over 20 years. Under the prevailing conditions, extensive animal husbandry is economically sound practice.

4.3.4 Agrarian structure and agrarian reform

The latest available figures on the size of production units, dating back to 1946, are given in Table 4.32. They show a marked polarisation of hold-

Table 4.30

Agricultural means of production

		1948/49–1952/53 ('000 tonnes pure nutrient)	1971
N	Production	–	10·3
	Consumption	22·1	100
P₂O₅	Production	6	6·7
	Consumption	21·3	65
K₂O	Consumption	16·4	100
Tractors in use		8,963	37,700[1]

[1] FAO estimate; during the period 1960–66 23,900 wheeled and 5,600 caterpillar tractors were imported.

Source: FAO, *Production Yearbook.*

Table 4.31

Livestock numbers (thousands)

	1947/48–1951/52	1970/71
Horses	410	750
Mules	33	39
Donkeys	3	6
Cattle	4,333	7,000
Pigs	1,315	1,460
Sheep	177	290
Goats	147	83
Poultry	7,190	10,500
Cow's milk ('000 tonnes)	180	480

Source: FAO, *Production Yearbook.*

ings, with four-fifths of the total number in the lowest category (up to 66 acres) holding between them no more than 15 per cent of the agricultural land, while the 3 per cent of the production units in the highest category (over 1,000 acres) have 57 per cent of the land. Even these figures still tend to understate the position, for within the top category

Table 4.32

Size of production units and production relations in 1946

	Number	%	Area (ha)	%	
− 2 cab.[1]	125,619	78·5	1,362,533	15·0	
2− 5 cab.	16,766	10·5	822,539	9·0	
5−30 cab.	13,150	8·2	1,728,241	19·0	
30−	4,423	2·8	5,163,842	57·0	
Total	159,958	100	9,077,155	100	
Social category of operator	Number	%	Area (ha)	%	ha per unit
Owners	48,792	30·5	2,958,700	32·4	60·6
Managers	9,342	5·8	2,320,000	25·6	248·3
Tenants	46,018	28·8	2,713,000	30·0	59·0
Subtenants	6,987	4·4	215,000	2·4	30·8
Share croppers	33,064	20·7	552,100	6·1	16·7
Peasants farming on owner's sufferance	13,718	8·6	244,600	2·7	17·8
Others	2,007	1·2	72,655	0·8	36·2
Total	159,958	100	9,076,458	100	56·7

[1]   1 caballería = 13·4 ha = 33·1 acres.

Sources: Gutelman, *Länderkurzberichte.*

22 sugar-cane plantations had aggregate holdings of 4,431,000 acres (1,793,020 ha) or 20 per cent of the total. Most of these giant estates were foreign owned. Under one-third of all production units – and the same proportion in the lowest category (under 66 acres) taken separately – were run by their owners; 6 per cent of the units, with one-quarter of the agricultural land, were run by managers, 29 per cent by tenants, 21 per cent by share croppers.

The separation of the sectors in agriculture and their completely different organisation and functions had a bearing on the aims of the agrarian reform, which proceeded in two stages, promulgated on 17 May 1959 and 13 October 1963 respectively. The first stage provided for the expropriation and nationalisation of the foreign-owned sugar plantations, as well as for the expropriation of Cuban-owned properties of over 1,000 acres (strictly 995 acres, equal to 30 caballerías).

The act of 1959 was designed to bring about a reforming rather than a revolutionary transformation of agriculture. Its aim was to abolish dwarf holdings as well as the latifundia. A holding of 66 acres (strictly 66·32 acres, or 2 caballerías) was regarded as the minimum required for subsistence, and land distribution was organised accordingly. Division or sale of land acquired under the land reform was banned. During the first stage, farms of up to 995 acres were not affected, provided they were farmed by the owner. Land in excess of that limit as well as any areas leased to tenants were expropriated and turned over to persons with no or little land. Each peasant who did not own the land he farmed received a plot of 2 cab. free of charge, with the option (rarely taken up) of up to 5 cab., to be paid off.

Two further steps along the road of expropriation were taken in 1960, though these had not been planned or foreseen by the government. It was the worsening of relations with the USA and the hostile attitude of some of the remaining landowners which prompted the passing of two Acts (Laws 851 and 890) providing for the nationalisation of all US-owned properties and of some Cuban-owned sugar estates.

Finally, the second stage of the land reform in 1963 brought the expropriation of the remaining Cuban-owned owner-managed properties in the range of 166 to 995 acres.

To forestall a drop in production, the following three measures were taken:

(a)   model enterprises of up to 3,316 acres (100 cab) were exempted from expropriation, provided their yields were 50 per cent above the national average;
(b)   some of the expropriated land was taken over by the state sector;
(c)   the National Institute for Agrarian Reform (INRA) combined its land distribution activities with the organisation of an agricultural advisory (extension) service.

Among the motives that prompted the agrarian reform, social and national considerations were closely linked. The land was acquired at a fraction of its commercial value, since the expropriated owners were compensated on the basis of the valuations given in their own tax returns. Compensation was effected by the issue of agrarian reform bonds carrying a rate of interest of 4 per cent and redeemable after 20 years. In this way the cost of the operation was kept low, inflationary effects were avoided, and payment was to all intents and purposes deferred.

Figures on the composition of the land fund and the impact of the two stages of the reform on the state and private sectors are set out in Tables 4.33 and 4.34.

Table 4.33

The land fund

	ha	%
Agrarian Reform Act	1,199,184	27·0
Law on the sequestration of dishonestly acquired estates	163,214	3·7
Gifts to land reform agency (INRA)	322,590	7·3
Voluntary sales	581,757	13·1
Nationalisation Law 851	1,261,587	28·4
Nationalisation Law 890	910,547	20·5
	4,438,879	100
End of 1962		
State sector	3,903,300	44
Private sector	5,173,800	56
under 5 cab.	3,331,000	36
5–30 cab.	1,863,000	20
End of 1963		
State sector	5,513,700	60
Private sector	3,563,100	40

Source: Gutelman.

Table 4.34

Small peasant holdings after the first stage of the land reform: independent peasant farms up to 5 caballerías in 1961

	Number	Area (ha)	Received through land reform (ha)	Total area
Old owners	48,315	805,493	—	805,493
New owners	101,805	—	2,725,910	2,725,910
Number of holdings up to 5 cab.	150,120	805,493	2,725,910	3,531,403

Source: Gutelman.

Thus, in November 1963 60 per cent of the country's agricultural land was in the hands of the state, and no small peasant had been expropriated. On the contrary, the reform established for the first time a large number of independent peasant farms. Table 4.33 shows that in 1961, after the first stage of the reform, two-thirds of the small and medium peasants (holdings up to 166 acres), with three-quarters of the total peasant land in this category, had owned no land before the reform. In the final stage, the limit of private land holdings was set high enough (at 166 acres, or 5 cab) to preserve the medium-sized private farms. The peasant farms' share in agricultural production (in 1965) is set out in Table 4.35. They contributed one-third of the sugar-cane and rice crops and most of the coffee, tobacco, fruit and vegetables grown on the island.

On the other hand, the large production units expropriated under the reform were not broken up, but retained by the state to avoid production losses. The state now holds half the island's horned cattle, especially fat stock. Most of the sugar crop, the entire cotton crop as well as other commercial crops are grown in the state sector.

In favour of the agrarian reform, then, it is to be noted that it was efficient in achieving its social and national aims; caused no major drop in production; was not costly or inflationary; and was swift and effective in execution, so that obstruction was not possible.

In 1960 a beginning was made with the formation of sugar co-operatives, which enjoyed a measure of self-government through the institutions of co-operative democracy, while their operation was in the hands of a manager appointed and constantly guided in his decisions by the INRA. In August 1962 the sugar co-operatives were officially converted into state sugar-cane farms. The state then controlled 280 'people's farms' with a total acreage of 7,028,000 acres (2,844,000 ha) and 600 sugar-cane farms

Table 4.35

Share of private sector in the production of selected products, 1965
(percentages)

Sugar-cane	32	Coffee	83
Rice	32	Tobacco	89
Tubers	58	Beef	21
Vegetables	69	Pork	22
Fruit	68	Milk	40

Source: Gutelman.

totalling 2,224,000 acres (900,000 ha). The size of the units ranged from 500 to 220,000 acres (200 to 90,000 ha). In 1962, the people's farms had a permanent labour force of 200,000 and the sugar-cane farms one of 120,000. In 1963 the state sector was reorganised according to a uniform pattern in which the state farms — the new name given to both sugar-cane farms and people's farms — formed part of a four-tier structure. They were, on the one hand, divided into departments and subdivided into 'lots', the functional production units, and, on the other, grouped in larger regional administrative units, called 'agrupaciones'. In 1966, there were 575 state farms administered through 58 agrupaciones, each of which controlled an area ranging from 32,000 to 250,000 acres (13,000 to 100,000 ha) of agricultural land.

The collective sector is very small and is, if anything, held back rather than promoted by the state. There was no forced collectivisation. The formation of collective farming enterprises was left to the voluntary imitation of good examples, which, however, have not so far been forthcoming. In 1963, there were 230 crop-farming and livestock co-operatives with a total area of 42,000 acres (17,000 ha), of which 17,300 acres (7,000 ha) was brought in by the members, while the remainder came from the land fund. By 1966 the number of producer co-operatives had risen to 270, with a total of about 50,000 acres (20,000 ha).

The more general type of agricultural service co-operative is represented by 537 credit co-operatives, which in 1967 had a combined membership of about 50,000.

In addition, the following agricultural organisations were set up to help the peasant farmer.

1   In 1960, the National Association of Small Peasants was set up. This dealt with technical aid, credit, supply of production equipment and materials and services.

2   In 1963, the National Institute for Agrarian Reform, INRA, took over the technological tasks from the peasant organisation. INRA discharged many functions, some of them outside agriculture. It dealt with land reform, management of state-owned land, capital aid for new and established peasants, and the development of certain industries. After 1969 the Institute was relieved of its political functions and of its tasks of structural reform in agriculture and was reorganised as a body exclusively concerned with agricultural advice and instruction.

3   Machine stations (SMAP) were set up and equipped with about 1,500 tractors, in order to carry out the heaviest work on the peasant farms. They have not so far been successful.

Mechanisation of agrarian production is necessary, in order to cope with the enormous seasonal peak demands for labour.

Summing up, two main considerations have determined the specific character of the Cuban agrarian reform.

(i)   political: weakness of the industrial working class and the urban proletariat, hence the need to win over the rural proletariat and the small peasants;

(ii) functional: shortage of modern production equipment aggravated by the US economic blockade. To overcome this is a long-term task: without modern means of production large production units can only apply pre-industrial methods and can scarcely benefit from economies of scale.

4.3.5   *Economic policy: assessment of the Cuban model*

Cuba's economic policy is determined by its geographical and political position and by the political character of the state. The trade partners within easy reach from the point of view of communications are boycotting Cuba and are trying to impose a blockade. A Central Planning Commission, Juceplan, was set up. The general planning objectives are as follows:

1   Moderate industrialisation, making allowance for the small size of the domestic market and the long haul for imports of raw materials. Industry is therefore to be based chiefly on domestic agricultural products. Priority is to be given to the production of fertilisers for agriculture and to electrification. The production of fertilisers had a slow start: whereas the plan envisaged an output of 1 million tonnes of nitrogenous fertilisers in 1970, rising to 2 million tonnes in 1975, the figure actually achieved in 1971 (Table 4.30) was some 10,000 tonnes of pure nutrient, corresponding to roughly 50,000 tonnes gross. All in all, economic planning in Cuba derives from a model of industrialisation adapted to the country's specific conditions, and therefore different from the Soviet model.

2   Diversification of foreign trade relations: trade with the Soviet Union, Britain, France, Spain, Czechoslovakia and other countries improves Cuba's bargaining position in price negotiations. Economic relations between socialist countries, too, are not entirely free of problems (rice from China, Soviet experts, etc.). Payment in freely convertible currencies would be desirable as it would widen the country's freedom of manoeuvre in foreign economic relations.

3   Renewed promotion of sugar-cane cultivation (see below, subsection 4.3.6, and Table 4.36).
4   Moderate measures to reduce the country's dependence on imports, in keeping with improved export prospects.

Table 4.36

Cuba's share in world production of sugar-cane and raw sugar, 1948–1972

	1948/49 –1952/53	1961–65	1970	1971	1972
Sugar-cane area ('000 ha)					
Cuba	1,204	1,103	1,455	1,160[1]	1,000[1]
World	6,584	9,566	11,400	11,194	10,864
Cuba's share (percentage)	18·3	11·5	12·8	10·4	9·2
Raw sugar ('000 tonnes)					
Cuba	5,786	5,254	8,538	5,924[2]	4,400[2]
World	32,322	56,917	74,178	75,194	73,799
Cuba's share (percentage)	17·9	9·2	11·5	7·9	6·0
Sugar-cane yield (q per ha)					
Cuba	419	384	557	466	450
World	422	492	545	533	535

[1]   FAO estimate.
[2]   Unofficial figure.

Source: FAO, *Production Yearbook.*

The share of agricultural development in the total expenditure of the state is again on the increase. In 1961–65 $ 232 million was invested in agriculture. The plan target for 1965–70 was $ 1,000 million. (Figures on actual performance during that period do not appear to have been released so far.)

Relative investment expenditure on the various sectors for the years 1962 to 1964 is set out in Table 4.37.

Gutelman has given the following analysis and interpretation of the Cuban economic model:

The first lesson of the development of the agricultural sector in Cuba is that the classical formulation of the theory of underdevelopment ceases to be valid the moment the existing structures are overthrown by a genuine and profound social-political revolution. According to that theory, capital is in short supply, whereas labour is relatively abundant. In actual fact [as a Cuban author has pointed out], there

228

Table 4.37

Allocation of investments (percentages)

	Agriculture	Industry	Other sectors	Total
1962	27·7	21·6	50·7	100
1963	21·5	30·4	48·1	100
1964 (plan)	25·2	30·8	44·0	100
1964 (actual)	33·2	27·4	39·4	100

Source: Gutelman.

is no shortage of capital resources: what happened is simply that they were wasted by the big landowners, sterilised by the hoarding of wholesale merchants, speculators and other parasites, and finally channelled into the imperialist mother countries. Careful investigation has shown that many Latin American countries are at present net exporters of capital to the USA. The same is likely to have been the case in the past as regards Cuba ... .

The decision to give priority at first to the development of agriculture and the industries connected with agriculture, in order to establish sound foundations for a subsequent industrial development, was the right decision under the specific conditions prevailing in Cuba. It broke with the traditional notion that immediate industrialisation must of necessity come first in the development programme of an economically underdeveloped country. The period 1959–63 has shown in this respect that historical factors can act as formidable obstacles, and that it is necessary to come to terms with the facts, even if one refuses to accept them as inexorably ordained by destiny.

Cuba has recognised on the one hand the advantages stemming from its favourable natural conditions, and on the other the limitations imposed by the historical deformations of its economy. It may be said that the country has taken the line of least resistance in its development. In spite of the magnitude of the targets, Cuba's sugar and livestock breeding will not be turned into a counterpart of the role of steel in the first Five-Year Plans of the Soviet Union. Cuba will in this way undoubtedly avoid the very heavy sacrifices which the socialist states in Europe took upon themselves. Tensions are nevertheless sure to arise owing to the rapid growth rhythm.

4.3.6 Agrarian policy

The main lines of agrarian policy that can be discerned are discussed below.

As regards structure, the two sectors — state and peasant farming — are to continue to exist side by side. The independent peasants are not being absorbed into collectives. So far (up to 1973) there have been no indications of any intention on the part of the government to introduce collectivisation through administrative measures. Since, however, the government is not in a position to offer the producers substantial price incentives as an encouragement to higher production, other methods have to be used to integrate the private sector with the planning of agricultural production and food supplies. Peasant farms integrated into the urban production belts are presented with 'micro-plans', operational plans adapted to the capacity of the individual peasant farm and at the same time dovetailed with the overall plan. There are other measures, such as the offer of old-age pensions for old peasants parting with their land; leasing of peasant land to the state, with the peasant either keeping a household plot or accepting employment as an agricultural worker; or cultivation under contract.

There is no likelihood of collectivisation on the Soviet model, compressing a radical structural transformation into four or five years. For one thing, it is not needed economically: the state has many other instruments at its disposal to enforce its policy, notably the dominant state sector. For another, the modern means of production required to utilise large-scale farming methods in the peasant fields are not available.

The large estates are placed under estate managements and divided into smaller units. Supplies are organised on a regional basis; farm and food supply belts are formed round the main centres of consumption. This general relaxation and devolution of central authority was occasioned by excessive demands on the transport system, especially during the sugar-cane harvest, and by distribution difficulties.

As for agricultural production, a moderate degree of diversification is to be introduced as well as regional specialisation. Earlier efforts to diversify Cuba's agriculture and promote food production for domestic consumption were attended by very limited success (see Table 4.38 for figures concerning rice and cotton). As a result, the authorities reverted to the cultivation of the traditional crops and launched a drive for the expansion of sugar-cane growing in particular. Most promising among the new crops are rice and oil palms. In 1960/61, under a pioneer scheme, 800,000 oil palm saplings were imported and planted. A number of reasons can be given for the moderate success of attempts at diversification:

(a)   the natural conditions are not suitable for the new crops;

(b)   the producers lack experience and are hampered by traditional attitudes;

(c)   if the terms of trade shift, it may be more advantageous economically for Cuba to continue playing her part in the world-wide division of labour – in fact, the world market price of sugar has been going up again since 1961.

Accordingly the following priorities were laid down for the agricultural production sector:

1   Sugar: a target of 10 million tonnes of raw sugar was set for 1970. It was to have been achieved by substantially raising yields per acre through the extended use of fertilisers and machinery and by increasing the permanent labour force of agriculture. Table 4.36 shows that the 10 million mark was missed by nearly 1·5 million tonnes in 1970, and that production dropped to near half the 1970 target figure in the following two years.

The decline in the Cuban position on the world sugar market is due to the fact that the sugar-cane acreage dropped and yields stagnated in Cuba, while both went up in the rest of the world, and sugar beet production increased even more.

On 24 October 1968 a new World Sugar Agreement was concluded. Cuba would like to regain its former position on the world market. Out of a maximum of 8·5 million tonnes to be sold in the 'free' world market, Cuba was allocated a quota of 2·5 million tonnes. This entails higher export proceeds in convertible currencies and an improved bargaining position in price negotiations with the Soviet Union.

2   The cattle population is to be increased from 6·6 million head in 1964 to 12 million head in 1975. Total animal production is to include 4 million head of fat stock a year and 10 million litres of milk a day.

3   Measures to raise production of other export goods.

4   Safeguarding of food supplies, as far as possible from domestic production.

Industrial development, scheduled to proceed at a relatively slow pace, is to be linked in two ways with the agricultural sector: on the one hand by processing agricultural products, on the other by supplying production equipment and materials to agriculture. The following measures are envisaged to accelerate the advance of agricultural production:

(a)   mechanisation and establishment of machine brigades;

Table 4.38

Attempts at diversification of agricultural production, 1952–1971

Year	Rice			Cotton		
	Area ('000 ha)	Production ('000 tonnes)	Yield (q per ha)	Area ('000 ha)	Production ('000 tonnes)	Yield (q per ha)
1948/52	61	106	17·4	–	–	–
1962/66	95	141	14·9	13	3	2·1
1967	60	93	15·5	4	1	2·9
1969	146	293	20·1	4	1	2·9
1971	180	452	25·1	4	1	2·9

Source: FAO, *Production Yearbook.*

(b)   extension of irrigation;
(c)   action to check harvest risks and lessen the fluctuations in crop production, in particular for sugar-cane and rice;
(d)   a ban on the slaughter of female calves, with a rapid increase in the cattle population.

As for the means of production, the use of equipment and production materials is to be intensified, and the production units are to be technologically modernised. Food imports are to be kept low.

Cuban agricultural policy has introduced a novel element, the militarisation of agricultural labour. Beginning in 1968, labour brigades were formed – both from army units and from civilian volunteers – especially for the operation of agricultural machinery and tractors. The brigade members work under military discipline for equal pay. This set-up is to cope with a situation in which mechanisation advances swiftly and expensive equipment is deployed, while manpower is short, experience slight and standards of technological training are low. It is hoped to achieve in this way the optimum utilisation of equipment and a rapid transfer of specialised knowledge under conditions of military discipline with no or little material incentives.

Gutelman has analysed this development in the following terms:

> The ostensibly critical point of view, according to which Cuba could readily emerge from underdevelopment if only things were better organised, gives rise to a tendency to isolate organising ability from its cultural environment and turn it into a fetish. Underdevelopment, then, is looked upon merely as a technological problem, forgetting its

cultural aspects, of which the ability to organise is one. On the other hand, the militarisation of labour, operating with simple and clear-cut rules, constitutes a rapid method of inculcating in the workers the discipline that is called for by modern technological developments. During the current stage of technological and cultural under-development it undoubtedly offers the most effective way of raising labour productivity, for it helps to focus all individual efforts upon a limited number of clearly defined objectives. It further makes it possible to keep strict checks on performance, and it establishes clearly bounded spheres of responsibility. This is particularly important in agriculture, where the process of mechanisation and the use of capital equipment are rapidly advancing. Generally, it can be said that as the interests of the individual cease to be paramount and as men's social duties come to the fore, so, and to the same degree, will it be appropriate to abandon and replace an organisation of work that has outlived its usefulness because it belongs to a waning socio-economic order geared to the satisfaction of individual interests by a system of wages, prices and bonuses. The militarisation of organisation, in which group interest, the principle of authority and above all the group's social consciousness are the dominating influences, represents the logical alternative to an organisation founded on the interest of the individual.

Alternatively it may be argued that the militarisation of labour can be relaxed as soon as the country is rich enough to be able to offer material incentives and provide better training facilities. Once that point is reached, it will be possible to look upon militarisation as a passing phase in which a virtue (or theory) was made of necessity.

5 On the Agrarian Policy of Socialist States

The specific forms of agrarian policy depend on a multitude of data, the most important factors being the state of economic development, the agrarian structure and the natural conditions of production. Since there are wide variations in these vital factors within the communist world, generalisations must not be lightly made.

5.1 The four stages of agricultural development

Current policies cannot be understood unless attention is given to the distinction between the various stages of development. It is possible to discern four main stages of socialist agrarian policy.

The first stage is that of disinvestment. A high contribution to overall economic development is forcibly exacted from agriculture by a variety of methods, such as taxation in cash and in kind, unfavourable terms of trade, compulsory deliveries, and legal regulations on the distribution of revenues and surpluses of collective farms. State funds are allocated almost exclusively to the economically and politically decisive sectors: the basic industries and the cultural infrastructure. Agriculture is the most important sector of the economy and has made the largest contribution to these objectives without getting anything in return. Eventually a state of affairs is reached in which even the modest inherited level of agricultural productivity seems threatened with exhaustion.

The second stage is a battle for production. Great efforts are made to increase the output of agriculture through the allocation of production equipment and materials made by industry, and through direct subsidies, increased producer prices and other incentives. The purpose of the new measures is to meet the growing demands of the non-agricultural population and of the processing industries. Naturally, some time elapses before the planned new factories are able to deliver their products, and more time before their influence on agricultural production comes to be felt. Considerations of economical production — to the extent that such a concept makes sense under conditions of scarcity — are brushed aside, in order to catch up with the arrears of the agricultural sector. Under conditions of a general shortage of foodstuffs and a lack of foreign exchange, the marginal utility of any additional domestic production is very high. Price—cost analyses from countries where different conditions prevail are therefore of little relevance in assessing the economic soundness or otherwise of the expenditure incurred to attain a specific increase in production.

The third stage is characterised by a new economic system, a change-over from physical and direct to indirect and flexible planning by means of economic and financial controls. At this stage the socialist market is to play a growing part as a link connecting outline and long-range plans with detailed enterprise and regional plans, or in other words macro-planning with micro-planning. The allocation of production equipment and materials is superseded by the purchasing decisions of managers of agricultural enterprises.

In this context the market is conceived as a meeting place where social production is matched with the aggregate collective needs of society as well as with the individual needs of all its members. Seen in this light, the market is not an alien body in the fabric of socialist economic planning, but one of its integral parts, having specific regulating and control functions to perform in relation to the plan. During the initial stages of development, under conditions of war communism and general shortages, the regulator cannot function. Since socialist economic planning is impelled not by the profit motive but by the total needs of society, planned production and aggregate demand must be in line at least in the long term. If this condition is not met, the plan is inadequate.

The fourth stage is that of surplus production. The increased inputs are taking effect. The agricultural production pattern is changed by increasing the relative importance of animal husbandry and taking up export production. Surplus production, of course, is a relative concept, depending on price levels and the incomes of the mass of consumers.

The industrialised capitalist states, of course, never passed through stage three, which is peculiar to planned socialist economies. They have forgotten that they themselves emerged quite recently from stage two — the battle for production — and moved straight into the surplus production of stage four. Most communist states are at present in stage three and are about to achieve for the first time a bare satisfaction of their physiological needs. Some of them — such as Hungary, Bulgaria and Romania — are producing agricultural surpluses due in part to a slower pace of industrialisation. In the Soviet Union the second phase ended around the beginning of the 1960s.

236

5.2 Structural policy: economic planning and free enterprise elements

Structural policy has to deal with two types of units of production, which respond in different ways to measures of agricultural policy: on the one hand socialised elements, such as state farms, machine and tractor stations, and producer co-operatives of various types; on the other hand private elements, in the form of peasant farms and household plots.

These different elements tending in opposite directions live in a dialectical symbiosis and division of labour. The functions assigned to the contrasting structural elements are clearly differentiated. Thus, the state farms are to ensure the satisfaction of certain essential consumer demands and to safeguard supplies of agricultural means of production, such as seed crops and pedigree stock. They concentrate at first on lines of production easily adaptable to mechanisation, above all in arable farming. The collective farms and the household plots of their members have pooled their production equipment and their labour. The household plots iron out the seasonal fluctuations in the collective farms' demand for labour; they provide supplementary incomes for the members; they produce the most labour-intensive products; and they add to the food supplies of the population. In terms of macro-economics the two elements are complementary, while at the level of micro-economics they compete for the factors of production, notably animal feeds, labour and tractive capacity.

The agrarian structure of every communist country contains both elements, but the mixture varies from case to case. There may be regional variations within the same state in the relative strength of one element or the other, as for instance the preponderance of kolkhozes in the areas of old settlement, and that of state farms in uninhabited and virgin land regions. It is the mixture of the two elements on which the instruments and methods of agrarian structural policy depend. The most important instruments of policy are described below.

1 *Nationalisation of land.* Only in the Soviet Union was all land nationalised. This has obviated unproductive payments to big landowners as well as ground-rent due to peasants on joining a collective farm.

2 *Changes in the size of production units.* The pattern of farm sizes must be assessed in relation to ecological conditions, natural fertility and population density. Marked variations are manifest within and between the various countries. Figures for the European communist countries, with the exception of Yugoslavia, are given in Table 5.1 in respect of agricultural producer co-operatives and state farms. The belief that maximum

237

Table 5.1

Characteristic data of producer co-operatives and state farms in European communist countries
(Yugoslavia excepted)

(a) *Producer co-operatives*

Country	Year	Number	AL ('000 ha)	Members ('000)	AL (ha) per co-operative	Members per co-operative	Members as a percentage of economically active population
Albania	1964	1,064	365[1]	302·0[1]	343	248[1]	44·2[2]
Czechoslovakia	1971	5,871	4,241·3	876·2[3]	675	149	12·3[4]
GDR	1972	7,574	5,405·1	877·6[3]	714	115	7·9[5]
Rumania	1969	4,655	9,070	3,456·4[6]	1,948	74	–
USSR	1971	32,800	96,900[7]	18,100·0[8]	3,200	439	17·5[9]
Hungary	1969	2,678	4,853	851·2[10]	1,812	318	14·7
Poland	1972	1,081	293	28·4[6]	271	26	–

(b) *State farms*

Country	Year	Number	AL ('000 ha)	Work force ('000)	AL (ha) per farm	Work force per farm	Work force as a percentage of economically active population
Czechoslovakia	1971	326	1,428	146·7[11]	4,380	450	2·1
GDR	1972	500	446·7	73·4[12]	893	147[12]	0·9[12]
Rumania	1969	359	2,112	–	5,883	–	–
USSR	1971	15,502	94,400[13]	9,212	6,100	594	–
Hungary	1969	192	1,004	154	5,229	802	–
Poland	1972	4,941	2,896	392	586	79	–

1   Work force.
2   1960.
3   Permanent work force substantially less.
4   Number and proportion of regularly working members are substantially lower.
5   Proportion of regularly working members substantially lower.
6   Families.
7   Sown area.
8   Inclusive of collective farmers doing military service.
9   1968.
10 Average number of work force.
11 Permanently employed.
12 1971.
13 Cropland.

Source: Statistical Yearbooks of socialist countries.

size means optimum size has generally been abandoned, and a more pragmatic approach has been adopted. The position is summed up as follows in *Grundriß der Kooperation* (Döring, 1967):

> The creation of large-scale production units as part of the system of socialist agriculture does not automatically entail the superiority of the large units. One of the problems that must be solved if an effective and well-planned social organisation of production is to be assured is the question of the most economic size of the socialist agricultural production unit ... . Technologies of production and machine systems have been developed, which necessitate a degree of concentration and centralisation going well beyond the unit sizes of 3,500 to 5,000 acres of agricultural land hitherto accepted as standard. In his investigation of the application of industrial production methods in agriculture, Gruner arrives in this context at the following conclusion:
>
> 'An agricultural enterprise in which all branches of production can be carried out at the optimum scale, so as to warrant the economical introduction of industrial methods in the use of technology, would need to have a size of up to 25,000 acres of agricultural land. However, production units of that order of magnitude are uneconominal in view of increasing transport costs.'

3   *Co-ordination.* While decentralisation is helping to render the largest production units more manageable, attempts are being made to achieve economies of scale through the co-ordination of several large production units in particular spheres. The gigantomania that was rampant in the Soviet Union in the 1920s and 1930s seems to have been overcome.

4   *Expansion of state farms at the expense of other sectors.* On financial grounds alone, such schemes – also known as 'sovkhozisation' – are likely to be opposed by the Ministers of Finance. The question as to whether two different types of large-scale production units – producer co-operatives and state farms – ought to go on existing side by side was at one time answered by the theoretical proposition that co-operative ownership of the means of production represented a lower stage in the development towards socialism than did state ownership. Since the end of the 1960s, however, the two forms of common ownership of the means of production have been held, in the Soviet Union itself, to be of equal value. Thus a formula was found for the continuation of the collective farms on a long-term basis.

5   *Encouragement or lack of toleration for private sector.* It appears that

240

a tolerant attitude has carried the day in all communist countries. The complementary character of this sector and its important functions within the framework of the economy as a whole have come to be appreciated.

6   *Legal provisions on the income distribution of producer co-operatives.* The amounts to be transferred to each of the funds of a co-operative and their order of priority are laid down by law. This means enforced formation of capital and reduced consumption. Originally, the remuneration of the members ranked lowest. If the amounts of the compulsory transfers are reduced and if the order of priorities is modified it is possible to improve the remuneration for work even without state subsidies. In recent years the ranking of wages in the order of priorities has been substantially raised.

One of the basic theses of Stalin's planning policy said that planning presupposes control of *all* means of production. But to the Soviet Union, too, the lesson was brought home that the complete or near-complete socialisation of the means of production is not in itself a guarantee of plan fulfilment. Private production can supplement the plan and can to some extent be harnessed to the satisfaction of social needs, though by indirect means.

5.3   Use of the means of production and methods of raising production

During the first stages of planning, the basic and heavy industries as a rule received preferential treatment, while agriculture was neglected to the point of disinvestment. The scant stocks of machines, concentrated deployment of which allows substantial savings in production costs, were administered by the state. Eventually a point was reached where it was no longer possible to exact from agriculture a higher contribution to production and to the market without making new investments. The weakness of agricultural production acted as a brake on the rest of the economy, the advance of which was slowed down by the shortage of raw materials and foodstuffs. The order of priorities had to be readjusted in favour of agriculture and the production of equipment and materials for agriculture. Yet, it takes years before a planning decision in favour of setting up a fertiliser industry leads to actual production, and a further two years at least before the result shows in higher yields. A great deal of leeway has to be made up in respect of harvest combines, mechanisation of indoor processes in animal husbandry, fertilisers and plant-protection agents.

During the first stage, the scarce means of production were centrally administered and deployed, or allocated according to plan, with priority in supplies being granted to enterprises producing directly for the state-controlled market. Gradually, as the supply increased, it became possible freely to purchase agricultural production equipment and materials. A third possibility is production under contract and vertical integration, which may involve, for instance, the supply of feeds in return for the delivery of pigs.

5.4 Marketing policy

Corresponding to the various elements making up the agrarian structure, the market for agricultural products is — and remains for a considerable time — divided into three sectors.

1   As regards the staple foods produced by state farms and collective large-scale production units, a system of compulsory deliveries is in force, which, with the given agrarian structure, is relatively easy to supervise. Producer prices are fixed by the state at a low level. This constitutes a convenient and effective method of exacting the factor contribution of agriculture through the price scissors, the imposition of unfavourable terms of trade.
2   Surplus produce in excess of the delivery quota is taken up by the state purchasing enterprises at substantially higher prices, and the same applies to certain products offered by individual members of collective farms, notably bread grain, which of course is not grown on the household plots, but comes out of the members' remuneration in kind.
3   Products of the household plots — fruit, vegetables, eggs, milk, cheese, meat, flowers, etc. — may be freely sold by the producers at the peasant markets.

During the second stage, marked by the expansion of economic exchanges between industry and the agricultural sector, compulsory deliveries are reduced and eventually abolished. Prices of products in sectors (1) and (2) are then unified at an intermediate level.

Since the state controls all the means of production, it also fixes prices in this sector.

The instruments of agricultural marketing policy are not very different from those in use in Western countries: raising of producer prices, modification of agricultural price patterns to boost high-grade animal husbandry, price reductions for industrial products, dismantling of quota deliveries and state allocation of materials and equipment, contract production. In some countries uniform consumer prices are maintained for a number of basic products, while a differentiation of producer prices is effected by the payment of delivery bonuses and by tax concessions depending on the quantity of deliveries and on regional factors, such as transport costs and conditions determining yields.

5.5 Welfare policies

At the beginning there were few machines to replace human labour. Accordingly, in the state-managed and collective large-scale farming enterprises the labour force was deployed in large groups (brigades) working under close supervision. This organisation of labour corresponds to the pre-industrial stage of manufacture. As mechanisation advances, the operational working groups are progressively reduced in size. In some cases the operational units are teams linked by kinship, who take charge of a branch of production in a particular area of agricultural land in return for a direct share in the proceeds. The demand for labour on the part of the large-scale production enterprises is subject to wide seasonal fluctuations due to the low degree of mechanisation, the limited development of high-grade animal husbandry, and – as far as large regions of the Soviet Union are concerned – a shorter growing season. In summer the demand is very high, while in the winter many people are underemployed or unemployed.

Different working conditions apply respectively to state farm workers and collective farmers. The state farms employ their regular labour force throughout the year and pay wages laid down in collective agreements. The workers are organised in unions. The collective farmers until recently had to bear great risks arising from the uncertainty of harvest yields. This situation was changed not very long ago, and the collective farmers now have a guaranteed minimum wage that is fixed in relation to the sovkhoz workers' wages. There is no social organisation or representative body for the collective or co-operative farmers. It is only now that some efforts are being made in some of the countries to establish such bodies. Whereas state farm workers were from the outset fully covered by social insurance, the kolkhozes were brought step by step into the system. Until the middle of the 1960s each collective farm in the Soviet Union was to a limited extent made responsible for the living costs of its old members. In the GDR the co-operative farmers were integrated into the general social insurance as early as 1955/56.

For a long time there was no freedom of movement for people working in agriculture. A peasant was neither able to leave his collective farm nor

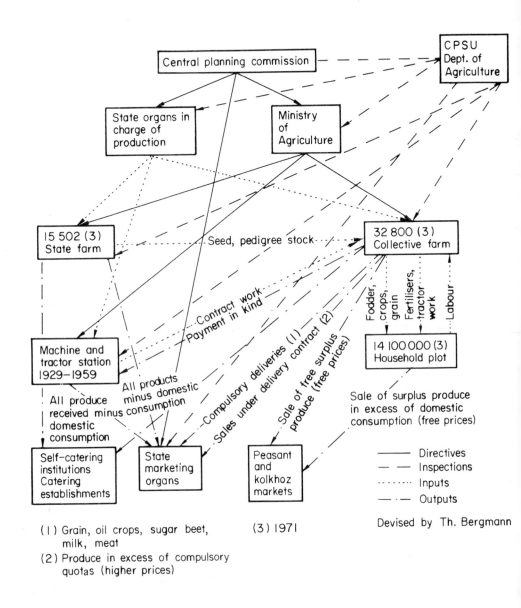

Fig. 5.1 Structural elements of collectivised agriculture and their inter-action: USSR (See also subsection 2.1.4, pp. 27–42 above)

could he be dismissed. Although great efforts were made to improve standards of training, the lack of mobility depressed the social level of state farm workers and pushed that of collective farmers below that of industrial workers. This fact, together with the lack of mechanisation, accounts for the low productivity of labour. Here it must be borne in mind, however, that an assessment of labour productivity solely in terms of acreage per worker can be misleading. Due allowance must be made for the substantial production of the household plots, the labour of which is pooled with that of the producer co-operative. Moreover, the large-scale enterprises in the communist countries have a great deal of work carried out by their own labour, which in West European agriculture, with its small production units, is left to specialised trades and industries, enterprises or institutions. This applies to building work, machine repairs, contract work, agricultural advice, and so on.

The difference in social conditions is reflected in the composition of the labour force in state farms and co-operatives respectively, a contrast that is particularly striking in Czechoslovakia. The state attracts the most active workers, younger and technically more qualified people, whereas the older age groups and women are disproportionately represented in the labour force of the agricultural producer co-operatives. As people are able to move more freely and industry needs more labour, the stream of migrants increases again. At this point, it becomes vital to improve incomes and working conditions.

In all socialist countries the producers are offered material and moral incentives to higher and better production and productivity. Material incentives take the form of wages, bonuses, new housing and extra leave, while moral incentives may consist of appeals for work on special tasks, public commendation, distinctions and orders. The combination of the two elements, however, varies from country to country. The extent to which either of the two types of incentives is more prominent than the other depends not so much on the ideological purity of the socialist system in question as on the stage of development. In the early days following the revolution, enthusiasm is great and extra work is performed voluntarily. High material incentives are precluded by the general poverty. In the later stages enthusiasm subsides, but the higher level of production makes it possible to offer higher wages, more bonuses and so on, and to combine moral incentives such as orders with material rewards. From then on, differences between the various stages in each country and between the various countries are reduced to a matter of degree, depending on the relative size of the income differentials.

6 Marxist Agrarian Theory

Marxism consists of several parts of which the most important are:

(a)   analysis and social critique of the existing (capitalist or socialist) social order;
(b)   political theory of the Marxist (workers') movement;
(c)   doctrine (or dogma) of countries with communist governments.

The pronouncements of Marxism on the agrarian question can be grouped accordingly.

6.1   Analysis of agriculture under capitalism

Marx looked upon the development in the rural areas which led to a labour surplus, to the 'flight from the land', as a historically inevitable counterpart, concomitant and prerequisite of industrial expansion:

> The expropriation and eviction of a part of the agricultural population not only set free for industrial capital the labourers, their means of subsistence and material for labour; it also created the home market. (Marx, *Capital*, I, p. 747.)

The absorption of part of the rural population into the industrial reserve army is a necessary process in every capitalist country:

> As soon as capitalist production takes possession of agriculture, and in proportion to the extent to which it does so, the demand for an agricultural labouring population falls absolutely, while the accumulation of the capital employed in agriculture advances, without this repulsion being, as in non-agricultural industries, compensated by a greater attraction. Part of the agricultural population is therefore constantly on the point of passing over into an urban or manufacturing proletariat, and on the look-out for circumstances favourable to this transformation. (Manufacture is used here in the sense of all non-agricultural industries.) This source of relative surplus-population is thus constantly flowing. But the constant flow towards the towns presupposes, in the country itself, a constant latent surplus population, the extent of which becomes evident only when its chan-

nels of outlet open to exceptional width. The agricultural labourer is therefore reduced to the minimum of wages, and always stands with one foot already in the swamp of pauperism. (Ibid., p. 642)

In agriculture as in manufacture, the transformation of production under the sway of capital means at the same time the martyrdom of the producer; the instrument of labour becomes the means of enslaving, exploiting and impoverishing the labourer; the social combination and organisation of labour-processes is turned into an organised mode of crushing out the workman's individual vitality, freedom and independence. The dispersion of the rural labourers over larger areas breaks their power of resistance while concentration increases that of the town operatives. In modern agriculture, as in the urban industries, the increased productiveness and quantity of the labour set in motion are bought at the cost of laying waste and consuming by disease labour-power itself. Moreover, all progress in capitalistic agriculture is a progress in the art, not only of robbing the labourer, but of robbing the soil; all progress in increasing the fertility of the soil for a given time is a progress towards ruining the lasting sources of that fertility. The more a country starts its development on the foundation of modern industry – like the United States, for example – the more rapid is this process of destruction. Capitalist production, therefore, develops technology and the combining together of various processes into a social whole only by sapping the original sources of all wealth – the soil and the labourer. (Ibid., pp. 506 ff.)

While Marx had no doubt that capitalism invariably seizes control of agriculture – although there are differences of degree, depending on specific circumstances – he did not look upon this process in a onesided manner as nothing but an increase in the area of the production units. He regarded such an increase merely as one type of the concentration of capital (here in the shape of land) in fewer hands. A different type of capital concentration (now in the shape of machines and working capital) entails a diminution of the area. Thus he cites with approval a remark by the economist Richard Jones:

In the progress of culture 'all, and perhaps more than all, the capital and labour which once loosely occupied 500 acres, are now concentrated for the more complete tillage of 100'. Although 'relatively to the amount of capital and labour employed, space is concentrated, it is an enlarged sphere of production, as compared to the sphere of production formerly occupied or worked upon by one single independent agent of production'. (Ibid., p. 329.)

Marx was able to study the eviction of peasants from their holdings in England and Ireland and to observe the consequences.

These results of the agricultural revolution – i.e. the change of arable into pasture land, the use of machinery, the most rigorous economy of labour, etc. – are still further aggravated by the model landlords who, instead of spending their rents in other countries, condescend to live in Ireland on their demesnes. In order that the law of supply and demand may not be broken, these gentlemen [according to a report by the Dublin Poor Law Inspectors] draw their 'labour supply ... chiefly from their small tenants, who are obliged to attend when required to do the landlord's work, at rates of wage in many instances considerably under the current rates paid to ordinary labourers, and without regard to the inconvenience or loss to the tenant of being obliged to neglect his own business at critical periods of sowing and reaping'. (Ibid., p. 708)

After 1850 Marx was in a position to follow in terms of statistics the development that led up to the concentration of tenant farms and the destruction of the small farmers. In his attempt to generalise the English experience in a scientific manner, Marx did not by any means shut his eyes to the fact that the peasant farm still existed and would continue to survive for a considerable time. He saw the reason in the peasant farmer's readiness to forgo a part of his wage (comparable to the workers in the cottage industry, who were obliged to compete with modern industry at its prices):

One portion of the surplus labour of the peasants, who work under the least favourable conditions, is bestowed gratis upon society and does not all enter into the regulation of price of production or into the creation of value in general. This lower price is consequently a result of the producers' poverty and by no means of their labour productivity. (Ibid., III, p. 786.)

Marx was fully aware of the distance that separated highly developed Britain from her European neighbours:

England, with her concentration of the ownership of land – that tool of agricultural labour – also has a division of labour in agriculture and uses machinery for tillage. France, where the tool – that is to say, the land – is divided through the system of smallholdings, as a rule neither has a division of labour in agriculture nor does she use machines for tillage.

Thus it took a long time before the feudal tenant was replaced by the industrial capitalist. In Germany this transformation started only in the last third of the eighteenth century. In England alone is this relationship between industrial capitalists and landowners fully developed. (Marx, *Elend der Philosophie*, 1895, pp. 124 and 146.)

And in *Capital* Marx underlines:

The expropriation of the agricultural producer, of the peasant, from the soil is the basis of the whole process [of primitive accumulation]. The history of this expropriation, in different countries, assumes different aspects, and runs through its various phases in different orders of succession, and at different periods. In England alone, which we take as our example, does it have the classic form. (*Capital* I, p. 716.)

Marx endorsed Ricardo's theory of agricultural prices (though only for a capitalist economy):

In the agricultural industry, on the other hand [in contrast to the manufacturing industry discussed in the preceding passage], it is the price of the product produced with the greatest quantity of labour that regulates the price of all equivalent products. First, in contrast to the manufacturing industry, it is not possible to increase the instruments of production of equal productivity, i.e. pieces of land of the same fertility, to any desired degree. Instead, to the degree necessitated by population growth, production is raised either by taking land of lesser quality into cultivation or by putting fresh capital into the same field, which is relatively less productive than the capital first invested. In either case a larger quantity of labour is applied to obtain a relatively lower output. Since the needs of the population have made the increase in labour necessary, the produce of the land cultivated at greater cost will find buyers as readily as that of the land that can be farmed at lower cost. Since competition equalises the market price, the produce of the better soil will be as dear as that of the inferior soil. (*Elend der Philosophie*, pp. 144 f.)

Thus arises the differential ground-rent for the producers farming the better land.

The agrarian theory of Marx and Engels fits into their general concept of economic development: the same tendency towards a concentration of production units and a concentration of invested capital, diversified by a number of features peculiar to agriculture and by the specific circumstances of each country. In contrast to the utopian socialists, they looked upon the contemporary private acquisition of the means of production as a historically progressive step by comparison with the preceding stage of primitive common production and common consumption (agrarian communism, various forms of communal land use, notably the German 'Allmenden'). There was no way under the old village constitutions of fully utilising the discoveries of agricultural chemistry and the other agro-technical sciences. Thus, the contemporary private economy, acquiring a more and more pronounced capitalist character, constitutes the dialectical negation of the preceding collective economy. According to the Hegel— Marxian dialectic, this negation must in turn be 'lifted' in the dual sense of the dialectic: removed and elevated, superseded, yet with its progressive content preserved. Thus,

> ... capitalist production begets, with the inexorability of a law of Nature, its own negation. It is the negation of the negation. This does not re-establish private property for the producer, but gives him individual property based on the acquisitions of the capitalist era: i.e. on co-operation and the possession in common of the land and of the means of production. (*Capital* I, p. 763.)

The demand for the socialisation of the land stands logically as the conclusion of Marx's agrarian theory, a conclusion arrived at by the use of the dialectical method.

Friedrich Engels sought to fit the successive stages of development in the history of agrarian constitutions into a dialectical sequence:

> All civilised peoples start with the common ownership of land. For all peoples that have passed beyond a certain primitive stage in the development of agriculture, this common ownership becomes a fetter impeding production. It is abolished, negated, and, following a more or less prolonged series of intermediate phases, turned into private ownership. Yet, the higher development of agriculture initiated by the private ownership of land causes that very private ownership to become in turn an obstacle to production, as is the case today both with small and with large-scale landed property. This of necessity gives rise to the demand for the negation of this form of ownership, for its reconversion into common ownership. Yet, this demand does not imply the restoration of the original ancient form of land owner-

ship, but the creation of a much higher and more advanced form of common ownership. So far from acting as an obstacle to production, this new form for the first time frees production of all fetters and enables the modern chemical discoveries and mechanical inventions to be fully utilised. (Engels, *Anti-Dühring*, 1948, p. 169.)

Marx at the time analysed primarily the contemporary situation, illustrated in particular by the examples of England and Ireland, but he did not devise any plans for an agrarian structure that might suit future socialist societies or economic systems.

6.2 The agrarian debate within the West European social democratic movement

Since Marx's forecasts were not borne out immediately or to the letter, doubts as to the correctness of the Marxian analysis began to emerge, especially among German social democrats. The social democratic agrarian debate before the First World War was in part a scholastic quarrel over the correctness or fallacy of a Marxian thesis. At the same time, however, the controversy turned also on topical issues: on the methods to be adopted to enlist the political support of farmers and agricultural workers and on an adequate model of a modern agrarian structure. The German social democrats pleaded for the co-operative large-scale production unit to be formed by small farmers pooling their holdings or through the take-over of expropriated estates by agricultural workers. The French socialists did not go to such lengths in their reform proposals, but made greater allowances for the mentality of the French farmer. Engels, while accepting the co-operative large-scale production unit as a long-term objective, urged that the working peasants should be given a long time in which to make up their minds and be allowed to decide in complete freedom. They should first be able to find out to their own satisfaction, as demonstrated by practical examples, that they stood to benefit from large-scale production units with their modern labour-saving machines, their improved social conditions, and so on. Any haste or coercion would be unnecessary as well as harmful.

In his essay of November 1894 on 'The peasant problem in France and Germany', Engels outlined some basic propositions on the agrarian question and pointed to possible Marxist solutions. He suggested that socialists, after taking power in a country, should nationalise large estates and let them be managed as co-operatives by the agricultural workers previously employed there. There should be a measure of public supervision over the use of the land. Engels did not go into detail on this point, but he went on:

> The example of such agricultural producer co-operatives will later on convince the last remaining small farmer, who may be hesitant, and some big farmers, too, of the advantages of the large-scale production unit in agriculture ... . We shall do all that can be done to ease the lot of the small farmer and smooth his way during the transition to co-operation, once he has decided to adopt this course. And even if he still has not made up his mind, we will grant him a prolonged period for reflection, sitting on his own land ... . (Engels, 1970.)

In Western Europe, where this debate was conducted, it concerned the approach to free and liberated farmers who did not wish to suffer a drop in social status. Moreover, the social democratic parties were able to fall back on their urban-proletarian mass basis for support.

6.3 The role of the peasants before, during and after the revolution

A completely different political task confronted the Russian, Chinese and other Marxists operating in agrarian countries. Even here, the interests of peasants and industrial workers were not identical. Nevertheless, the peasants, economically and socially unfree, had an interest in the overthrow of the existing order. An anti-feudalistic agrarian programme had to lay bare the latent social conflicts in the village and to appeal to the lowest strata in the village, who were mostly not workers in the industrial sense. Hence, in his first draft of a party programme in 1896, Lenin demanded the following reforms in favour of the Russian peasants:

(a) abolition of the redemption payments (exacted from the peasants to pay off the land handed to them on the abolition of serfdom in 1861) and compensation of peasants for payments already made; return of the amounts overpaid by the peasants to the state;
(b) return to the peasants of the land 'cut off' from peasant land in 1861;
(c) parity of status for peasant and estate land as regards liability to imposts and taxes;
(d) abolition of collective liability and all laws restricting the peasant's right to dispose of his land.

Communist parties have seized power in the aftermath of revolution in developing countries where peasants form a majority of the population.

Contrary to Marx's predictions, they have so far failed to achieve success in highly industrialised capitalist countries. To gain mass support, the communist leaders in the agrarian countries had to turn to the oppressed and exploited peasants, to analyse their wants and wishes and to formulate a policy that would mobilise their social forces and energies for the overthrow of the old order. Lenin, Bukharin, Preobrazhenskiy and Mao Tse-tung conscientiously examined Russia's and China's agrarian problems before the revolution.

The peasants played a decisive part in the Russian and Chinese revolutions, and also in other revolutions. Their short-term aims were identical with those of the revolutionaries; in Russia these were peace and land. It was in keeping with the yet more pronounced relative weakness of the Chinese industrial proletariat that the Chinese communists went further in modifying the Marxist theory and declared the peasants to be the main force of the revolution.

In building up the economy, the communist planners endeavoured to extract a maximum factor contribution from the agrarian sector in return for minimum contributions to agriculture from the other sectors. The peasants' wishes tended in the opposite direction. Thus, the transient identity of interests and aims during the revolution was bound to be shattered in a dialectical process and to give way after the revolution to complete antagonism. Stalin's ruthless methods of government brooked no compromise and led to a head-on clash.

In the development process of agrarian countries it is agriculture which is called upon to create the basis for the expansion of the other sectors by

(a)   supplying manpower and capital − its factor contribution;
(b)   raising market production − its production contribution;
(c)   taking up goods and services from the other sectors − its market contribution.

None of these three contributions could be forthcoming without the other two, and the size of each depends on that of the others: no goods can come from the other sectors, nor can agricultural production be raised except on on the basis of prior capital formation. Conversely it can be said that the higher the factor contribution, the lower the production contribution.

After the revolution, new tasks gradually emerged. In an agrarian country, rapid modernisation implies the expansion of the cultural and technological infrastructure, industrial development and urban construction. The factor contribution of agriculture is decisive. At the same time the urban masses are expected to put up with shortages, owing to the low agricultural production contribution, while compulsory deliveries are imposed on the rural masses without any quid pro quo and enforced through the transformation of agriculture. As early as 1925 – four years before the first Five-Year Plan – these necessities were clearly stated by Preobrazhensky:

> We can formulate a law, or at any rate that part of a law that relates to the distribution of the material means of production. The more backward economically a country is that has made the transition to a socialist organisation of production, the stronger its petty-bourgeois and peasant elements are and the smaller the socialist accumulation fund of the working class which the social revolution inherits; the greater in relative terms will be the extent to which socialist accumulation has to depend on the alienation of the surplus value of pre-socialist branches of the economy (agriculture) and the smaller will be the relative importance of the formation of capital by the socialist economy's own production base; that is to say, the less will capital formation derive from the surplus value created by the workers in socialist industry. Conversely, the more developed economically and industrially a country is in which social revolution triumphs, and the greater the material assets in the form of a highly developed industry and capitalistically organised agriculture, which the proletariat in such a country inherits by nationalisation when taking over from the bourgeoisie, the smaller will be the significance of pre-capitalist forms in the country in question. And furthermore, the more the proletariat in such a country is obliged by necessity to curtail the non-equivalent exchange of its products for products of former colonies, the more will the main weight of socialist accumulation shift to the production base of the socialist forms; that is to say, the more will it have to rely on the surplus value of its own industry and its own agriculture. [Preobrazhensky's footnote:] This law must of course be modified in the event of a transfer of means of production from an advanced to a very backward socialist country. (Preobrazhensky, 1965, p. 124; in this and a subsequent quotation from Preobrazhensky's book the English translation has been slightly edited.)

Preobrazhensky arrived at the conclusion that the socialist state would have to tax the small producer more heavily than capitalism had done. However, that heavier tax burden was to be levied on a growing income, such growth being expected to follow modernisation, which would be bound to affect the agrarian sector as well. Accordingly, Preobrazhensky and his supporters advocated a slow pace of industrialisation and a slow

255

transformation of the agrarian sector.

The process of the socialist transformation of agriculture and the agricultural population is generally marked by one decisive turning point, which may occasion profound crises of the communist regime. The peasantry shows enthusiasm in making its political contribution to the overthrow of the old feudal order. It is a contribution that is welcome to the revolutionary leadership and indispensable for the victory of the revolution. The dialectical leap from enthusiasm to aloofness and opposition occurs as soon as the factor contribution is exacted from agriculture. The more quickly the contribution is wanted, the fewer benefits are granted in return, and the more abrupt will be the cooling off of relations between the revolutionary party and the peasantry. Control of the soil as their means of production is not enough for the peasants: they want to control the product as well.

This fundamental change in political–social needs was not analysed or explained during the Stalin era. Western agrarian politicians have overlooked, misunderstood or ignored it, and have fastened on the subsequent tension between the peasants and the socialist planners as evidence of a supposed inherent hostility of communist parties to the peasants. Accordingly, the peasants' enduring support for the (agrarian) revolution in Yugoslavia, China, Cuba and North Vietnam is a constant surprise to them.

Soviet economists and politicians recognised the problem, and warnings against rash economic policies (against all too great a 'leap forward') were uttered especially by Preobrazhensky and Trotsky. Lenin had estimated that under the most favourable conditions the co-operative transformation of adjustment more concentrated and more painful. The persons affected ated the radical transformation through harsh administrative measures without offering any economic incentives. The process and the traditional stages were duly compressed and shortened. This also made the difficulties of adjustment more concentrated and mor painful. The persons affected by change were scarcely allowed time to adjust to the new set-up. New production relations were created, but without new productive forces. This was one of the main reasons for the slight economic impact of the new agrarian structure and its failure to attract support through the force of example. The formal process of the transformation of millions of individual peasant farms into 35,000 collective farms is completed. The corresponding technological development and provision of equipment as well as the social readjustment of the peasants and the transformation of their consciousness cannot be effected by administrative ukase, cannot even be accelerated to any substantial extent.

6.4 The role of the agrarian sector in economic planning and society

The general aims of the agrarian policies of socialist countries have seldom been formulated in precise statements. Despite the wide divergencies in the agrarian structures, the social relations and the cultural traditions of these countries, Šuvar and Puljiz have attempted a general formulation of these aims under five headings:

(i)   socialisation of agrarian production;
(ii) expansion of agrarian production;
(iii) industrialisation of production, combined with the centralisation and concentration of the means of production in agriculture;
(iv) peasant—worker alliance in the development of a new society;
(v)   reduction and gradual abolition of differential living and cultural standards between urban and rural population.

Points (ii), (iii), and (v) are in substance identical with the aims of capitalist countries. This does not apply to point (i), since capitalism is bent on preserving the basic principle of private ownership, nor to point (iv), concerning which the authors observe:

> The political alliance of peasants and workers was an essential requirement for the now socialist countries. This alliance was of decisive importance during the armed phase of the revolution. On the eve of the revolution most of those socialist countries had a large peasant population. Their involvement on the side of the workers was an indispensable condition for the successful overthrow of the capitalist system.

The low production contribution of agriculture may be accounted for by the following reasons:

(a)   high factor contribution (systematic disinvestment) forcibly exacted by the state;
(b)   no deliveries of means of production;
(c)   agrarian structure: accelerated transformation allows the people affected no time to adjust;
(d)   low remuneration, hence lack of identification, passive resistance on the part of the producers;
(e)   other causes of low productivity.

The deficiencies of rapid collectivisation in the Soviet Union led to peasant resistance, burying of grain stores, slaughter of animals, declining or stagnating production. But the greatest mistake of all was the proclama-

rence of political crises, some of which seriously jeopardised the communist governments. In Yugoslavia and Poland collectivisation was first launched, then reversed; in other countries the share of the household plot was increased, in order to adapt the model to specific national circumstances.

The position of agriculture changes under the new economic system. It seems likely, however, that in some countries this system represents a tendency rather than current reality. The economic importance of the agrarian sector is recognised, and this awareness is reflected in the plans, where a higher priority is now accorded to the needs of agriculture. More means of production come out of the new factories and are offered to the production enterprises. The production contribution of agriculture rises, the factor contribution drops, the market contribution increases. With central dirigism and central supervision abandoned, active participation on the part of the kolkhoz peasants, whose democratic rights had previously existed on paper only, is now possible and indeed required.

Disproportions between the agrarian and industrial sectors are due to several causes:

1 The extent to which the natural conditions of production can be controlled is still inadequate. Increased control requires substantially higher capital investments.
2 To achieve increases in agricultural production comparable to industrial growth rates requires preliminary investments as well as a regular supply of equipment and materials calculated to raise production.
3 The number of producers to be integrated into the planned process of economic development is very large. Owing to the peculiar effect of technology in agriculture — dispersal of individuals, social isolation, absence of a division of labour and of a concentration of masses of workers — new socio-technical instruments must be found for the management of production.

Since fluctuating harvests due to natural conditions cannot be entirely eliminated, only mitigated, planning must be generous and operate with wide safety margins. Attentive and critical monitoring of planning progress should give early warning if and when the need for a major change in economic policy arises.

6.5   The collective farm in the light of the theory of co-operation

It has been argued by some authors, in particular some of the older

tion of the Soviet model's universal validity, so that its imitation became compulsory in the countries conquered by the Red Army, in utter disregard of the great difference of the starting situations. The unmodified transfer of Soviet agrarian policy was largely responsible for the occurtheoreticians of the West German co-operative movement, that the collective farms cannot properly be described as co-operatives at all. Other definitions – for instance by Boettcher and some other authors – lead to the opposite result. Now, definitions are functional, determined by their purpose, and not free of value judgements. Which of the many acceptable definitions is chosen is a matter of personal judgement.

Undoubtedly, the organisational principles, working methods and functions of the socialist producer co-operatives are not in line with those of the West German service co-operatives. It would, however, be rather restrictive and scientifically sterile to elevate today's accepted principles of co-operatives to the status of an eternal and universal truth.

Judged by the degree of integration and the scale of co-operative activities, the collective farms of the socialist countries occupy an intermediate rather than an extreme position. They may be compared in the first place with some types of co-operatives with a low degree of integration established in many capitalist and a few socialist countries, and in the second place with more thoroughly integrated types of socialist and capitalist countries. Looking upon the currently existing forms of co-operatives as parts of a continuum characterised by a progressive integrative tendency, we find the auxiliary economic service co-operatives at the one end of the scale and the kibbutz, the complete co-operative in the narrower sense, at the other. The kolkhoz stands between the two extreme forms, being much less integrated and, as regards income distribution, much less egalitarian than the kibbutz and preserving elements of private enterprise. (See also section 7.4.)

The role of the co-operatives as agents of change is also disputed. Whereas some authors have attributed to the co-operatives an effective function as agents of social change, Preobrazhensky emphatically denies this:

> Co-operatives qua co-operatives are not bound by their inner logic to an active principle of social change leading towards socialist production relations. The utopians of the co-operative movement said the opposite, but their argument has been refuted by the entire practical experience of capitalism and the co-operatives. (Preobrazhenskiy, p. 219.)

Co-operatives, then, are to be regarded as ideologically neutral social-

259

technical institutions, the specific forms, methods and functions of which largely depend on the social system within which they are operating, and which moulds them to a far greater extent than they can mould it. Co-operatives can be defined as follows.

A co-operative is a body of persons co-operating on equal terms according to binding rules in an institutional framework based on the forms of organisation of federated enterprise for the common good of the members. This requires an organisation which must have statutes defining its aims. The principal economic aim is the promotion of the members' economic interests through joint effort, mutual aid and self-help. The members, who enjoy complete equality, have to make a uniform minimum contribution, which is defined in specific terms (e.g. land, products, labour, money, livestock). The members exercise self-government from the start, or are gradually led towards that aim, if necessary with assistance from the state. The social and educational function is discharged by extending economic support.

A static or, on the global plane, parochial approach would be unproductive as far as the problems of the developing countries are concerned. In order to produce a generally valid definition, therefore, some features have been omitted because they are either controversial or associated only with specific manifestations of the concept. This applies, for example, to the stipulation that each member runs an independent enterprise and to the principles of open access to membership, voluntariness and freedom from state intervention. The stipulation of equality of rights for all members, on the other hand, sets the co-operatives apart from other forms of economic collaboration, where influence within the organisation depends on the capital brought into it by each member. This distinction brings out the social function of the co-operative.

Once this approach is adopted, the collective farm appears as a co-operative of a type peculiar to some socialist countries. Its problematic aspects are dealt with in another section.

6.6   Stages of reform within the agrarian revolution

A comparison of the processes involved shows that, like most historical categories, an agrarian revolution is not a single act completed at a stroke, but comprises a large number of steps and measures spread over a prolonged period. Thus the crucial difference distinguishing agrarian revolution from agrarian reform is not the absence of the small steps, but the immediate radical upheaval transforming social relations in the village,

Chart 6.1

Comparison of the main features
of the service co-operative and collective farm

	Service co-operative	Collective farm
Economic system	capitalist	socialist planning
Functions		
internal (affecting members)	subsidiary function in support of private production	confined to sphere of production, no bearing on consumption
external (affecting society)	may help to strengthen small producers' position against monopoly tendencies	integration of small producers into the planned economy
Importance to members	subsidiary	main source of income, role of private holdings (household plots) subsidiary
Occurrence	in many non-socialist, some socialist countries	in socialist countries with a collectivised agriculture, chiefly in areas of old settlement
State influence	moderate, indirect	initially very strong and direct, later gradually relaxed and indirect
Co-operative democracy	impaired by members' economic inequality	impaired by state directives
Factors of production		
land ownership	individual	co-operative
work	co-operative	co-operative
Redistribution of income	slight	more pronounced, but not egalitarian
Membership	formally open, sometimes impaired by economic constraints	formally voluntary, becoming effectively so only at late stage

where the big landowners are expropriated without compensation and banned from further residence and land is distributed forthwith and unbureaucratically. As a result of this radical upheaval, the existing economic, social and political power positions are liquidated at the very outset. Thus, resistance against the subsequent reform measures is made impossible. The order and speed of the later steps depend on a number of circumstances, notably:

(a) stage of economic development or, respectively, degree of underdevelopment;
(b) the framework of national economic planning;
(c) effectiveness of the administration and strength of the revolutionary party;
(d) cultural and psychological effects and after-effects of the revolutionary struggles on the peasantry.

The individual steps of which the transformation consists can be most clearly discerned in China, where they effected a gradual development spanning the time before as well as after the revolution, and in Czechoslovakia, where the various types of agricultural producer co-operative represent the formal and psychological steps which after the revolution led up to the complete integration of the formerly independent peasants.

New means of production can serve as economic incentives and help to avoid slumps in agricultural performance. An extension of the time scale of the follow-up measures and the interposition of intermediate stages in the course of the transformation enable the peasant to adjust himself gradually. Democracy in the shape of active participation avoids the alienation of the peasantry.

6.7 Criticisms of communist agrarian policy

Non-communist criticisms are concerned above all with the following points:

1 Agricultural production, productivity per unit area, labour productivity and food supplies are unsatisfactory. Some countries which had been traditional exporters of agricultural products became net importers after the transformation of their agrarian structure. Production and deliveries slumped.
2 Agriculture is backward in terms of technology of production and does not reach the standards of the highly industrialised countries.

3   The peasants have been deprived of their economic freedom; their status has been downgraded to that of agricultural workers without a stake in their work. Peasant individualism resists uncongenial co-operative labour. Communist economic planning does not suit the agrarian sector.

4   Many state-managed and collective large-scale production units are working at a loss and need state subsidies. The advantages of large-scale production in agriculture are questionable.

Communist critics accept the necessity of planning and social change and the goal of a technologically and socially modern agriculture based on large-scale production units. They also grant that a high factor contribution on the part of agriculture is necessary for rapid economic development, that indeed development could not have got off the ground, had that contribution not been forcibly exacted. The criticism from within the system is addressed above all to the following points:

1   The formation of large-scale co-operative production units not accompanied by supplies of the means of production suited to this type of agriculture is doomed to failure. Mechanisation first, and, after that, voluntary collectivisation may follow (argued Trotsky in the Soviet Union and Liu Shao-ch'i in China), or different forms may have to be found for the integration of the small producers (suggested Kardelj in Yugoslavia).

2   Ruthlessness, coercion and speed of the social transformation have aroused the resistance of the peasants. Bureaucratisation prevents democratic participation and supervision from below.

3   Planning has become an end in itself and ignores the wishes of producers and consumers (Šik). Planning in detail from above by the state is inconsistent with the nature of co-operative enterprise, which is thus turned into a part of the state apparatus (Mysliveček).

4   It was wrong to have proclaimed the universal validity of the Soviet model and disregarded the specific conditions in which it was conceived (Mieszczankowski, Poland). Communist agrarian policy and collectivisation are not synonymous; rather collectivisation is but one of a number of possible variants.

5   The social needs of the producers were not considered, partly for the reason that they had no recognised body to represent their interests. Trade unions as well as representative peasant organisations are vital as a countervailing force against a power-drunk planning bureaucracy. Promises of future benefits cannot supply a sufficient impulse for strenuous efforts over prolonged periods. If the producers notice no material improvements for a considerable span of time, their resolution will falter. Central planning without participation of the producers leads to alien-

ation. The construction effort and the goals of planning are placed in jeopardy by such methods.

6   The original form of Soviet planning may have suited the conditions, needs and technical resources in the Soviet Union at the time, but planning itself is not exempt from the need for modernisation. The change-over to new stages of development and new planning methods must be foreseen and initiated in good time.

7 Comparative Performance and Development Prospects

7.1 The concept of efficiency

Efficiency, as defined by Webster, is the generation of the desired result with a minimum of effort, expenditure or loss. According to this definition, then, efficiency can be measured only in terms of specific means and known ends. Seen in this way, socio-economic efficiency cannot be taken for granted by any means, even where purely economic efficiency is undisputed. Shatil selects three main criteria:

(i)   efficiency of settlement;
(ii) technological and economic efficiency;
(iii) efficiency of individual and group welfare.

Each of the three criteria has its economic component. In making such assessments, a distinction must be drawn between micro and macro-economics. Some forms are micro-economically inefficient, but macro-economically necessary and efficient. Conversely, it may happen that micro-economic efficiency is achieved at the cost of macro-economic inefficiency, for instance when a large number of small-scale production units is maintained by state subsidies. Production optimum and financial optimum may be far from coinciding.

7.2 Problems of comparative indicators

Many indicators may be used for purposes of comparison:

1   Productivity per unit area. This depends on the climate, use of production equipment and materials, population density (governing demand), and so on. So long as the available area is relatively large, intensive land use is uneconomic.
2   Productivity of labour. This depends on technological re-equipment, size of production unit, availability of manpower.
3   Per-capita production.

4   Productivity of capital: production per unit of means of production employed (input—output analysis).

5   Money incomes of producers. However, purchasing power is not reflected in the exchange rates and depends on price policy and social priorities.

6   Satisfaction of producers' material needs. This criterion ignores all the other wants arising in a modern society, wants which take on increasing importance as material living standards go up. Once a certain material standard has been reached, for instance, the following alternatives may present themselves: higher income, better education for the children, regular working hours, more leisure.

7   Growth rate of the economy.

Every one of the above indicators, considered in isolation, is onesided and questionable. Only if all the indicators are considered together and judiciously weighed can it be at all possible to arrive at an exhaustive and valid measurement.

7.3   Problems of comparative assessment

All the indicators taken together represent only the quantifiable part of the performance, by no means the performance as a whole. An extension of the range of quantifiable aspects of performance would be of great advantage. And yet it has not been possible to express in quantitative terms the following contributions of agriculture to the national economy and to society:

(a)   financial contribution to overall development, capital formation over 150 years for the non-agricultural sectors;

(b)   discriminatory terms of trade ('price scissors');

(c)   mobilisation of intellectual reserves;

(d)   cost of food supplies, assuming the entire domestic needs are met through imports under conditions of an ideal international division of labour.

In the communist countries, contributions have been rendered to society and the economy which still elude measurement. In the Soviet Union collectivisation was the instrument by which domestic capital formation was compressed from 150 into 15 years, a deliberate and planned step taken to eliminate the development lag and prepare for the military conflict with Hitler. In China, the peasant masses in their millions were shaken out of their lethargy and mobilised, and their labour potential, until then lying waste, was used for the first time. In all communist countries the people have been made literate and modern systems of education have been set up. In the producer co-operatives, the agricultural producers are able to benefit from the social norms of a modern society.

Pure comparisons of production performance thus ignore the aims and achievements of society and the economy as a whole, though admittedly their social cost is no more amenable to quantitative measurement than are the achievements themselves. Cost assessments would have to compare the cost of agricultural policy in a country with an agrarian structure based on peasant farming (subsidies for a multitude of unprofitable small production units, advice, price support, storage, other state measures in aid of peasant farming) with the corresponding cost in a country with a collectivised agriculture (state support, subsidies for relatively few unprofitable large-scale production units). New methods need to be elaborated to measure these factors and include them in a comprehensive comparison. The unprejudiced critic will seek to perceive the social aims of a system and will take them into account in his comparative assessment of agricultural performance.

7.4   Comparisons

Comparisons between the agrarian systems of various countries have been attempted on a number of occasions. P.K. Raj made such an assessment for India, Pakistan and China, Lazarcik for Czechoslovakia and Western Europe (see subsection 2.2.1 (vi) above). The GDR and West Germany were compared by Tümmler, Merkel and Blohm in the Federal Government's report on the state of the nation. These two countries lend themselves most readily to a comparison, since up to 1945 they constituted an economic and political entity, and 'only' the agrarian structure was changed. The results of this comparative assessment can be summed up in brief by saying that in the early years the agricultural production achievement of the GDR lay below that of West Germany, whereas in recent years the GDR has achieved standards of production close to those of West Germany, but with lower inputs. This comparison, however, takes no notice of the performance of the economy as a whole and makes the implicit assumption that in West Germany changes in the agrarian structure are either not needed at all or are effected painlessly and without cost. All in all, the comparative assessments that have been made so far are methodically unsatisfactory and therefore inconclusive.

An international comparison of the various types of producer co-operatives brings out a number of salient facts, notably:

Chart 7.1

Kolkhoz, people's commune and kibbutz: a comparison

Aspect	Kolkhoz	People's commune	Kibbutz
Tasks	basic production, mainly crops; marketing; remuneration	all functions in production, administration and planning	all functions in production, administration and planning
State influence	very strong	strong	moderate
Co-operatives' economic scope	production of staple foods; management; work planning	bulk of market production; small share in producing basic food supplies for members	entire production and food supplies for home use
Members' economic scope	household plot: use of wages in kind (fodder crops) and feeds for high-grade animal production	as kolkhoz, but household plots smaller	residual functions of individual households
Inter-unit co-ordination	processing and marketing of agricultural products	nil	processing and marketing of agricultural products
Land	state-owned before and after collectivisation	privately owned land brought into co-operative becomes collective property	collective ownership
Membership	open; in theory voluntary, in fact compulsory	as kolkhoz	open or limited; voluntary
Co-operative democracy	formal	slight	far-reaching
Social influence	slight	moderate	out of proportion to numerical strength or economic importance
Proportion of population	30 per cent	about 80 per cent	3-4 per cent

Chart 7.1 continued: collective (C) and individual (I) decision-making

Sphere	Kolkhoz	People's commune	Kibbutz
External and market relations	C	C	C
Production planning	C	C	C
Production:			
use of machinery	C	C	C
crop farming	C	C	C
stock farming	C/I	C/I	C
Household plot	I	I	nil
Household	I	I/(C)	C/(I residual)
Social services:			
education	I	I	I
welfare	(C)/state	C	state/C
Industry:			
paid outside work	I	I	C
development of village industry	nil (so far)	C	C

1   The kolkhoz and people's commune do not have precisely the same functions. The Chinese commune copes on behalf of the state with general economic and administrative tasks. The basic economic unit is substantially larger than the village. The weakness of the central administration and of the communications system and the low level of productivity rule out a greater measure of centralisation.

2   Both forms retain a private-enterprise sector.

3   The kibbutz represents the highest stage of social integration. There is no private sphere in production. Consumption is egalitarian, but here the private sphere expands with growing affluence. (See Chart 7.1.)

Comprehensive assessments comparing the agricultural performance of different communist countries as well as of the different regions within the large communist countries might cast a revealing light on the crucial factors by which development is determined. The undeniable fact that in quantitative terms the agricultural performance of the communist countries lies below that of the highly industrialised capitalist countries cannot be attributed to the revolutionary transformation of the agrarian structure alone, but is due also to the stage of economic development, to the natural and demographic conditions, and so on. One should ask, and if possible measure, if and to what extent the development lag was reduced as a result of the planned mobilisation of resources after the revolution. Most observers answer the question in the affirmative.

7.5   Development trends

No fundamental changes in the agrarian structure are to be expected. In the countries with a collectivised agriculture, reorganisations within the production units and minor land transfers between collective farms and state farms may well occur, but a liquidation of the collective farms — either through absorption into the state sector or through a return to independent peasant farms — is inconceivable. No second attempt at collectivisation will be made in Yugoslavia or Poland. The private-enterprise elements are tolerated and allowed to develop within limits. What changes there may be will be effected within the present agrarian structure. The more the mechanisation of animal production advances, the greater will be the part that state-managed and co-operative large-scale production units will be able to play in this branch by the application of near-industrial production methods.

Within the new economic system a higher priority must be accorded to agriculture. Industries supplying agriculture with the means of production are being expanded. The stock of machines is being increased in terms of quantity and at the same time diversified. Most production processes are being fully mechanised by stages. The use of fertilisers is being increased and land use intensified. Advanced animal husbandry is being expanded both in the large production units and on the household plots. Individual production units, or numbers of them linked by co-ordination, are embarking on the processing of agricultural products.

The hidden unemployment of the agricultural population is reduced by a movement of manpower into industry and by the diversification of the village economy. Social conditions are being improved and the differential in incomes and social status between industry and agriculture is being pared down. A measure of democracy is being introduced in state farms and kolkhozes. The collective farmers are recognised as a social stratum that has its own needs and interests and is entitled to representation. Organisations of collective farmers are about to be set up.

New models of communist agrarian policy are being developed.

Bibliography

Abosch, H., 'Nordvietnam – Der Staat im Schatten' *Frankfurter Hefte* vol. 21, no. 5, 1966, pp. 335–40.

Adams, A. E. and J. S., *Men versus Systems*, New York 1971.

Alavi, H., *Theorie der Bauernrevolution*, Stuttgart–Hohenheim 1972.

Arlt, R., *Fragen des Rechts der LPG in der DDR*, [East] Berlin 1955.

Barkin, D., 'L'agriculture, pivot du développement à Cuba' *Revue Tiers-Monde* vol. 11, no. 44, October–December 1970, pp. 643–74.

Beauvoir, S. de, *La longue marche: essai sur la Chine*, Paris 1957.

Belden J., *China Shakes the World*, New York 1949.

Benary, A., *Aktuelle Probleme der Agrartheorie des Marxismus–Leninismus*, [East] Berlin 1955.

Bergmann, Th., 'Die Rolle der landwirtschaftlichen Genossenschaften in Jugoslawien' *Archiv für öffentliche und freigemeinwirtschaftliche Unternehmen* vol. 3, no. 1, 1957, pp. 63–72.

Bergmann, Th., 'Die landwirtschaftlichen Genossenschaften in Ostdeutschland' *Archiv für öffentliche und freigemeinwirtschaftliche Unternehmen* vol. 3, no. 4, 1958, pp. 361–79.

Bergmann, Th., 'Agricultural co-operation in Poland – the new system' *Yearbook of Agricultural Co-operation*, London 1960.

Bergmann, Th., 'Neue Aufgaben der Genossenschaften in der jugoslawischen Agrarpolitik (Zu einem Buch von E. Kardelj)' *Archiv für öffentliche und freigemeinwirtschaftliche Unternehmen* vol. 6, no. 1, 1962, pp. 81–5.

Bergmann, Th., 'Die Agrarfrage bei Marx und Engels – und heute' in *Kritik der politischen Ökonomie heute – 100 Jahre Kapital*, Frankfurt/Main 1968, pp. 175–94.

Bergmann, Th., 'Der Kolchosbauer – sozioökonomische Merkmale und Problematik' *Sociologia Ruralis* vol. VIII, no. 1, 1968, pp. 22–47.

Bergmann, Th., 'Agrarproduktion und Agrarstruktur in der ČSSR' *Osteuropa-Wirtschaft*, vol. 14, no. 1, March 1969, pp. 63–84.

Bettelheim, Ch., et al., *Zur Kritik der Sowjetökonomie*, Berlin 1969.

Bettelheim, Ch., J. Charrière, H. Marchisio, *La construction du socialisme en Chine*, Paris 1965.

Bettelheim, Ch., et al., *China 1972 – Ökonomie, Betrieb und Erziehung seit der Kulturrevolution*, Berlin 1972.

Bianco, L. (ed.), *Das moderne Asien*, Frankfurt 1969.

Biehl, M., *Die chinesische Volkskommune im „Grossen Sprung" und danach*, Hamburg 1965.

Biehl, M., *Die Landwirtschaft in China und Indien*, Frankfurt/Main etc., 1966.

Blumer, G., *Die chinesische Kulturrevolution 1965/67*, Frankfurt/Main 1968.

Boettcher, E., *Die sowjetische Wirtschaftspolitik am Scheideweg*, Tübingen 1959.

Boettcher, E., 'Genossenschaft und Kolchose' *Zeitschrift für das gesamte Genossenschaftswesen* vol. 14, Göttingen 1964, pp. 370–84.

Bossung, J.-P., *Die Betriebsgrösse in der grossbetrieblichen Landwirtschaft Sowjet-Russlands in ihrer Beziehung zu den wirtschaftsgeographischen Verhältnissen*, Diploma thesis, Hohenheim 1970.

Broadbent, K., 'Two decades of social and economic development in Chinese communist agriculture, 1949–1969' *World Agricultural Economics and Rural Sociology Abstracts* vol. 11, no. 4, December 1969, pp. 1–21.

Brunner, G., and K. Westen, *Die sowjetische Kolchosordnung*, Stuttgart 1970.

Bucharin, N., *Ökonomik der Transformationsperiode*, Hamburg 1922.

Bucharin, N., et al., *La question paysanne en URSS (1924–1929)*, Paris 1973.

Burchett, W. G., *Schatten über dem Dschungel*, Berlin 1963.

Burian, A., 'K charakteru práce a ke společenskému postavení žen pracujících v našem zemědělství' (On the character of labour and on the social position of working women in our agriculture), *Sociologie a historie zemědělství*, vol. 3, no. 1, Prague, July 1967, pp. 1–16.

Burki, S. J., *A Study of Chinese Communes, 1965*, Cambridge (Mass.) 1969.

Černin, R., 'Rozbor výsledků dosahovaných v růžných formách doplňkových hospodářství' (Analysis of results of various forms of farming as a supplementary source of income), *Zemědělská ekonomika* vol. 12, no. 7, Prague, July 1966, pp. 447–55.

Chaliand, G., 'Les paysans du Nord-Vietnam et la guerre' *Cahiers Libres* nos 130–131, Paris 1968.

Chao Kuo-Chün, *Agrarian Policies of Mainland China: A Documentary Study (1949–1956)*, Cambridge (Mass.) 1957.

Châu, Lê, *Le Viet nam socialiste – une economie de transition*, Paris 1966.

Chesneaux, J., *Geschichte Vietnams*, Berlin 1963.

'China' I and II, *Staatsbürgerliche Informationen*, Bonn 1962.

China und die Revolution in der Dritten Welt, Frankfurt/Main 1971.

Chinese People's Republic, *Le Soleil rouge éclaire Tatchai dans sa marche en avant*, Peking 1969.

Choląj, H., *Planning of Agriculture in People's Poland*, Warsaw 1970.

Ciháková, K., 'Rozdíly ve společenské spotřebě obyvatelstva mezi hlavními skupinami domácností' (Differences in social consumption between the main social groups of households), *Sociologie a historie zemědělství* vol. 2, no. 2, December 1966, pp. 85–99.

Clecak, P., 'Moral and material incentives' *Socialist Register*, London 1969, pp. 101–35.

Communist Party of the Soviet Union, *The 23rd CPSU Congress*, Moscow 1966.

Conklin, D. C., *An Evaluation of the Soviet Profit Reforms*, New York 1970.

David, E., *Sozialismus und Landwirtschaft*, Leipzig 1922.

Davídek, V., 'Problémy současné populace zemědělského obyvatelstva ČSSR' (Problems of the present agricultural population of Czechoslovakia), *Sociologie a historie zemědělství* vol. 3, no. 1, July 1967, pp. 17–34.

Delayne, J., *Die chinesische Wirtschaftsrevolution*, Reinbek 1972.

Democratic Republic of Vietnam, 'Regierungserlass No. 239/B.TLP' *Ost-Probleme* vol. 6, no. 23, pp. 909–14, 12 June 1954.

Democratic Republic of Vietnam, *Le Vietnam d'aujourd'hui*, Hanoi 1965.

Democratic Republic of Vietnam, 'Problèmes agricoles (2): Le riz' *Études Vietnamiennes* no. 13, Hanoi 1967.

Democratic Republic of Vietnam, 'Economic progress in 1970' *Vietnam-Courier* vol. 8, no. 305, January 1971.

Deutscher, I., *The prophet outcast: Trotsky 1929–1940*, Oxford 1963.

Döring, H. (ed.), *Grundriss der Kooperation in der Landwirtschaft*, [East] Berlin 1967, pp. 15–85.

Dumont, R., *Cuba – Socialisme et développement*, Paris 1964.

Dumont, R., *Sovkhoze, kolkhoze ou le problématique communisme*, Paris 1964.

Economic Policy of the State in Czechoslovak Agriculture during the Period 1945–1969, Prague 1970.

Engels, F., 'Die Bauernfrage in Frankreich und Deutschland' in K. Marx and F. Engels, *Werke* vol. 22, [East] Berlin 1970, pp. 483–505.

Engels, F., *Herrn Eugen Dührings Umwälzung der Wissenschaften*, reprint, [East] Berlin 1948.

Fall, B. B., 'Ho Chi-minhs Bodenreform' *Ost-Probleme* vol. 6, no. 46, 19 November 1954, pp. 1842—80.

Fedorenko, N. P., P. G. Bunitsch and S. S. Schatalin, *Effektivität in der sozialistischen Wirtschaft*, [East] Berlin 1972.

Fitzgerald, C.P., *Revolution in China*, London 1952.

Flek, J., 'Počet pracovních sil v čsl. zemědělství a faktory ovlivňující jejich potřebu' (The size of the labour force and factors influencing demand), *Zemědělská ekonomika* vol. 11, no. 9, 1965.

Frenkel, I., 'Dynamika zatrudnienia v polskim rolnictwie w latach 1950—1960 w świetle porównán miedzynarodowych' (Employment trends in Polish agriculture 1950—1960 in the light of international comparisons), *Zagadnienia ekonomiki rolnej*, no. 1, Warsaw 1966, pp. 11—34.

Freyberg, Jutta von, and Kurt Steinhaus (eds.), *Dokumente und Materialien der vietnamesischen Revolution* vol. 2, Frankfurt/Main 1969.

Galeski, B., *Basic Concepts of Rural Sociology*, Manchester 1972.

Giap, Vo Nguyen, *Guerre du peuple, armée du peuple*, Paris 1966.

Gordon, A., 'Debate on agriculture in North Vietnam', *New Left Review* no. 68, July—August 1971, pp. 72—82.

Griesau, H. D., 'Strukturwandlungen in der Landwirtschaft und dem agrarischen Aussenhandel Jugoslawien' *Berichte über Landwirtschaft* vol. 31, no. 3, 1953, p. 402.

Grossmann, B., *Die wirtschaftliche Entwicklung der Volksrepublik China*, Stuttgart 1960.

Gumpel, W., 'Fortschritte und Grenzen der Zusammenarbeit im Rat für gegenseitige Wirtschaftshilfe' *Osteuropa-Wirtschaft* vol. 12, no. 3, September 1967, pp. 208—31.

Gumpel, W., et al., *Die Sowjetwirtschaft an der Wende zum Fünfjahresplan — Rückblick und Ausblick*, Munich—Vienna 1967.

Gutelman, M., *L'agriculture socialisée à Cuba*, Paris 1967.

Gutelman, M., 'L'agriculture cubaine en 1968—1969' *Études rurales* no. 33, Paris, January—March 1969, pp. 27—42.

Hartmann, Th. T., *Die Kooperation in der sozialistischen Landwirtschaft der DDR*, Berlin 1971.

Healey, D. T., 'Chinese real output 1950—1970', *Bulletin of the Institute of Development Studies*, vol. 4, no. 2/3, June 1972, pp. 49—59.

Henle, H., *Chinas Schatten über Südost-Asien*, Hamburg 1964.

Heuer, K., 'Zur Entwicklung der genossenschaftlichen Demokratie im neuen ökonomischen System' in: Autorenkollektiv unter Leitung von Gert Egler, *Zum neuen ökonomischen System in der Landwirtschaft*, [East] Berlin 1965, pp. 232—361.

276

Hidasi, G., 'China's economy in the early 1970s' *Acta Oeconomica* no. 1, Budapest 1972, pp. 81–94.

Hinton, W., *Fanshen, a Documentary of Revolution in a Chinese Village*, New York 1967.

Ho Chi Minh, *On Revolution*, London 1967.

Holzer, W., 'Reiseberichte aus der DRV' *Frankfurter Rundschau*, 1, 3, 12, 15 and 23 December 1970.

Honley, P. J., 'Agricultural collectivization in North Vietnam' *China News Analysis*, Hong Kong (undated).

Horlemann, J., 'Vietnam' *Rote Presse-Korrespondenz* no. 30, Berlin 12 September 1969, pp. 10–12.

Horlemann, J., and P. Gäng, *Vietnam – Genesis eines Konflikts*, Frankfurt/Main 1966.

Huber, B., *Vietnam*, [East] Berlin 1968.

Huberman, L., and P. M. Sweezy, *Cuba – Anatomy of a Revolution*, London 1960.

Ishikawa, S., *Factors Affecting China's Agriculture in the Coming Decade* Tokyo 1967 (duplicated).

Jahn, G., *Die Wirtschaftssysteme der Staaten Osteuropas und der Volksrepublik China*, Berlin 1961.

Jasny, N., *The Socialised Agriculture of the USSR – Plans and Performance*, Stanford 1949.

Johnston, J. A., and M. Williams, *The New China*, Sydney, etc., 1971.

Kakiel, R., *Landwirtschaft Polens*, Warsaw 1969.

Karcz, J. F. (ed.), *Soviet and East European agriculture*, Berkeley–Los Angeles 1967.

Kardelj, E., 'Problems of socialist policy in rural areas' *Bulletin of Information and Documentation* vol. 7, no. 2, 1958.

Kardelj, E., *Les problèmes de la politique socialiste dans les campagnes*, Paris 1960.

Karger, A., *Die Sowjetunion als Wirtschaftsmacht*, 2nd ed., Frankfurt/Main 1968.

Kautsky, K., *Die Agrarfrage*, Stuttgart 1902.

Kaye, W., 'A bowl of rice divided: The economy of North Vietnam' *China Quarterly* no. 9, London, January–March 1962.

Kemper, M., *Marxismus und Landwirtschaft*, Bonn 1929 (reprinted, Stuttgart–Hohenheim 1973).

Kerblay, B., 'Du mir aux agrovilles (L'expérience agricole soviètique)' *Structures agraires, systèmes politiques et économiques, Colloque de Venise 14–18 Oct. 1967* (duplicated).

Kiernan, V. G., 'The peasant revolution – some questions' *Socialist Register*, London 1970, pp. 9–37.

Kohn, P., 'Socialní struktura družstevního rolnictva a negativní jevy ve vztahu družstěvniků k prací v JZD' (The social structure of the co-operative farmers and the negative aspects of their attitude to work in the unified agricultural producer co-operatives), *Sociologie a historie zemědělství* vol. 3, no. 2, December 1967, pp. 113–24.

Kôi, Lê Thành, *3000 Jahre Vietnam,* Munich 1969.

Kolesnikov, L., 'Agriculture of the Soviet Union' *XIV International Conference of Agricultural Economists*, Moscow 1970.

Komitee für wissenschaftliche Zusammenarbeit mit Cuba, *Cuba – 14 Jahre revolutionäre Entwicklung in Wissenschaft, Erziehung, Wirtschaft und Gesellschaft. Dokumentation zur Ausstellung des Komitees für wissenschaftliche Zusammenarbeit mit Cuba*, Bielefeld, January 1973.

Kosta, J., J. Meyer and S. Weber, *Warenproduktion im Sozialismus*, Frankfurt/Main 1973.

Kramer, F., 'Kollektivwirtschaftliche Ursprünge des Sozialismus in China und Russland' in K. Meschkat and O. Negt (eds) *Gesellschaftsstrukturen*, Frankfurt 1973.

Kramer, M., *Die Landwirtschaft in der sowjetischen Besatzungszone*, Bonn 1953.

Kuznets, S., 'Economic growth and the contribution of agriculture' *Proceedings of the International Conference of Agricultural Economists*, London 1963.

Laird, R. D. and B. A., *Soviet Communism and Agrarian Revolution*, Harmondsworth 1970.

Lane, D., *The End of Inequality? Stratification under State Socialism*, Harmondsworth 1971.

Lanoue, H., 'L'Indochine d'hier' *Cahiers Internationaux* vol. 12, no. 19, Paris, January–February 1958, pp. 12–24.

Lantsev, M., 'Progress in social security for agricultural workers in the USSR' *International Labour Review* vol. 107, 1973, pp. 239–52.

Lazarcik, G., 'The performance of Czechoslovak agriculture since World War II', in Jerzy F. Karcz (ed.), *Soviet and East European Agriculture*, Berkeley–Los Angeles 1967, pp. 385–410.

Lehmann, H. G., *Die Agrarfrage in der Theorie und Praxis der deutschen und internationalen Sozialdemokratie*, Tübingen 1970.

Lenin, V. I., *Collected Works*, Moscow–London 1963–70.

Lichnowsky, L., 'Agricultural policy in mainland China since 1949' *Monthly Bulletin of Agricultural Economics and Statistics* vol. 11, no. 10/11, October–November 1962.

Loncarevic, I., *Die Landwirtschaftlichen Betriebsgrössen in der Sowjet-union in Statistik und Theorie*, Wiesbaden 1969.

Manteuffel, R., 'Grösse der landwirtschaftlichen Staatsbetriebe in Polen' *Das Problem der Betriebsgrösse in der Landwirtschaft, Symposium der landwirtschaftlichen Fakultät der Karl-Marx-Universität 1959*, Leipzig 1960, pp. 125–40.

Mao Tse-tung, *Selected Works* I-IV, Peking 1961–65.

Marchisio, H., 'Communes populaires chinoises. La contradiction, moteur de développement dans une Commune populaire chinoise' *Archives Internationales de Sociologie de la Coopération et du Développement* no. 20, Paris 1966, pp. 76–132; no. 23, 1968, pp. 173–214.

Maretzki, H., *Was suchen die USA in Vietnam?* [East] Berlin 1967.

Markert, W. (ed.), *Osteuropa-Handbuch, Jugoslawien*, Cologne 1954.

Marx, K., *Capital* I–III, Moscow 1961–62.

Marx, K., *Das Elend der Philosophie* (translated by E. Bernstein and K. Kautsky), Stuttgart 1895.

Meissner, B., *Sowjetgesellschaft im Wandel – Russlands Weg zur Industriegesellschaft*, Stuttgart 1966.

Mellor, R. E. H., *Geography of the USSR*, London 1964.

Menclová, J., and Stoces, F., *Les reformes foncières en Tchécoslovaquie*, Prague 1963.

Merkel, K., and H. Immler, 'DDR-Landwirtschaft – eine Herausforderung?' *Deutschland-Archiv* no. 8, December 1968.

Merkel, K., and H. Immler (eds), *DDR-Landwirtschaft in der Diskussion*, Cologne 1972.

Mieszczankowski, M., 'Zarys historii teorii uspolecznienia rolnictwa' (A brief history of the theory of the socialisation of agriculture), *Zagadnienia ekonomiki rolnej* no. 6, 1962, pp. 23–38 and no. 1,1963, pp. 15–34.

Misiuna, W., 'Weclowe problemy rozwoju rolnictwa do 1980 roku' (Basic problems of agricultural development up to 1980) in *O socjalistyczny rozwój wsi – dyskusja*, Warsaw 1964, pp. 60–82.

Mus, P., *Viêt-Nam. Sociologie d'une guerre*, Paris 1952.

Myrdal, J., *Report from a Chinese Village*, London 1965.

Myrdal, J., *China: the Revolution Continued*, New York 1970.

Mysliveček, F., 'Metodologické otázky zkoumání charakteru a postavení družstevního vlastnictví' (Methodological questions concerning the character and status of co-operative property), *Politická ekonomie* vol. 14, no. 6, Prague 1966, pp. 452–63.

Nguyen Khac Vien (ed.), *Vietnamese Studies. Agricultural Problems (3): Some Technical Aspects*, Hanoi 1971.

279

'North Viet-Nam: A profile' *Problems of Communism* vol. 14, no. 4, 1965.

Nove, A., *An Economic History of the USSR*, London 1969.

Novosti Press Agency, *Third All-Union Congress of Collective Farmers*, Moscow 1969.

Okuniewski, J., 'Revolucja techniczna w rolnictwie i jego tendencje rozwojowe' (The technological revolution in agriculture and its developmental trends), *Zagadnienia ekonomiki rolnej* no. 1, 1963, pp. 3–13.

Osadjko, M., 'Die persönliche Hilfswirtschaft der Kolchosangehörigen und Sowchosarbeiter' *Aus der sowjetischen Landwirtschaft* vol. 17, no. 15, August 1967.

Osipov, G. V. (ed.), *Town, Country and People – Studies in Soviet Society* 2, London 1969.

Periodicals:

Archiv Friesdorf, Bonn;
Current Scene – Developments in Mainland China vol. 6, no. 17, Hong Kong, October 1968;
Informationsbulletin, Botschaft der Demokratischen Republik Vietnam in der DDR, [East] Berlin;
Internationale Zeitschrift der Landwirtschaft, Berlin–Sofia;
Kooperation, [East] Berlin;
Osteuropa, Stuttgart;
Osteuropa-Wirtschaft, Stuttgart;
Roczniki socjologii wsi (Yearbooks of rural sociology), Warsaw 1970;
Vietnam-Courier, Hanoi;
Wieś Wspólczesna. Pismo ruchu ludowego (The modern village), Warsaw;
Zemědělská ekonomika, Prague;
Zemědělská ekonomika, Statistická Příloha, Prague.

Pham Van Dong, 'La réforme agraire' *Cahiers Internationaux* no. 58, Paris, July–August 1954, pp. 89–93.

Pokšiševskij, V. V. (ed.), *Sowjetunion, regionale ökonomische Geographie*, Gotha/Leipzig 1967 (Russian edition Moscow 1964).

Popovic, S., *La politique agraire de la Yougoslavie*, Belgrade 1964.

Preobrazhensky, E., *The New Economics*, Oxford 1965 (translation of 1st Russian edition, Moscow 1926).

Raj, K. N., *India, Pakistan and China – Economic Growth and Outlook*, New Delhi 1966 (duplicated).

Raupach, H., *Geschichte der Sowjetwirtschaft*, Reinbek 1964.

Raupach, H., *System der Sowjetwirtschaft*, Reinbek 1968.

Rauth, M., *Raumgliederung, Raumordnung und Regionalplanung in der Sowjetunion aus landwirtschaftlicher Sicht*, Wiesbaden 1967.

Richman, B., 'Economic development in China and India – some conditioning factors' *Pacific Affairs* vol. 45, no. 1, 1972, pp. 75–91.

Robinson, J., *The Cultural Revolution in China*, London etc., 1969.

Rochlin, R. P., *Agrarpolitik und Agrarverfassung der Sowjetunion*, Berlin 1960.

Rochlin, R. P., and E. Hagemann, *Die Kollektivierung der Landwirtschaft in der Sowjetunion und der Volksrepublik China – eine vergleichende Studie*, Berlin 1971.

Roll, Chr., 'Nordvietnam auf der chinesischen Linie' *Aussenpolitik* vol. 16, no. 2, 1965, pp. 129–33.

Romanow, A., *Agricultural Circles and the Process of Structural Changes in Private Farms*, paper submitted to the FAO World Land Reform Conference 1966, Warsaw 1966 (duplicated).

Rosenkranz, O., 'Zur Problematik der Betriebsgrösse in der Landwirtschaft' in *Das Problem der Betriebsgrösse in der Landwirtschaft. Symposium der landwirtschaftlichen Fakultät der Karl-Marx Universität*, Leipzig 1960, pp. 14–34.

Rosier, B. (ed.), *Agriculture moderne et socialisme. Une expérience yougoslave*, Paris 1968.

Roy, M. N., *Revolution und Konterrevolution in China*, Berlin 1930.

Sagara, D., 'Teoretické předpoklady iniciatívy družstevných rolníkov' (Theoretical preconditions for a display of initiative on the part of the co-operative farmers), *Sociologie a historie zemědělství* vol. 3, no. 2, December 1967, pp. 93–104.

Sakoff, A., 'The private sector in Soviet agriculture' *Monthly Bulletin of Agricultural Economics and Statistics* vol. 11, no. 9, Rome, September 1962, pp. 1–12.

Sakoff, A., 'Production brigades: organizational basis of farm work in the USSR' *Monthly Bulletin of Agricultural Economics and Statistics* vol. 17, no. 1, January 1968, pp. 1–8.

Sakoff, A., 'Soviet agriculture and the new model constitution of the Kolkhoz' *Monthly Bulletin of Agricultural Economics and Statistics* vol. 19, no. 9, September 1970, pp. 1–9.

Sakoff, A., 'Rural and urban society in the USSR – Comparative structure, income, level of living' *Monthly Bulletin of Agricultural Economics and Statistics* vol. 21, no. 10, October 1972, pp. 1–13.

Schiller, O., *Die Kollektivbewegung in der Sowjetunion. Ein Beitrag zu den Gegenwartsfragen der russischen Landwirtschaft*, Berlin–Königsberg 1931.

Schiller, O., 'Die Landwirtschaftspolitik der Sowjets und ihre Ergebnisse' *Berichte über Landwirtschaft* 150, special issue, Berlin 1942.

Schiller, O., *Ziele und Ergebnisse der Agrarordnung in den besetzten Ost- gebieten*, Reich Ministry for the Occupied Eastern Territories, Berlin 1943.

Schiller, O., 'Die Problematik der jugoslawischen Agrarpolitik' *Berichte über Landwirtschaft* vol. 32, no. 3, 1954, p. 461.

Schiller, O., *Das Agrarsystem der Sowjetunion*, Tübingen 1960.

Schinke, E., *Die Mechanisierung landwirtschaftlicher Arbeiten in der Sow- jetunion*, Wiesbaden 1967.

Schinke, E., 'The Organisation and Planning of Soviet Agriculture' *World Agricultural Economics and Rural Sociology Abstracts*, March 1970.

Schlesinger, R., 'Zur Frage der Verwandlung von Kollektiv— in Sowjet- wirtschaften' *Osteuropa* vol. 11, no. 7–8, 1961, pp. 511–15.

Schweizer, H., *Sozialistische Agrartheorie und —praxis*, Bern—Frankfurt 1972.

Shanin, T., *The Awkward Class*, London 1971.

Shillinglaw, G., 'Traditional rural cooperation and social structure – the communist Chinese collectivization of agriculture' in P. Worsley (ed.), *Two Blades of Grass*, Manchester 1971.

Šik, O., 'Ein Beitrag zur Analyse der tschechoslowakischen ökonomischen Entwicklung' *Neue Richtungen in der tschechoslowakischen Ökonomie* no. 1, Prague, March 1966, pp. 1–70 (duplicated).

Šik, O., *Ökonomie-Interessen-Politik*, Berlin 1966.

Šik, O., *Fakten der tschechoslowakischen Wirtschaft*, Vienna 1969.

Šima, J., 'Some background figures on social and technical development of Czechoslovak agriculture' *Für die sozialistische Landwirtschaftswis- senschaft* vol. 16, no. 2/3, Prague 1967, pp. 265–72.

Simonis, U.-E., *Die Entwicklungspolitik der Volksrepublik China 1949–1962, unter besonderer Berüksichtigung der technologischen Grundlagen*, Berlin 1968.

Simonis, U.-E., 'Die gesamtwirtschaftliche Entwicklung der Volksrepublik China' *Gewerkschaftliche Monatshefte* vol. 21, no. 2, Cologne 1970, pp. 84–96.

Sobottke, I., 'Formen sozialistischer Agrarwirtschaft am Beispiel Jugosla- wiens' in *Von der Agrar- zur Industriegesellschaft. Sozialer Wandel auf dem Lande in Südosteuropa*, Wiesbaden 1971.

'Die Sowjetunion – Land und Wirtschaft' *Informationen zur politischen Bildung* no. 139, Wiesbaden 1970.

Sowjetunion von A bis Z, [East] Berlin 1958.

Die soziale Sicherheit in der Tschechoslowakei, Prague 1966.

282

Stalin, I. V., 'Concerning questions of Leninism' *Works* vol. 8, Moscow–
London 1954, pp. 11–97.
Statistics, official agencies, etc.:

Czechoslovakia, *Statistická ročenka 1964*, Statistical Yearbook of the
Ministry for Agriculture, Forestry and Water Resources, Prague
1965;
Czechoslovakia, *Statistická ročenka ČSSR 1972*, Prague 1972;
FAO, *Production Yearbook*, Rome;
GDR, *Statistisches Jahrbuch der DDR*, [East] Berlin 1970;
GDR, *Statistisches Jahrbuch der DDR 1972*, [East] Berlin 1972;
GDR, *Statistisches Taschenbuch der DDR 1973*, [East] Berlin 1973;
Poland, *Kleines statisches Jahrbuch Polens 1970*, Warsaw 1970;
Poland, *Rocznik statystyczny 1972*, Warsaw 1972;
Poland, *Maly rocznik statystyczny 1973*, Warsaw 1973;
USSR, *Narodnoe khozyaystvo 1922–1972*, Moscow 1972;
West Germany, *Länderberichte, Jugoslawien 1962*, Stuttgart 1962;
West Germany, *Länderberichte, Nord-Korea, Nord-Vietnam*, Stuttgart
1963;
West Germany, *Länderberichte, Volksrepublik China 1969*, Stuttgart–
Mainz 1969;
West Germany, *Länderberichte – Länder im Rat für gegenseitige Wirt-
schaftshilfe*, Stat. Bundesamt, Stuttgart–Mainz 1970;
West Germany, *Länderkurzberichte, Nord-Vietnam*, Stuttgart 1969;
West Germany, *Länderkurzberichte, Jugoslawien 1971*, Wiesbaden
1971;
Yugoslavia, *Statistički Godišnjak SFRJ 1965*, Belgrade 1965.

Steinhaus, K., *Vietnam. Zum Problem der kolonialen Revolution und
Konterrevolution*, Frankfurt/Main 1966.
Stern, K. and J., *Reisfelder – Schlachtfelder*, Halle 1967.
Strauss, E., *Soviet Agriculture in Perspective. A Study of its Successes and
Failures*, London 1969.
Strauss, E., 'Die Milchwirtschaft in der Sowjetunion' *Berichte über Land-
wirtschaft* no. 2, November 1970, pp. 338–72.
Struzek, P., *Agricultural Development in the Polish People's Republic*,
Warsaw 1970.
Summit Conference of Indochinese Peoples, 'Joint Declaration of the
Summit Conference of the Indochinese Peoples of April 28th 1970'
Peking Review, special issue, 8 May 1970.
Šuvar, S., and V. Puljiz, 'The role of rural sociology in Yugoslav agrarian
policy' *Sociologia Ruralis* vol. XI, no. 1, pp. 66–74.

Szewczyk, W., 'Koszty zastosowania róznych form mechanizacji' (Comparative cost of various forms of mechanisation in agriculture; English summary) *Wieś wspolczesna* no. 11, Warsaw 1965, pp. 22–7.

Tretiak, D., and B. H. Kang, 'An assessment of changes in the number of livestock in China, 1952–1970' *World Agricultural Economics and Rural Sociology Abstracts*, December 1972, pp. 1–32.

Truyen, Doan Trong, and Pham Thanh Vinh, *Building an Independent National Economy in Vietnam*, Hanoi 1964.

Tümmler, E., K. Merkel and G. Blohm, *Die Agrarpolitik in Mitteldeutschland und ihre Auswirkung auf Produktion und Verbrauch landwirtschaftlicher Erzeugnisse*, Berlin 1969.

Turski, R. (ed.), *Les transformations de la campagne polonaise*, Wroclaw 1970.

US Department of Agriculture, *The Europe and Soviet Union agricultural situation. Review of 1966 and outlook for 1967*, Economic Research Service, Foreign No. 185, Washington 1967.

O socjalistyczny rozwój wsi – dyskusja (On the socialist development of the village – a discussion). Warsaw 1964.

'Una evaluacion de la reforma agraria en Cuba' *Revista latinoamericana* no. 29/30, October–December 1972, pp. 187–205.

Unger, H., *Merkmale und Besonderheiten der chinesischen Ackerbaugebiete*, Report no. 2/56 of the Institut für Agrarraumforschung der Humboldt-Universität, [East] Berlin.

United Nations, Economic Commission for Asia and the Far East, *Economic Survey of Asia and the Far East 1966* vol. 7, no. 4, Bangkok 1967.

Varga, G., 'The household plot' *The New Hungarian Quarterly* no. 23, Budapest 1966, pp. 7–23.

'Le Viet-Minh – La République Démocratique du Viet-Nam 1945–1960' *Cahiers de la Fondation Nationale des Sciences Politiques* no. 106, Paris 1960.

Volin, L., *A Century of Russian Agriculture. From Alexander II to Khrushchev*, Cambridge (Mass.) 1970.

Volksrepublik China – ein wirtschaftlicher Überblick, Hamburg 1959.

Voss, W., 'Probleme und Möglichkeiten der Entwicklungsprognose für die Volksrepublik China' *Asienforum* vol. 2, no. 3, July 1971, pp. 349–60.

Wädekin, K.-E., *Privatproduzenten in der sowjetischen Landwirtschaft*, Cologne 1967.

Wädekin, K.-E., 'Die Expansion des Sovchoz-Sektors in der sowjetischen Landwirtschaft' *Osteuropa-Wirtschaft* vol. 13, no. 1, March 1968, pp. 1–25.

Wädekin, K.-E., *Führungskräfte im Sowjetischen Dorf*, Berlin 1969.

Wädekin, K.-E., *Die Bezahlung der Arbeit in der sowjetischen Landwirtschaft*, Berlin 1972.

Wädekin, K.-E., *The Private Sector in Soviet Agriculture,* Berkeley 1973 (translation of Wädekin 1967, revised and amplified by the author).

Wagener, H.-J., 'Die RSFSR und die nichtrussischen Republiken: ein ökonomischer Vergleich' *Osteuropa-Wirtschaft* vol. 14, no. 2, June 1969, pp. 113–29.

Weinschenck, G., and Th. Heidhues, 'Probleme der Betriebsplanung und Betriebsorganisation in landwirtschaftlichen Grossbetrieben der UdSSR', *Agrarwirtschaft* no. 7, 1965, pp. 289–300.

West German Federal Government, *Bericht der Bundesregierung und Materialien zur Lage der Nation 1971.*

Wheelwright, E.L., and B. McFarlane, *The Chinese Road to Socialism,* New York–London 1970.

Wilmanns, H., 'Zur Struktur und Faktoranalyse bei der Wirtschaftsregionalisierung in der Sowjetunion' *Osteuropa-Wirtschaft* vol. 14, no. 3, September 1969, pp. 161–82.

Weidemann, D., 'Die Entstehung der Volksmacht in Vietnam' *Staat und Recht* vol. 15, no. 10, 1966, pp. 1671–89.

Wiznitzer, L., 'Der Premier gewann die Wette' *Der Spiegel*, Hamburg, 22 February 1971, pp. 110–16.

World 'University Service, 'Vietnam' *WUS-Nachrichten*, special issue, Bonn, November–December 1969.

Yamamoto, H., *Development of Agricultural Collectivization in China*, Tokyo 1961.

Zagreb University, Department of Rural Sociology, *The Yugoslav Village*, Zagreb 1972.

'Zwölf Karten und Textbeiträge zur Landes- und Wirtschaftskunde der Sowjetunion' *Informationen zur politischen Bildung* no. 78/79, Wiesbaden 1959.

Index

Indexer's note: For easier reference, the book dealing with comparisons of countries, many heads will be found under the individual country concerned, cross references also being made to the subject and sub-divided by countries. Thus, Crops will be found both under crops and as a sub-head of the country itself. Where a subject head is not divided into countries, the subject is dealt with as a generality.
The terms USSR and Russia are not used, all entries being under Soviet Union.

tural performance, assessment of 96—7; crops 92, 96; fertiliser 93; future prospects 98—100; historical data 77—8; incomes 97—8; input and output 92—6; labour force 82—5, 91; land usage 92; livestock 96; new agrarian structure 79—86, in private sector 86; population and occupation structure 86—91; social security 97—8

Developing countries, *see* China; Cuba; North Vietnam
Development prospects, *see* Comparative performance
Dumont 14

Economic systems: China 194—6; Cuba 227—33; North Vietnam 200—3; Soviet Union 25—7, 44—50; Yugoslavia 130; *see also* under Agrarian theory
Engels, Friedrich 250—1, 252, 253

Fertilisers: China 183; Czechoslovakia 93; GDR 112; Poland 166; Soviet Union 50, 51
Future prospects, *see* Trends in agricultural policies

German Democratic Republic (GDR), collectivised agriculture in 100—28: agrarian structure at outset 101—2; appraisal 123—8; as compared with West Germany 118—21; crops 108; historical data 100—1; labour force 113—18; livestock 109—10; machine and tractor stations 106—7; productive performance 108—13; resources 108—13; transformation, three stages of 102—8; trends in policy 122—3
Gutelman 228, 232

Historical data: China 175—6; Cuba 217—18; Czechoslovakia 77—8; GDR 100—1; Poland 152—3; Soviet Union 13; Yugoslavia 129—30

Incomes: China 189—90; Czechoslovakia 97—8; GDR 117; Soviet Union 58—62

Jones, Richard 248—9

Kardelj 148—50, 263
Kibbutz 259, 268—70

Kolkhozes (collective farms in Soviet Union) 24—5, 36—9, 59—67, 76, 268—70

Labour force: China 179, 180, 186; Czechoslovakia 82—5, 91; GDR 113—16; Soviet Union 30, 37, 53; Yugoslavia 141
Land use: China 181, 193; Cuba 224; Czechoslovakia 92; North Vietnam 203, 211; Poland 163—4; Soviet Union 49, 237; Yugoslavia 135, 139, 145
Lazarcik 267
Livestock: China 184; Cuba 221; Czechoslovakia 96; GDR 109—10; North Vietnam 214; Soviet Union 57, 72—3; Yugoslavia 151

Marketing policy 242
Marxist agrarian theory, *see* Agrarian theory
Mellor 14
Merkel 267
MTS, *see* Machine and tractor stations *under* Soviet Union, collective agriculture in, and *under* German Democratic Republic
Mysliveček 263

Non-collectivisation countries, agriculture in, *see* Agriculture non-collectivisation in
North Vietnam 197—216: agrarian reform and structure 203—10; agricultural production, and marketing 210—16, animal production 214—15, crop production 210—14; economic structure 200—3; geography, terrain and climate 197—8; land usage 203, 211; livestock 214; population 199—200; summary 215—16

Pokšiševskij 14
Poland 152—73: agrarian policy 170, 173; agrarian structure 153—66; agricultural circles 162—5; co-operatives 157—8, 160—1, 165—6; fertilisers 166; historical data 152—3; land usage 163—4; marketing 168—70; means of production 166—8; trends in future 170—3; yields and efficiency 166
Population: China 176—9, 186; Czechoslovakia 86—91; GDR 114; North

288